Neil Sperry's

Lone Star Gardening

Texas' Complete Planting Guide
and Gardening Calendar

Neil Sperry's

Lone Star Gardening

Texas' Complete Planting Guide and Gardening Calendar

NEIL SPERRY
TEXT AND PHOTOGRAPHS

A publication of
Neil Sperry's GARDENS Magazine
McKinney, Texas

All text by Neil Sperry and all photographs, except where noted, by Neil Sperry

Editor: Carolyn Skei
Graphic artist: Cynthia Smith
Printing consultant: Collin Flood
Printer: Clear Vision, Inc., San Antonio, TX

Printed in the USA. ISBN 978-0-9916207-0-8.

Additional copies of this publication are available from

Neil Sperry's GARDENS
400 West Louisiana Street
McKinney, TX 75069
www.neilsperry.com
800-752-4769

To my wife and the love of my life, Lynn

To our children, Brian, Todd and Erin

To our grandchildren (left to right),
Lauren, Nolan, Audrey, Ella, Sam, Joseph and Alex

To my dad and mom, Omer and Lois

And most of all, to my God, for His glorious garden…

With deepest gratitude.

Contents

Acknowledgments

I was working at the State Fair of Texas in October 1980 when I was handed a note to call a Dallas publisher. One call, many meetings and 14 months of typewriting later, I completed the first edition of *Neil Sperry's Complete Guide to Texas Gardening* (1982).

A second edition followed nine years later (1991).

Carolyn Skei, Neil Sperry and Cyndy Smith

And that is where the story paused. But in July 2013, I met with the extremely accomplished editor of my magazine, Carolyn Skei, and Cyndy Smith, the supremely talented graphic artist who had designed my eight most recent Texas Gardening Calendars. The topic of that meeting was a new book with a new title and a new approach to helping Texas gardeners succeed with their favorite hobby.

For nine months, I have awakened each day with a sense of excitement, thinking about what tasks were at the top of my list. The amazing talent and inspiration these two women brought to this project have made it the most fulfilling work of my life. Thank you, Carolyn and Cyndy. You are the best.

Thank you to all the men and women of the Texas A&M AgriLife Extension Service for what you have shared with me, both online and in person. Special thanks to Dr. George Ray McEachern for his extensive help in the Fruit chapter.

I took all but four of the photos in this book. Carolyn's photograph of the Festival Hill herb garden in Round Top (page 315) was too gorgeous not to include. Our son Brian took the photo of me on the back cover. And the photos you see on these pages of my family and my publication team were taken by Joe Ownbey, Ownbey Photography in McKinney. Joe has been my friend and photographic mentor for many years. His guidance made that part of this book possible.

Thanks many times over to Steven Chamblee for advising me without making me feel under-prepared. What a great friend. Thanks, also, to Bob Brackman, Jimmy Turner and Tucker Reed for helping me prepare the details in our Annuals and Perennials charts and to Richard Hartman for his consultation on Palms.

To all who have listened to me, read me, watched me and come up to me on the street, thank you. I am incredibly humbled. You are really the ones who gave me the reason to spend nine solitary months preparing this volume.

We, the Team of Three, hope you think our baby is wonderful!

Neil Sperry

March 1, 2014

Preface

You are holding in your hands the book that I've always wanted to
write. In fact, it's the best representation of this one man's life experiences
that I can offer you. I've given it my best horticultural, journalistic and
photographic efforts based on half a century of communicating about
gardening in our wonderful state. I've been truly blessed, and I am
grateful each day for the opportunities I've been given. I have tried
never to abuse your trust.

It is my most sincere hope that you will enjoy *Lone Star Gardening*
and use its information to create a more beautiful corner of Texas for
you and those around you.

The second thing I hope is that you will help me spread *The Gospel
of Common Sense* as it relates to Texas gardening. Hold others
accountable for what they say, what they sell and what they do in the
name of horticulture.

There is no one clear and right path through successful gardening in
Texas – but if there were such a path, I am certain that it wouldn't be
along the extreme boundaries. We would use adapted plants, whether
they were native or not. We would use properly tested and legally
labeled products to feed and protect the plants around us. We would use
water-conscious plants, and we would use them in responsible ways – but
we wouldn't limit ourselves to xeriphytic plants that might or might not
be able to tolerate times of rainfall in Texas.

The message in all of that, in my opinion, is that we need to find and
follow the middle course. I have done my very best in preparing this
volume to do exactly that.

Happy reading, and happy gardening!

N.S.

A note about my opening photographs

With the rest of the book devoted to Texans' home landscapes and gardens, I thought it was only fitting that these opening pages feature a couple of my favorite photographs that I've taken in God's natural gardens right here in the Lone Star State.

I remember the first photo I ever took. I was about 7, and my dad, Omer, and I were somewhere on US 90 between Valentine and Marfa, Texas. He let me hold his camera to take a picture of the Davis Mountains. From 30 miles away. That was a coming of age for young Neil – getting to use my dad's camera. (The photo wasn't nearly as good as the memories.)

Dad founded the Biology Department at Sul Ross State University in Alpine. He spent many years combing what would become Big Bend National Park, eventually co-authoring the 1951 book *Plants of Big Bend National Park*.

There is a joy in sharing my own photographs of that same glorious corner of Texas. I'm looking closely. I think I can see some of his footprints.

N.S.

Pages ii-iii: Big Bend's desert bursts into bloom mere days after a spring rainstorm.

Page vi: Bold texture of cannas' leaves provides backdrop to purple coneflowers and reseeding larkspurs at the Antique Rose Emporium, Independence (Brenham).

Page ix: Ocotillo celebrates a spring rain against Casa Grande in Big Bend National Park.

Page x: Roadside meadow, Central Texas in April

Page xi: Sawtooth Mountain, Davis Mountains State Park

*This page: Mexican feather grass (*Nassella tenuissima*)*

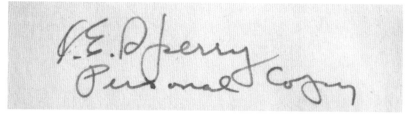

My prized possession: my dad's personal copy of the book he co-authored.

Basics

"Basics?" You're hoping this book will show you the way to the Texas gardening Promised Land, and I label my first chapter "Basics?" Well, that doesn't sound very exciting. But let me lay just a little groundwork before our journey takes off. I promise – there's plenty of good stuff to come. Follow me!

South of the Denison Dam at Lake Texoma

I'm a Native Texan. Born in San Antonio (just like this book), raised in Alpine (OK, for only two early years), Bryan and College Station. I've traveled the entire state, and I've lived my professional life in DFW as I continued to travel (and write and broadcast) across Texas. It's my opinion, and I'll bet you agree, Texas is a pretty fabulous place.

Gardening abounds here in Texas. Oh, it's different to garden in Borger or Beaumont, Houston or El Paso. Every region has its own assets – and liabilities. You'll see that as we lay out descriptions, maps, charts, lists and zones for each part of Texas. We'll get into all the specifics, but our travels have to begin with the first simple steps. I call them the "Basics."

This chapter, brief as it is, will be about building blocks – the pieces that fit together to make up the science of gardening in Texas. There are important concepts and facts that encompass all of our other chapters. They're so critical to our success that they demand explanation before we proceed any further.

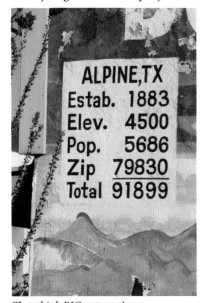

Omer, young Neil and Lois Sperry

They think BIG out west!

Mural circa 2004
Alpine, Brewster County, Texas

Alpine is the county seat of the largest county in Texas. Surrounded by mountain peaks, it is the heart of the Big Bend Country. After I was adopted at age 6 weeks, Alpine was our family's home for two years. It remains one of my favorite places to be!

Collin County barn, circa 2008

It Begins with Our (Crazy) Weather

I've observed that when people move to Texas from some other part of the world, they tend to hang onto their old gardening calendars. "I planted my peas in early May up North, so I'll plant them in May here in Texas." What they don't realize (but soon will) is that they should be *harvesting* those peas in May, not thinking about *planting* them then. Give up that old calendar or the seasonal tips in the big national magazines, and read on just a little more. The next section of the book will give you monthly gardening guides (for Texas!), and our planting charts for flowers and vegetables in later chapters will fine-tune the information still more.

I love weather statistics. (I know – you always wanted to meet somebody odd like that.) Texas is replete with weather phenomena. I offer examples:

- It rarely freezes in Brownsville, yet on February 8, 1933, the temperature dropped to -23 F in Seminole. Just 42 months later (August 12, 1936), it was a toasty 120 F in Seymour. And those two towns aren't that far apart (only 205 miles). A 143-degree swing! It's tough to be a native plant in Texas!

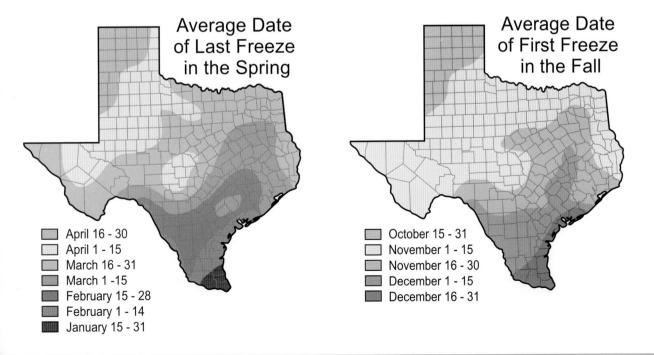

Average Date of Last Freeze in the Spring

- April 16 - 30
- April 1 - 15
- March 16 - 31
- March 1 -15
- February 15 - 28
- February 1 - 14
- January 15 - 31

Average Date of First Freeze in the Fall

- October 15 - 31
- November 1 - 15
- November 16 - 30
- December 1 - 15
- December 16 - 31

Dynamite red crape myrtles are framed by an Allen, Texas, rainbow in June.

Mist settles in after summer shower.

Texas rainstorms can soak the soil quickly.

Clay soils drain slowly in Lucas.

- My dad was a range ecologist with Texas A&M, and as we drove those long miles from College Station to Mentone or Valentine or Paisano Pass for his work, he would remind me that you lose, on average, one inch of rain for every 17 miles you go west in Texas. Rainfall averages 65 inches in Orange compared to 9.7 inches in El Paso – fractional inches matter in El Paso. (By the way, that distance is 852 miles, so it looks like my dad was right – as usual.)

- Starting in the Rio Grande Valley and heading halfway to Canada, you lose about a week on each end of the growing season for each 100 miles you go north. (Brownsville to Dalhart: 862 miles. That's about nine weeks later for spring plantings in the Panhandle and nine weeks earlier for their first freeze in the fall.) That's not a precise measurement, but you'll be amazed at how often that little week-per-hundred-miles tidbit will come in handy.

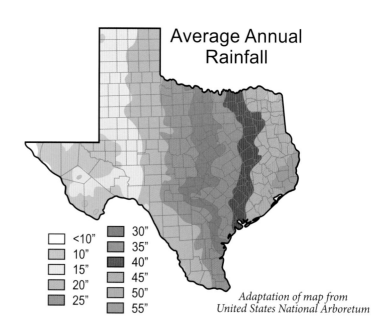

Average Annual Rainfall

<10"	30"
10"	35"
15"	40"
20"	45"
25"	50"
	55"

Adaptation of map from United States National Arboretum

Hardiness Zones

I warned you that a bunch of this stuff was going to be very important. Well, get ready to plow into some really critical information if you're going to call yourself a Lone Star Gardener. Professor Neil on duty here, and I've brought my facts and maps.

The United States Department of Agriculture periodically issues Hardiness Zones maps, most recently with the help of researchers at Oregon State University. Built on exhaustive stores of data, the maps show the minimum temperatures that might be expected in each county of the U.S. each winter.

I've chosen to show both the most recent 2012 Hardiness Zones map and the 1990 map it replaced. It's just one guy's personal opinion, but those 22 years between maps included many very warm winters, and because the data have been collected only since the 1930s, those warm winters may have skewed the figures. You'll notice that some of the northern boundaries of the Zones have shifted northward by several counties from the 1990 map to the 2012 one.

Garden Tip

Beware of choosing plants from much colder (far northern) Hardiness Zones. While they may be tolerant of any winter weather Texas might have, they frequently can't handle our prolonged summer heat. You're usually safest if you choose plants from your Zone and the one or two to the north of you. (Example: If you're in Zone 7, plants listed for Zones 7, 6 and 5 should be your best bets.) Your nurseryman will be able to help you fine-tune your choices.

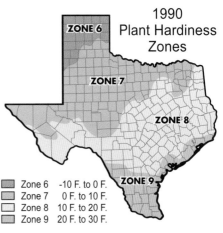

1990
Plant Hardiness
Zones

Zone 6   -10 F. to 0 F.
Zone 7   0 F. to 10 F.
Zone 8   10 F. to 20 F.
Zone 9   20 F. to 30 F.

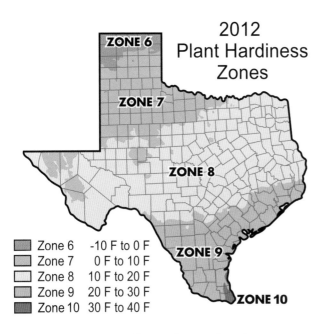

2012
Plant Hardiness
Zones

Zone 6   -10 F to 0 F
Zone 7   0 F to 10 F
Zone 8   10 F to 20 F
Zone 9   20 F to 30 F
Zone 10   30 F to 40 F

Ranges of average lowest annual temperatures Compiled by U.S.D.A.

Note from Neil

If you live near the northern edge of one of the Zones in the 2012 map, compare where your county was shown in 1990. Be cautious in choosing plants that are marginally hardy to your area under the 2012 ratings. One severe winter could cause major plant loss.

Aspidistra plantings, one left uncovered and the other covered with frost cloth December through late February.

Windbreak grows near Sul Ross State University in Alpine.

Nandina berries find themselves encased in ice.

Navigating the Hardiness Zones Map

The chapters that follow offer Hardiness Zone ratings for hundreds of plant varieties. Here's how to use those charts and this map to best advantage:

- Locate your county and determine which Hardiness Zone you are in.

- As you buy landscape plants, choose only types listed as being winter-hardy in your Zone or northward. (Example: if the map shows your county to be Zone 7, choose only plants listed as Zones 7, 6, 5 and colder.)

- Limit the numbers of plants that you try from warmer Hardiness Zones, since those plants will be at greater risk of damage or death in average winters in your area.

"Hardening" vs. "hardened"

In answering gardeners' questions (*lots* of questions!) since I got out of college, I've found that there is great confusion between these two terms. I'm going to give you the horticultural explanation, then I'll give you a more familiar comparison to which you'll probably relate.

In gardening, these terms refer to a plant's ability to withstand a weather extreme such as heat, wind, or (usually) cold. "Hardening" is a progressive event, where the plant becomes toughened to progressively more challenging conditions over a course of repeated exposures. "Hardened" means that the process has been completed, that the plant is as resilient as it can ever become.

Now, to bring all that to human terms. Remember how cold that first 60-degree Friday night football game was in September? How much more comfortable might that same 60 F temperature have felt in the playoffs in mid-December? You have it in you to be a "hardy" gardener, but you usually aren't "hardened" when the first cold front of the fall rolls through. Plants, like gardeners, toughen up with repeated exposures.

Oleander tissues are frozen (again).

Holding winter damage to a minimum

Even in balmy old Texas, winters can occasionally get dicey. Smart gardeners start planning years ahead. Here are some of the things that they've learned and that you can do to lower the winter risks to your plants.

- Choose plants that are winter-hardy to normal winters in your area (as per the Hardiness Zone ratings).

- Keep plants properly watered, especially when cold temperatures are expected. Dry plants suffer more serious cold injury.

- Mulch planting beds. Mulches don't really "keep the soil warm." It's more that they moderate the rate at which soil temperatures fluctuate. Rapid temperature changes in plant tissues (as in human tissues) are most damaging.

- Avoid practices that might stimulate premature new growth during winter warm spells, most notably late fall pruning and fertilizing.

- Cover vulnerable plants prior to the arrival of cold with a lightweight frost cloth. Secure it to the ground with weights or pegs. Leave it in place until the extreme cold subsides. It can remain over the plants for many weeks without damaging them if necessary. Do not cover plants with plastic film. It heats up too rapidly on sunny, cold mornings. Plants thaw too rapidly, and they almost always end up with scorched leaves.

- Wait to remove browned tissues until you can determine the extent of the dieback. Sometimes new leaves will replace old, dead leaves. Other times, you'll have to trim plants back completely to the ground. You usually can't tell until it's almost time for new spring growth.

Bark mulch not only makes a good path, but it also protects plants from weather extremes.

Pine bark mulch is excellent.

Gardenia twig has been damaged by cold.

Frost cloth protects large planting of aspidistra in author's landscape.

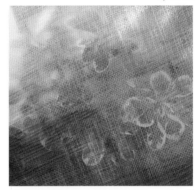

Variegated pittosporum is alive and well thanks to protection of frost cloth.

Texas Soils: How to Survive Them

Still with me? You've made it through weather, and now we're into everyone's favorite: the topic is "soils." (Stifle that yawn!)

Texas soils are as varied as our people. We have acidic (East Texas) soils, and we have alkaline (most of the rest of Texas) soils. Brazos River bottomland soil is hundreds of feet deep, and there are parts of Texas where you can't find any soil at all (any town with "rock" in its name). Rich and highly organic soils in the prairies and forests contrast with white sands and chalky caliche. Yep. We pretty much have 'em all. And you're going to have to figure how best to cope with what came with your property.

Texas soils aren't always ideal.

Soil depth

As you begin your gardening endeavors, be sure that you have enough soil for the plants that you want to grow. Smaller plants with more limited root systems (turfgrass, annuals, perennials, vegetables, groundcovers and small shrubs) can get by with as little as 12 to 24 inches of soil. Larger plants need deeper soils. For large shrubs and small trees, you'll want to have up to 3 feet of topsoil, and for large trees, 4 to 6 feet is ideal.

If your house is sitting atop a bald knob, with little more than a skiff of what someone calls "soil," does that mean that you can't garden there? Not at all, but it does mean that you'll have to be much more careful in choosing the types of plants that you grow under those circumstances, and in how you maintain them. If you're unable to haul in more topsoil, you may be limited to smaller species of plants (less extensive root systems) and you may find yourself committed to more frequent waterings and feedings.

Piles of compost and landscaping mix ready as crew heads home.

Raised beds

The old axiom is that you can always add water when the soil is dry, but it's much more difficult to remove water when the soil is too wet. Elevating beds, even by only a few inches, assures quick drainage for better root growth.

But wait! There's more! If you're in one of those shallow-soil spots we referred to earlier, building beds above-grade gives you that much more soil in which to garden. Either way, raised beds are great investments.

Raised beds provide drainage, set plants off visually.

Best soil amendments

Wherever you live, the best thing you can add to improve your soil is organic matter. It comes in many different forms. For best results, use a blend of compost, well-rotted manure, finely ground pine bark mulch, sphagnum peat moss and others. As the organic matter decays, it will help loosen tight clay soils. It will help sandy soils hold moisture and nutrients.

If you are preparing a flower or vegetable garden's soil, add 5 or 6 inches of organic matter and rototill it into the existing topsoil to a final depth of 12 to 15 inches. Additionally, if you are amending a heavy clay soil, add 1 inch of expanded shale along with the organic matter. Each time that you rework the bed, rototill 2 or 3 inches of additional organic matter into the ground to maintain the tilth of the garden. Replenish the expanded shale every three or four years.

This intensity of soil building is primarily intended for smaller plants such as flowers, vegetables, dwarf shrubs and groundcovers. It is impractical to think of doing this amount of work for shade trees and large shrubs. Their root systems are far too extensive. In those cases, choose types that can survive the soils you can provide for them.

Soil pH, its effects and remedies

Acidity and alkalinity are measured on a scale of 1 (extremely acidic) to 14 (extremely alkaline). Neutral is 7. Minor elements such as iron become insoluble in alkaline soils, so iron chlorosis (deficiency) may develop. You can add agricultural sulfur to acidify alkaline soils for small plants. However, that's not practical when trees and large shrubs are involved. To the other extreme, when soils are too acidic, lime will raise the pH.

Tiller poised to blend organic matter into native topsoil.

Garden Tip

Expanded shale is a clay-based material that is heated until the grains pop. It becomes a very stable and porous soil amendment that has been shown, through Texas A&M research and years of applied use by Texas horticulturists, to loosen tight clay soils much better than sand. So, for any old recommendation calling for "washed brick sand" in a planting mix, substitute an equal amount of expanded shale. It's available both in bag and in bulk from nursery and landscape contractor suppliers.

Fringe flower with iron deficiency

Severe iron deficiency on pin oak

Pin oaks declining due to iron deficiency

SPECIAL TLC FOR ACID-LOVING PLANTS

Azaleas need special bed preparation in much of Texas.

Most plants that we grow prefer slightly acidic soils (pH of 6 to 6.5). Some, such as gardenias, azaleas, camellias, wisterias, blueberries, water oaks, pin oaks, dogwoods and many pines require strongly acidic soils (pH of 4.5 to 5.5). Iron becomes insoluble in alkaline soils and with alkaline irrigation water, so these are the plants that first show signs of iron deficiency when they're grown in alkaline conditions. They'll exhibit yellowing leaves with dark green veins, most prominently on the newest growth at the ends of the twigs.

Where it's practical, as with azaleas and gardenias, you might consider planting acid-loving plants in beds filled to 18 to 20 inches deep with only organic matter (equal parts of sphagnum peat moss and finely ground pine bark mulch). Sure, you'll have to redo the beds and replace the plants after 10 or 15 years, but the results in the meantime will be lovely.

A critical fact to remember: *This extreme soil replacement program is practical only for plants that stay relatively small. If you're gardening in alkaline soils, you'll be wasting a bunch of time, effort, hope and money if you plant large shrubs and trees that require acidic soil. About the time the plants grow and begin to attain good size, their temporarily acidic planting mix will have run out of steam, and iron deficiency will inevitably take over. Adding iron won't solve the problem – you wouldn't be able to supply enough. Your only solution will be to replace the plants, that is, start over.*

FAQ

Q Is it good practice to add fireplace ashes to my garden?

A Only if your native soil is acidic (East Texas, for example). Ashes are highly alkaline, and that is not a good thing to be adding to soils that already tend to be alkaline anyway. It's better to send the ashes off to the landfill.

Visit Neil's FAQ pages at www.neilsperry.com

Choose the Best Fertilizers

It's time for a short reading lesson: how to navigate your way through the large and small print on plant food labels.

- Products sold as fertilizers in Texas are required by law to list a precise measure of their contents. It will be expressed as the "analysis" of the product.

- Three numbers will make up each product's analysis. They are required to be conspicuously visible on the bag, box or bottle.

- Those numbers are percentages. They identify the percent of nitrogen (for leaf and stem growth), phosphorus (for roots, flowers and fruit) and potassium, or potash (for summer and winter hardiness) that the product contains.

- If trace elements are included, they will be listed on the label as well.

- If other non-nutritional components such as insecticides or herbicides are included in the product, the label must tell you that, too.

- The label will also show the total weight or volume of the container, and it should give you instructions for proper application of the fertilizer.

Fertilizer "analysis" vs. fertilizer "ratio"

Here comes the math class! The product's "analysis" is the actual percentage of the three major nutrients. Let's use 20-5-10 as a real-life example. Add the numbers and you'll determine that that product is comprised of 35 percent actual nutrients.

The "ratio" is the proportion of one nutrient to the next and to the third. Divide our 20-5-10 analysis by 5, and you have a fertilizer with a 4-1-2 ratio. You would have the same 4-1-2 ratio with a 16-4-8 product, although you would need to apply 25 percent more of the 16-4-8 to get the same total amount of nutrients you would be applying with the 20-5-10. Still with me?

Soil tests

So now that you've had your reading lesson (fertilizer labels) and math class (understanding analyses and ratios), your soil gets to take the test for you!

To monitor the progressive changes brought about by your feeding program, have your landscape and garden soils tested every couple of years through the Texas A&M Soil Testing Laboratory or other reliable agency. Basic tests will usually indicate relative nutrient levels of the major elements, soil pH and accumulations of mineral salts. More extensive tests can be performed when necessary.

Oh, this part is important! Don't be surprised if your soil test results suggest low levels of nitrogen and extremely high levels of phosphorus and potassium. Phosphorus is slowly soluble, so it tends to accumulate in soils, particularly in clays.

The soil test will very possibly indicate that there are excessive levels of phosphorus and that you should use only a high-nitrogen or even an all-nitrogen fertilizer.

Add only nitrogen? To your *prize* tomato or rose garden? That's really shocking the first time you see that recommendation for a garden where you might otherwise have been tempted to apply one of the highly marketed flower-producing or fruit-setting plant foods. But you've paid for the test. Trust its results.

A Fact from Soil Science

Plants cannot and do not differentiate whether a fertilizer is "organic" or "inorganic." Nutrients enter plants' roots in elemental form in aqueous solution.

Learn to read the analysis of contents on fertilizer packaging.

Garden Tip

Ever hear the term "complete and balanced" referring to a fertilizer? It's actually two terms that may or may not apply simultaneously. A "complete" fertilizer contains N, P and K – all three major elements (without regard to relative amounts of each element). A "balanced" fertilizer contains equal amounts of the elements. So in reality, a fertilizer can be "complete" without being "balanced," but it cannot be "balanced" without being "complete." A product labeled as 20-20-20 would be a "complete and balanced" fertilizer. You might use a plant food like that for container plants or in sandy loam soils.

Q How often should I water my plants?

A For all my career, I have told people that that is the one question I will never be able to answer with any certainty. Plants are like people. No two people drink the same amounts of water daily. In fact, most individuals don't even drink the same amount of water from one day to the next. There are too many inconsistencies in our lives.

With plants, those variables include temperature, wind, humidity, sun/clouds, types of soil, types of plants, growth rate and more. Learn to watch your plants and their soil. They'll give you the clues to their water needs. Stick your finger into the ground or container. If the soil is dry an inch or more down, it's probably time to consider watering.

Garden Tip

With some plants, you dare not let them reach the point of severe wilting. Caladiums will lose leaves and not recover, and vegetable produce can be severely damaged ("hot" radishes and onions, bitter lettuce, and blossom-end rot on tomatoes and peppers).

What about those "trace elements"?

Most high-quality lawn and garden fertilizers contain trace element packages, and those supplements may be all that is needed. There are two common exceptions.

First, iron deficiency (yellowed leaves with dark green veins, most evident on the new growth at the ends of the branches) will be fairly common in alkaline soils, so you may need to add iron. If you add sulfur at the same time that you're adding the iron, the sulfur will lower the soil pH, and in doing so, it will keep the iron soluble for uptake by the plants' roots. Second and more specifically, pecans benefit from applications of zinc spray to counteract tip dieback known as pecan rosette. Otherwise, you probably won't need to add trace elements unless a soil test shows need.

Watering and Water Conservation

Many of us overwater our plants. That's not good for the plants, nor is it good for our state's limited water reserves. Here are some guidelines to help you enjoy gardening and conserve water at the same time.

- Choose water-efficient, drought-tolerant plants. That doesn't mean that you're limited to cacti and succulents, but it does mean that plants that "like wet feet" probably won't be your best choices unless your property has naturally occurring boggy areas.

Color Guard yucca is water-efficient.

Oakleaf hydrangeas are wilted due to exposure to sun, not because they are dry.

Proper use of water is every Texan's responsibility.

Garden Tip

If you are counting on an automatic sprinkler system, have a "smart" controller, also known as an ET (evapotranspiration) controller, installed. It will allow you to set each station based on the soil type, sun/shade, slope, type of plants being grown and other cultural considerations. The controller will also have some type of access to weather data such as temperature, wind and recent rainfall. Smart controllers are affordable, and they typically repay the cost of installation within just a couple of years. If you don't have a smart controller, leave the timer set to the "Manual" mode unless you're out of town for an extended period.

Water late in day to avoid evaporation.

- Learn to recognize early signs of dry plants. Wilting alone isn't an adequate indicator. Some plants will wilt even when their soils are still moist. That could be because they're suddenly exposed to hot sunlight after several days of cloudy conditions.

- When it's time to water, soak the soil deeply. That will encourage deeper root growth, which in turn will improve resistance to drought. Light sprinklings encourage shallow surface roots. After you have soaked the ground, wait until you see the symptoms of dry plants before you water again.

- Water in the early morning hours. There is less wind then, so there will be more uniform coverage and less loss to evaporation.

- Invest in soaker hoses and drip irrigation lines, where possible and practical. They are always the most water-efficient ways to irrigate.

- Keep lawn sprinkler sprays low to the ground, and choose large droplet sizes whenever you can. Again, that will provide more uniform coverage and less loss to evaporation. Special low-throw heads are available for automatic sprinkler systems as well.

- Mulch all bare ground in landscape and garden beds to limit the soil-to-air contact. That will reduce evaporation, and the mulches will also slow the runoff, so that more water will soak into the ground.

FAQ

Q How much mulch should I put out on top of my beds?

A Normally not more than 1 inch. Were you to spread more than 1 inch of organic mulch on top of the ground, it would possibly soak up too much water during irrigations and rain showers. Add more than 1 inch of gravel or other inorganic mulch, and it will look like you piled it on heavily.

Too much mulch actually causes trees harm.

Garden Tip

If you're applying mulch around a newly planted tree, don't pile it up several inches thick around the trunk. "Mulch volcanoes" steal water from the plants' roots. They can even be homes to rodents, insects and decay organisms that could damage the trees.

Mulching: Essential for Texas!

A mulch is a material used to cover the soil for any of a variety of reasons:

- To moderate rate of soil temperature change. Mulches don't "keep the ground from freezing" in winter. They prevent rapid and damaging freeze/thaw cycles. They keep the sun from heating up the exposed soil too rapidly in the summer.

- To reduce soil-to-air contact. In doing so, mulches reduce the rate of evaporation from moist ground into the dry summer air.

- To slow development of weeds. Mulches prevent germination of weed seeds, and they also keep weeds from receiving adequate light.

- To lessen run-off during rainstorms. Mulches slow the water flow, and that increases the amount that soaks into the soil.

- To reduce splashing. Without mulches, rainfall would splatter all over flowers and produce, even onto the house.

- To add a finishing touch to the landscape and garden. Most mulches look good!

Choosing the right mulch

- Organic mulches such as pine bark and hardwood mulches, compost, pine straw and even pecan hulls bring a wonderfully natural look to their surroundings. As they decay, they also improve the garden soil. They're comparatively lightweight, and they're easy to spread. It's easy for many of us to make a case in their support.

- Inorganic mulches such as gravel, lava rock, ground rubber tires and even roll-type weed-blocking fabrics don't look as natural and they can be very heavy, but on the positive side, they also hold up almost indefinitely – there is little or no decay. Beware of white stone (reflects sun's rays onto the backs of tender plant leaves) and black stone (soaks up hot summer sun excessively).

You're done! "Basics" training is completed, and you're ready to move on to the fun phases of gardening. But look back here once in a while, just to keep your mental tools sharp.

January

This month begins with anticipation and it ends with the start of the early spring rush. Enjoy it while things are still peaceful. Take a breath, and start planning for warmer days to come.

Garden art at rest in winter

Magnum Pink Shades pansy

Plant of the Month

Pansies are stars of our mid-winter gardens. Their history in Texas dates back beyond Grandma's era, when they were grown in the sandy soils of Lindale and shipped wrapped in wet newspapers via bus to nurserymen and landscapers all across the Lone Star State. Scores of varieties and mixes have been developed over the ensuing years. Small- and mid-sized varieties perform best in our gardens, as do their diminutive cousins, violas. Pansies and violas are our most cold-hardy winter annuals, suitable for beds and containers.

Garden Tip

Plants that are over-wintered in garages usually do not fare well due to cold conditions and low light levels. South windows, sunrooms and greenhouses are far better places to maintain them.

FAQ

Q Do "grow lights" work well for starting seedlings indoors?

A They can, but you must keep the tubes very near the young plants (within 3 or 4 inches). Keep them on for 18 hours per day. A sunny windowsill might be better, and a bay window or greenhouse would be better still. Grow most types cool (60 to 65 degrees), to keep them from getting lanky.

Visit Neil's FAQ pages at www.neilsperry.com

Planting List for January

- Seeds to produce spring flower and vegetable transplants for your garden. Most types do best with full sun and cool temperatures (60 to 65 degrees).

- Tulips, Dutch hyacinths and other spring bulbs (e.g., tulips that you have been pre-chilling in the refrigerator) very early in month into well-prepared beds. Close plantings (3 or 4 inches) give best impact.

- Cool-season annuals. Pansies, pinks, snapdragons, ornamental cabbage and kale. South Texans can also include English daisies, calendulas, petunias, sweet alyssum, ornamental Swiss chard, Iceland poppies, stocks and larkspurs.

- Locally recommended fruit and pecan trees, grapes and blackberries from containers or as bare-rooted plants. Check the Texas A&M "Aggie Horticulture" website for the latest variety recommendations.

- Asparagus from dormant 2-year-old roots. Plant roots 5 to 6 inches deep into well-prepared and highly organic soil.

- Snap peas and onions (mid-month in South Texas and by late in month in North Texas). Early planting is essential to avoid late-spring heat.

- Trees and shrubs. Digging and relocating of established trees and shrubs must be done during winter dormant season. Dig with ball of soil intact, and replant at the original depth.

Pruning Tasks of January

- Crape myrtles and other summer-flowering shrubs and vines. Never "top" crape myrtles. It does not improve their flowering, and it ruins their natural form forever.

- Evergreen shrubs as needed to reshape and remove damage. Avoid formal shearing whenever possible. Wait to prune spring-flowering shrubs until they have finished blooming.

- Shade trees. Remove dead or damaged branches. Have a certified arborist remove branches that are large or high in the trees.

- Mistletoe. Remove the parasite from tree limbs each winter, just as young clumps are starting to establish. There are no effective consumer sprays to control mistletoe. You will be forced to do more major (and less successful) pruning if you put off the removal.

- Peaches and plums. Remove strongly vertical shoots to encourage horizontal branching. Maintain bowl-shaped trees 10 or 12 feet tall.

- Apples to remove vertical shoots ("watersprouts"). Pears, pecans, figs and pomegranates need little pruning except to remove damaged or dead branches.

- Grapes to remove 80 to 85 percent of cane growth and maintain scaffold branches along supports. This keeps vine size manageable, and it also ensures maximum fruit size and quality.

It's Time to Feed

- Winter annual color plants. Apply diluted, water-soluble, high-nitrogen food to flower beds every two to three weeks during warm spells.

- Late-winter perennial color plants. Violets, hellebores and other cool-season bloomers with high-nitrogen or all-nitrogen fertilizer.

- Greenhouse plants with diluted high-nitrogen, water-soluble fertilizer weekly. Houseplants monthly with same food.

- Fescue lawns, also temporary ryegrass turf, with all-nitrogen food late in month to promote early growth.

- Asparagus beds with all-nitrogen fertilizer late in month to encourage vigorous new shoots.

- Plants that have suffered root loss or damage. Apply liquid root stimulator. Repeat monthly for new balled-and-burlapped or bare-rooted trees and shrubs for one year.

Garden Tip

Our best houseplants include some great plants with odd names. They include the various aglaonemas, sansevierias, pleomeles, dracaenas (except *D. marginata* – needs too much light), pony tail, spathiphyllum, pothos and vining philodendrons. (Shrub-form types that do not vine will need more light.)

A sunny outlook on winter

Garden Tip

Adding organic matter such as compost, bark mulch, rotted manure, leaf humus and sphagnum peat moss will be your best way of preparing any garden soil. Organic matter helps sandy soils retain moisture and nutrients, and it helps loosen tight clays. Avoid quack products with extravagant claims of "stimulating microbes" or "activating enzymes."

Colorful winter foliage and fruit of nandina

Garden Tip

Most urban landscapes of the past several decades have room for only one or two shade trees. If you plant too many trees, they end up ruining one another. If you're considering planting new trees to shade your house, know each tree's mature width. Most types need to be 35 to 40 feet from other trees – and from the roofline of your home.

Chinese photinia in full fruit in winter

Timely Troubleshooting

- Cold weather extremes. Frost cloth offers 4 to 8 degrees of protection. It also keeps blustery wind off the plants. Have pieces pre-cut and ready to drape over your plants. Store in bags for repeated use.

- Clover, dandelions, henbit, chickweed and other non-grassy winter weeds can be controlled with an application of a broadleafed weedkiller. Carefully follow label directions regarding temperature and rainfall.

- Scale insects. Hollies, euonymus, crape myrtles, camellias, oaks, pecans and fruit trees are all susceptible. You'll find the immobile adult scales affixed to leaves, twigs and branches. Apply horticultural oil spray. Read and follow label directions.

- Houseplant pests. Most probable types include mealybugs, scale insects and spider mites. Your nurseryman will help you identify them and find the best product to eliminate them. Do not expose the plant to freezing weather or direct sunlight while you treat. Your garage may be a suitable location.

- Sunscald. Apply tree wrap to trunks of Chinese pistachios, red oaks and other thin-barked trees for first two years to prevent sunscald and borer invasion.

Odd Jobs

- Mulch beds. Mulches moderate the rates at which soils freeze and thaw, reducing the likelihood of freeze damage. They also inhibit weed growth, and they conserve soil moisture.

- Take mowers, other power equipment in for repairs before spring rush.

- Work with landscape architect to develop plans for spring plantings.

- Have soils tested by Texas A&M Soil Testing Lab or other reputable service now.

- Water during dry spells. Cold damage is more severe for plants that are allowed to become too dry.

February

It can still be quite cold in February, so don't push forward too quickly. Finish the winter responsibilities, and then prepare for the spring.

Bright Lights Swiss chard

Plant of the Month

Narcissus, daffodils and jonquils start blooming this month in South and Central Texas, and they continue into March in North Texas. Their cheering flowers mark the coming end of winter and the promise of better weather soon to follow. However, not all plants in this group perform equally well after their first years. Small- and early-flowering varieties tend to colonize and rebloom better than the big, late-blooming hybrid types. Come fall planting season, concentrate your efforts on repeaters like Grand Primo, Ice Follies, Carlton, Geranium, Cheerfulness, Golden Cheerfulness, and Suzy.

Ice Follies daffodils rescued from an unusually late freeze

Garden Tip

Looking for localized gardening information on a specific fruit or vegetable crop? The Texas A&M Horticulture website is outstanding. Search for "Aggie Horticulture" plus the name of the crop, and you'll find a wealth of information on everything from asparagus to zucchini.

Naturalized jonquils in East Texas

Planting List for February

- Cool-season vegetables. Finish onion and snap pea plantings early in month. Cabbage, broccoli, Brussels sprouts and cauliflower, also Irish potatoes early in month in South Texas, mid-month in North Texas. Leafy and root vegetables (spinach, leaf lettuce, chard, carrots, radishes, turnips, beets and others) mid-month in South Texas, late in month in North Texas.

- Cool-season annual flowers. Pinks, snapdragons early in month. Larkspur, English daisies, sweet alyssum, ornamental chard, petunias, calendulas, Iceland poppies, stocks and others early in month in South Texas, later in month in North Texas.

- Summer- and fall-flowering perennials. Dig and divide mallows, gloriosa daisies, cannas, mums, fall asters and salvias before they start growing late in month.

- Established and native trees and shrubs. Dig carefully to hold soil in place around roots. Replant at the same depth, and trim to remove 40 to 50 percent of top growth to compensate for root loss.

- Fruit trees, grapes and berries. Independent retail garden centers and Texas-based mail order sources will have varieties recommended for your area. (See the Texas A&M AgriLife Extension horticulture website.) Prune trees by 50 percent after planting.

Pruning Tasks of February

- Bush roses. Remove half of top growth, both by reducing height and by removing weak, internal canes. Each cut should be just above a bud that faces out from the center of the bush to encourage open growth.

- Groundcovers. Beds of Asian jasmine, mondograss and liriope that are uneven can be cut at 4 or 5 inches with a line trimmer or mower early this month.

- Evergreen shrubs as needed to shape. If you need to reduce a plant's height, do so this month. Use lopping shears and hand pruners to achieve a more natural looking final result.

- Nandinas. Remove the tallest canes entirely to the ground this month. Leave a few shorter stems to nurse the plants back to compact and vigorous growth.

- Summer-flowering shrubs and vines, but only as needed to remove damaged or unwanted branches.

- Do not top crape myrtles as a way of reducing their height. Plants that have been previously so-mangled can be cut completely to the ground and retrained.

- Peach and plum trees early in month, before buds begin to swell. Remove vertical shoots and maintain bowl-shaped habit to 10 or 12 ft. tall and 15 to 18 ft. wide. Remove strongly vertical shoots ("water sprouts") on apples.

- Grapes by 80 to 85 percent. Maintain scaffold branching system along supports.

- Scalp lawn late in month to remove browned stubble. Drop the mower blade by one or two notches. Bag clippings and use in compost or as mulch. Do not send to landfill. Wear goggles and a good-quality respirator.

FAQ

Q How far back can I prune my shrubs, and when should I do it?

A That depends on the type of shrub, whether it's been pruned before, and how vigorous it is. If it would mean removing all of the foliage from a plant that has already been sheared many times, it probably would not be a good plan. You can usually maintain a plant at 75 to 80 percent of its natural size by pruning it selectively just before new buds begin emerging for spring. If you've done that and it's still too large, it's probably time to remove or relocate it.

Visit Neil's FAQ pages at www.neilsperry.com

Garden Tip

The biggest mistake people make in landscaping is in not having a plan – a roadmap for their journey. Draw it to scale, and consider everything – plants, "hardscaping," etc. It's critical that you know plants' mature sizes and growth forms.

Flowering quince

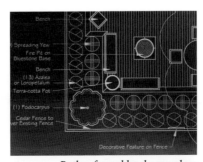

Rather formal landscape plans

Iceland poppies, pansies and sweet alyssum

Garden Tip

Using hybrid seed often results in several times the productivity. (Five or 10 times the weight in tomatoes with hybrids isn't uncommon.) Plus, hybrids are often bred to be disease-resistant, more flavorful, earlier, etc. If you're planting heirloom vegetables, be sure you include several hybrid types, too. You'll see the dramatic differences.

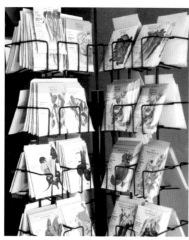

Start with top-quality seeds.

It's Time to Feed

- New trees and shrubs that were dug and transplanted. Apply a liquid, high-phosphorus root-stimulator fertilizer monthly for first year.

- Asparagus. Apply all-nitrogen fertilizer early in month to encourage strong new shoots. Harvest stalks for six to eight weeks, then feed again and allow the plants to grow untrimmed the rest of the year.

- Cool-season turf (fescue and ryegrass) late in month with an all-nitrogen fertilizer. Wait until late March (South Texas) or April to feed warm-season grasses.

- Pansies and other cool-season color plants. Apply high-nitrogen, water-soluble plant food every two to three weeks to keep plants growing and blooming vigorously.

Timely Troubleshooting

- Pre-emergent weedkiller granules for summertime weeds in late February in South Texas, early next month in North Texas. Repeat the treatment 90 days later for a full growing season of control.

- Cool-season non-grassy weeds, including clover, dandelions, henbit and chickweed. Apply broadleafed weedkiller spray when daytime temperatures will be above 70 degrees and when it is not expected to rain for 48 hours. Allow 10 to 15 days for complete kill. *(Note: it is too early to fertilize warm-season grasses. "Weed-and-feed" products are not a good idea.)*

- Scale insects on fruit trees, hollies, oaks, camellias, euonymus, crape myrtles and others. Apply horticultural oil spray very early in month. Follow label directions carefully for best results.

- Fruit and pecan trees. Apply insecticides and fungicides to protect produce from pests. Follow guidelines of Texas A&M (available online).

- Late frosts, freezes. Cover plants with frost cloth several hours before it turns cold. Secure the cloth to the soil to give your plants several degrees of protection. Wait until temperatures have risen well above freezing before you remove the covering.

March

March marks the beginning as gardens awaken. Your successes for the entire gardening year will be built on the foundation you lay during this pivotal month.

Solomon's seal is a handsome, low perennial for shade.

Every bluebonnet field comes complete with a child.

Plant of the Month

Bluebonnets begin to flower early in March in South Texas, finishing up in April along the Red River. Bluebonnets were named Texas state flower in 1901. Because the state is actually home to several species, the legislature voted in 1971 to select all five of the species as the official state flower. These annual lupines grow best in full sun and free of the competition of grasses. (That's why you usually find them growing natively in draws and on barren hillsides.) Buy acid-scarified seeds that have been specially prepared for the breakdown of their hard seed coats. That ensures quick and uniform germination as soon as the plantings are watered. Sow the seeds in late August or early September, so they can become established in fall and winter. Allow the plants to die and the seeds to dry before you mow down the stubble.

FAQ

Q Why doesn't my wisteria bloom?

A There seldom is one definitive answer. Wisterias need full or nearly full sun to bloom best. Do not prune them during the winter. (They set their flower buds in late fall, and winter pruning removes them.) Avoid high-nitrogen fertilizers near the plants from mid-summer on. You might try root-pruning by severing lateral roots with a sharpshooter spade 18 to 20 inches out from the trunk in September. That may trigger bud set.

Visit Neil's FAQ pages at www.neilsperry.com

Planting List for March

- Nursery stock is arriving in Texas nurseries daily. Buy while selections are best, especially if you're looking for an unusual or highly popular plant.

- Cool-season vegetables. Leafy and root crops must be planted early in month in northern half of state.

- Warm-season vegetables. Beans, tomatoes, corn, squash, cucumbers, melons and peppers should be planted one to two weeks after average date of last killing freeze in your area.

- Cool-season annual color. Use petunias, larkspurs, stocks, calendulas, sweet alyssum, foxgloves and other early-spring color plants for spots of color in pots and beds. Plant early in month for longest season.

- Warm-season annual color. Plant zinnias, marigolds, celosia, impatiens, wax begonias and coleus one to two weeks after average date of last killing freeze. Follow up with pentas, lantanas, moss rose, purslane, copper plants, purple fountaingrass, angelonias, fan flower and firebush as they become available, usually about one month after average date of last killing freeze.

- Summer and fall perennials. Know each plant's prime blooming season, height, width and color, and space accordingly into well-prepared garden soil. Plan for a sequence of color.
- New lawns. St. Augustine or bermuda from sod. Wait another month to plant bermuda from seed or zoysia from sod.

Pruning Tasks of March

- Scalp lawn early in month to remove winter-killed stubble. Wear respirator and goggles – it's a dusty job. (Note that scalping is optional – primarily aesthetic.)
- Evergreen shrubs before new growth begins. You can remove as much as 25 percent if you trim branch by branch with hand tools. Avoid formal shearing whenever possible.
- Spring-flowering shrubs and vines. Reshape immediately after these plants finish blooming.
- Trees to remove low-hanging, dead and damaged branches. To lessen likelihood of oak wilt fungus, do not prune oaks during spring,
- Recently dug and transplanted trees and shrubs by 30 to 40 percent to compensate for roots lost during the digging.

It's Time to Feed

- Lawngrasses. Apply a high-quality, all-nitrogen or high-nitrogen fertilizer to lawn mid-month in South Texas. Wait until early next month in North Texas.
- Pecans. Apply all-nitrogen food, 1 pound per inch of trunk diameter at ground level. Majority of fertilizer should be applied near the drip line (outer canopy of leaves). Repeat 30 and 60 days later.
- Trees, shrubs, groundcovers and vines. Apply lawn-type fertilizer to these plants as buds begin to swell. Avoid weed-and-feed products, since they can damage landscape plants.
- Spring-flowering trees, shrubs and vines. Wait to feed these plants until immediately after they finish blooming. Apply same lawn fertilizer to promote vigorous new growth this season.
- Annuals. Apply high-nitrogen or all-nitrogen fertilizer, as dictated by soil test, at half recommended rate one week after planting. Repeat at the recommended rate three weeks later.

Garden Tip

Large-fruiting tomato varieties such as Big Boy and Beefsteak are not productive in Texas gardens. They won't set fruit when night temperatures drop into the 60s, and they won't set when daytimes are over 90 degrees. Opt instead for small and medium-sized varieties.

Cool-season color of Lobelia Techno Blue

The best shade trees for large parts of Texas include live oak, Shumard red oak, chinquapin oak, bur oak, pecan, cedar elm and Chinese pistachio. Southern magnolias are also outstanding, just a bit slower. In East Texas, water oaks and willow oaks, too. All of these are large trees at maturity.

Syngoniums and wax begonias paired unexpectedly in a shade garden.

Garden Tip

When planting new trees and shrubs this season, remember that "heroic" soil preparation ought to be saved for small plants such as flowers, vegetables, groundcovers and low shrubs. When you're buying mid-sized and larger shrubs and shade trees (all with very large root systems), it's critical that you choose types adapted to your native soils.

- Perennials. Apply same lawn-type food to beds as growth begins. Water deeply after feeding.
- Patio pots, other container gardens. Apply diluted, water-soluble high-nitrogen fertilizer once a week.

Timely Troubleshooting

- Summer annual grassy weeds, including crabgrass and grassburs. Apply pre-emergent weedkiller granules two weeks prior to average last killing freeze date. Repeat 90 days later.
- Broadleafed (non-grassy) weeds. Mowing will remove many. Apply broadleafed herbicide spray containing 2,4-D to eliminate the others. Follow label directions carefully.
- Snails, slugs and pillbugs. These pests devour tender new growth. Sevin dust or snail/slug baits will control them.
- Caterpillars. Use *Bacillus thuringiensis* (B.t.) to control looping types ("inchworms"), including cabbage loopers and cankerworms (which hang from trees by single threads). Apply Sevin or B.t. to control all others.
- Fruit and pecans. Apply recommended insecticides and fungicides to prevent the common problems. Texas A&M spray guidelines are available online.
- Fire blight in pears, apples and other members of rose family. If you saw sudden die-back and blackening of twigs last spring, apply agricultural streptomycin when plants are in full bloom to lessen spread of the bacterium by bees.

Perennial candytuft is ideal for low borders.

Gardening Calendar
April

Set time aside to visit your favorite nurseries and botanic gardens several times this month. There's so much to see. It's the most fun a gardener has all year.

Riots of colors – they're the hallmark of coleus.

Plant of the Month

Lady Banksia rose was introduced into Texas gardens in the early 1800s, and it's still one of our finest choices for patio covers and fences. On its positive side, it's thornless, and it never shows traditional rose problems of black spot or powdery mildew. Down sides, perhaps, would be that it's not fragrant and it blooms only once each year (in April). It's a strong-growing plant, so give it a stout support and ample room (15 to 20 feet). It leans for its support, so you'll have to secure and train it properly from the outset. It must have full sun to bloom to its best potential.

Lady Banksia rose

Garden Tip

The potting soil you choose for your container garden is the foundation of your success. Try a soil that is 50 to 60 percent sphagnum peat moss, 25 to 30 percent pine bark, 10 to 15 percent perlite and 5 percent expanded shale.

Hardy amaryllis hybrid
Hippeastrum vittatum

Planting List for April

• Vegetables, including tomatoes, peppers, corn, beans, squash, cucumbers, melons and eggplant early in month in most of Texas, mid-month in Panhandle. Avoid large-fruiting tomatoes – they will not set fruit well in Texas' hot weather. Concentrate on small and mid-sized varieties instead.

• Herbs. Include attractive types such as sage, basil, parsley, rosemary, mint and thyme in color beds and pots. Others can be planted into vegetable garden.

• Summer annual color plants from 4-inch and quart pots. For sun: moss rose, hybrid purslane, trailing lantanas, Dahlberg daisies, cleome, fan flowers, pentas, firebush and angelonias for flowers, and purple fountaingrass, sun-tolerant coleus, copper plant, ornamental sweet potatoes and alternantheras for foliage. For shade: wax and Dragon Wing begonias and nicotianas for flowers, and caladiums and coleus for foliage.

• Perennials from quart and gallon pots. Know mature sizes, colors and blooming times to ensure the most attractive season-long arrangement.

• Roses from containers in bud and bloom. Earth-Kind® roses are those varieties that have been identified by Texas A&M as most environmentally responsible and requiring least maintenance.

- Turfgrasses. Bermuda from seed. Bermuda, St. Augustine, zoysia or buffalograss from sod. Ask plenty of questions, and do research ahead of time to choose best type for your needs.
- Nursery stock. Trees, shrubs, vines and groundcovers are in plentiful supply now. Let a Texas Certified Nursery Professional advise you as to plants' mature sizes and best types for your needs.

Pruning Tasks of April

- Mow lawn at recommended height. Letting grass grow tall weakens it.
- Spring-flowering shrubs and vines immediately after they finish blooming. Avoid formal shearing. Use hand shears, instead, to maintain natural form to the plants.
- Trees to remove lower branches that are casting excessive shade, causing turfgrass to struggle. To lessen chance of spreading oak wilt, do not prune oaks until mid-summer or mid-winter.
- Fall perennials to encourage branching. Included: Mexican bush salvia, fall asters and chrysanthemums.

It's Time to Feed

- Turf. Phosphorus accumulates in soils. Reliable soil tests usually call for an all-nitrogen fertilizer for clay soils and a high-nitrogen (4-1-2 ratio) fertilizer for sandy or loamy soils. Buy a high-quality product that has half or more of its nitrogen in slow-release form. Weed-and-feed products can be very risky if there are trees and shrubs nearby.
- Trees, shrubs, vines and groundcovers. The same all-nitrogen or high-nitrogen product you use on your turf will be fine.
- Vegetable and flower gardens. Use same product you're using on lawn and landscape plants. It will have instructions for rates of application for beds. Use a hand-held rotary spreader to distribute it.
- Container gardens. Apply a high-nitrogen, water-soluble plant food weekly. For sustained feeding, also apply timed-release product on soil surface.

FAQ

Q I didn't get my shrubs pruned in the winter like I wanted to. Can I still cut them back now, in the middle of spring?

A You can certainly trim them some, but if your goal is to do heavy pruning, you would be removing all of their new growth. That would set them back dramatically, and with some shrubs that have only marginal vigor left anyway, it might spell the end. Use lopping shears to remove the most unruly branches. Make your cuts flush with remaining branches so that no stubs will be visible. In terms of dramatic reduction of overall height or width, save that for early February so that the shrubs can put their full energy into new growth.

Visit Neil's FAQ pages at www.neilsperry.com

Garden Tip

Wind can blow new trees out-of-plumb unless they are staked and guyed carefully and tightly. Cables should be two-thirds of the way up the trunk, and the trunk should be padded.... Leave the guy wires in place for one to two years. If the tree has tipped, you must dig and reset it. Pulling or propping will not work.

Geranium

- Azaleas, gardenias, wisteria, hollies, ligustrums and other plants that are showing iron chlorosis – yellowing leaves with dark green veins, most prominent on newest growth at the tips of the branches. Use an iron/sulfur soil-acidifier product to correct the deficiency, and keep it off masonry or painted surfaces that could be stained.

Timely Troubleshooting

- Take-All Root Rot. This fungus causes St. Augustine to green up erratically or even die. Texas A&M research has shown that a 1-inch layer of sphagnum peat moss and the acidic layer it forms at the soil's surface will provide better control than any fungicide. Repeat as needed every two or three years.

- Black spot on roses. Lower leaves will yellow, then develop brown spots before the leaves fall entirely. Apply labeled fungicide, and repeat every seven to 10 days until summer.

- Snails, slugs and pillbugs. Apply labeled insecticide, or sprinkle bait around plants.

- Thrips. Tiny, sliver-shaped pests prevent roses from opening properly and cause browning around outer petals. They are visible within buds. A systemic insecticide can be used to prevent their outbreaks.

- Caterpillars, including cankerworms and cabbage loopers. Apply B.t. organic insecticide.

- Rose rosette virus. This fatal disease, for which there is no control, causes strong "bull canes" and abnormal bud development. It resembles damage of broadleafed weedkillers. Once confirmed, damaged plants must be removed and destroyed, roots and all, to keep the virus from spreading to other plants in the neighborhood.

Native wildflower Phlox drummondii

Gardening Calendar
May

May is transition time in Texas – spring into summer. Enjoy nature at its best. Plan for warm weather ahead, but relax enough to take in all you have already accomplished.

Victoria blue sage and pink pentas

Purple coneflower Mama Mia

Plant of the Month

I'm a big fan of purple coneflower (*Echinacea purpurea*). It's a dependable perennial that's been the object of much breeding work and varietal improvement over the past 10 to 20 years. First we saw a white form, then larger types and flowers with recurving petals. Most recently, our old lavender-pink favorite has shown up in every color of the sunset. Purple coneflower is actually a native wildflower along Texas highways. Garden forms tend to be short-lived perennials. They'll become crowded after a couple of years, at which point you'll want to dig and divide them, rework their soil and reset the divisions, all in the same day.

Garden Tip

Know your vegetable crops. Many should be harvested before they reach full maturity. Beans, squash, lettuce, cabbage, okra, etc., should be harvested when produce is half to three-quarters full size. Of course, tomatoes, peppers, corn, watermelons and others must be left on the plants until they're essentially full size and mature.

Sea hibiscus, a summer tropical

Planting List for May

- New lawns. This is the best month to plant new turf. Best choices for sun: bermuda, St. Augustine or zoysia. Best choices for shade: St. Augustine in southern two-thirds of state, fescue in Panhandle. (Both shade grasses require at least four to six hours of direct sunlight daily.)

- Trees, shrubs and other landscape plants. Have a landscape plan, and know each plant's potential size, then buy best plants for each purpose. Water by hand for first summer. Lawn irrigation will not be sufficient until roots are well established.

- Summer annual color. See list of best types in April planting tips. Buy "hardened" plants that are already acclimated to sun.

- Summer tropical annuals, including brugmansias, hibiscus, allamanda, mandevilla, Persian shield, crotons, plumbago and Gold Star esperanza.

- Summer- and fall-flowering perennials. Nurseries have good selections in quart and gallon containers. Buy types that will provide a sequence of continuous bloom.

- Summer vegetables. Plant sweet potatoes (sandy soils only), okra and southern peas early this month.

Pruning Tasks of May

- Spring-blooming shrubs and vines. Next year's flowers will be produced on shoots that develop this year.

- Shade trees. Remove low branches that cause visibility problems or that cast excessive shade on turf. Wait until mid-summer to prune oaks, to lessen likelihood of spreading oak wilt fungus.

- Peaches, plums. To produce highest quality, thin fruit very early in month to be 5 or 6 inches apart on the branches.

- Blackberries. Tip-prune new canes to encourage branching and to keep plants compact.

It's Time to Feed

- Turf. High-nitrogen or all-nitrogen fertilizer with half or more of that nitrogen in slow-release form.

- Trees, shrubs and groundcover beds. Apply same type of fertilizer as used on lawn. Be sure it does not contain a weedkiller.

- Annuals, perennials and vegetables. Apply the same all-nitrogen or high-nitrogen fertilizer unless a soil test suggests differently. Brush or wash granules off foliage, and water deeply after feeding.

- Pecans. If in lawn, fertilizer you're using for turf will suffice. Otherwise, apply all-nitrogen product, 1 pound per inch of trunk diameter. Apply near drip line and water deeply.

- Patio pots, hanging baskets. Apply water-soluble, high-nitrogen food with trace elements added. Repeat weekly. Supplement with encapsulated, timed-release fertilizer applied to soil surface.

Dwarf yaupon hollies topped by pots of hybrid purslane

It's amazing how sprinkler systems can develop problems over a winter. Heads become misaligned or even missing. Valves don't operate properly. Pipes may have been broken during winter's cold weather. You can do a quick inventory of your system's condition by running it through its stations manually. Look for problems, and repair the ones that you can. If more serious issues are found, schedule a visit from a licensed irrigation contractor soon – before the main summer watering season.

Monarda (bee balm)

Garden Tip

Plants are native only where they are found growing naturally. It's possible for a plant that is perfectly adapted in one location and growing natively there to be totally unsuited to soils just a mile or two away. I always recommend that people ask for "adapted" plants – native or otherwise.

Timely Troubleshooting

- Take-All Root Rot in St. Augustine. If turf is slow to green up for the spring, suspect TARR. Texas A&M research has shown that a 1-inch layer of sphagnum peat moss (any brand) applied over the lawn will give rapid results that are far more effective than any fungicide. Repeat every two or three years as needed.

- Black spot on roses. Yellowed lower leaves with large brown spots. Apply labeled fungicide. Keep foliage dry. When replanting, look for Texas A&M's Earth-Kind® roses that show superior resistance to common rose problems.

- Rose rosette virus. If you see strong-growing "bull canes" that flower abnormally, your plants may have this fatal virus. It is spread by a microscopic mite, and removing the plants (including roots) is your only remedy.

- Early blight on tomatoes. Lower leaves will develop fingerprint-sized yellow blotches. Disease will quickly progress up the stem, as older leaves turn brown and wither. Apply labeled fungicide, and keep foliage as dry as possible.

- Webworms in pecans, mulberries, persimmons and other trees. Use long-handled pole pruner to remove webs when they first appear (grapefruit-sized). Sprays are difficult to administer and not especially efficient. Be careful not to use pole pruner near power lines.

- Bagworms. These pests devour needles of junipers, arborvitae and cypress, among others. General-purpose insecticides or B.t. organic insecticide will eliminate them. Treat when they first begin feeding.

- Scale insects on crape myrtles, hollies, euonymus. Apply systemic insecticide Imidacloprid as drench around plants this month to limit extent of outbreaks.

- Non-grassy weeds. Apply a broadleafed weedkiller to eliminate clover, dandelions, dichondra, dollar weed, poison ivy and other unwanted plants. Read and follow label directions to ensure the best results.

- Nutsedge. Often called "nutgrass," it can be identified by its triangular stems. (Grass stems are round.) Apply Sedgehammer or Image according to label directions. Control is not fast, and you may need more than one application.

June

Plants are growing actively as June begins. By the end of the month, summer's stresses may be starting to take a toll. Give new plantings special attention during their first days and months in your garden.

Vitex and Tiger Swallowtail

Daylily Firestorm

Plant of the Month

Daylilies are Texas-tough, tried-and-true. From the handful of species and a few dozen original orange and yellow varieties that our grandparents grew, we're now blessed with tens of thousands of types in a huge and rich array of colors (every shade except blue), flower sizes/forms and repeat blooms. Daylilies have become truly mainstream perennials. The newest and most unusual varieties will always be sold from the gardens of private collectors. Watch for daylily society sales in large cities, usually in late September or October. Grow the plants in full sunlight and well-prepared garden soil, and their performance will only get better year after year.

FAQ

Q Why aren't my tomatoes setting fruit?

A There are a couple of possible reasons. Tomatoes are pollinated by vibration, primarily wind. If they're planted against a fence or other structure that blocks the wind, try thumping the flower clusters every couple of days to shake the pollen loose. Hopefully you're growing small and medium-sized types. Large-fruiting tomatoes like Big Boy and Beefsteak won't set fruit when temperatures climb into the 90s, regardless of whether you thump their clusters or not.

Visit Neil's FAQ pages at www.neilsperry.com

Planting List for June

- New lawns. Sow bermuda from seed, or plant any of the warm-season grasses (bermuda, St. Augustine, zoysia, buffalograss) from sod. Water daily (short intervals) for first couple of weeks to keep new grass from drying out.

- Landscape plants. Watch for end-of-spring sales. Have landscape plan in hand as you shop. Plant immediately. Hand-water the new plants every other day through the summer. Sprinkler irrigation will not be enough.

- Crape myrtles. Buy by variety and in full bloom, to be sure you're getting the colors you want. Know plants' mature sizes so you won't have to prune.

- Heat-tolerant annuals. Hybrid purslane, moss rose, pentas, lantanas, cleome, Dahlberg daisies, angelonias and gomphrenas for sun. Wax and Dragon Wing begonias and flowering tobacco for shade. For foliar color, use ornamental sweet potatoes, copper plants, firebush, purple fountaingrass, amaranthus and alternantheras for sun. For shade, include caladiums and coleus.

- Tropical annuals for flowers and foliage. Use tropical hibiscus, Gold Star esperanza, poinciana, allamanda, mandevilla and Mexican heather for flowers. Include bananas, variegated tapioca, variegated bougainvillea, sea hibiscus, ti plants and crotons for foliar color.

- Tomatoes. Sow seeds or take cuttings from your spring plants early in month, so that transplants will be ready the last week of June.

Pruning Tasks of June

- Shade trees if needed to admit more light to turf. Wait until mid-July to prune oaks, to minimize chance of spreading oak wilt fungus.

- Lawn. Mow at recommended height. If bermuda is browned for several days after each mowing, raise mower one notch. Drop mower back down for scalping next February.

- Spring-flowering perennials. Remove spent flowers, seed stalks and leaves as they brown. Garden mums to remove spring flowers and encourage regrowth for best fall bloom.

- Coleus, caladiums, lamb's ear, basil to remove flower stalks before buds open. These plants' flowers stop further leaf and stem growth.

- Blackberries. Remove canes that have just borne fruit by cutting completely to ground. Tip-prune new shoots to encourage branching.

It's Time to Feed

- Almost all lawn, landscape and garden plants. Apply all-nitrogen fertilizer in clay soils (which often accumulate phosphorus in excessive amounts) and high-nitrogen fertilizer in sandy soils. Half or more of nitrogen should be in a slow-release form. Water deeply after feeding.

- Hanging baskets and patio pots. Apply a timed-release food to soil. Use a high-nitrogen, water-soluble fertilizer weekly as well.

- Iron-deficient plants (yellowed leaves with dark green veins, most prominent on newest growth at ends of branches). Apply a combination iron/soil-acidifier product. Keep iron products off concrete and other surfaces that could be stained.

Garden Tip

When a red oak has yellowed leaves, it's usually due to iron deficiency, and it usually is a pin oak, not a true Shumard red oak. Adding iron is *not* a good option, as the tree will only need more every year. Buy oaks from local retailers.

Madame Legrelle ornamental pomegranate blooms beautifully each June.

Garden Tip

Buying new garden hoses? A 5/8-inch hose is best. Smaller hoses are cheap and don't hold up, and larger hoses are really heavy when full. Buy one that promises to remain flexible in cold weather. Measure distances in your yard and buy hoses 10 feet longer than necessary.

Garden Tip

"Smart controllers" monitor soil types, slopes, sun/shade, plant types, and other factors, then determine when sprinklers should run. They cost a few hundred dollars initially, but they usually pay for themselves within a year or two. They are among the best new products for gardeners.

Sunflower

Garden Tip

To cope with hot weather – (1) water deeply, less often; (2) hand-water new trees, shrubs; (3) pay special attention to needs of potted plants; (4) eliminate water-grabbing weeds; (5) mulch beds; (6) be on lookout for insects that attack stressed plants; (7) fertilize to perk up plantings.

Timely Troubleshooting

- Red oak, Chinese pistachio trunks. Wrap trunks of new trees to prevent sunscald and borer invasion.

- Crabgrass and grassburs. If you applied pre-emergent weedkiller granules to prevent these in March, you will need a second application in early to mid-June.

- Webworms in pecans, mulberries, persimmons. Remove with a long-handled pole pruner while webs are small (5 or 6 inches in diameter). Sprays are difficult and inefficient.

- Bagworms in redcedars and other junipers, cypress and arborvitae. Apply *Bacillus thuringiensis* (B.t.) or other control as soon as you see activity.

- Leafrollers. Apply systemic insecticide to prevent larvae of insects from rolling up foliage of vinca groundcover, pyracantha, sweetgum, cotoneasters, cannas and others.

- Lace bugs. Leaves of Boston ivy, pyracanthas, bur oaks, boxwood, azaleas and others turn tan with black specks on backs. Treat with systemic insecticide as preventive, before problem becomes unsightly.

- Chinch bugs in St. Augustine. Yellowed turf; soon thereafter dead spots appear, always in hot, sunny locations. Insects are BB-sized, black with irregular white diamonds on their wings. Apply a labeled insecticide immediately.

- Spider mites. Leaves of marigolds, beans, tomatoes and many other species will develop fine tan mottling. The nearly microscopic mites will be visible if you thump affected leaves over white paper. Apply labeled insecticide.

- Early blight on tomatoes. Lower leaves will develop bright yellow blotches. Keep foliage dry, and apply labeled fungicide.

- Blossom-end rot on tomatoes. Appears as sunken, browned tissues at the flower end of the fruit. Almost always caused by letting plants become excessively dry before watering.

July

Much of this month will be spent mulching, watering and protecting your plants. This is when it really pays to have used Texas-tough plants in your landscape and garden. Check on them daily, and care for them regularly.

Mixture of types of copper plants

Tuscarora crape myrtle

Plant of the Month

How could we have summer in Texas without our glorious crape myrtles! They date back to our earliest settlers, but most of the big news has happened in the past several decades. Prior to 1960, most crape myrtles were large shrubs, and they were sold only by color (red, pink, white, lavender and purple). But in the 1960s, nurseries began to offer dwarf crape myrtles and named varieties that allowed us to buy the same plant time after time. In the '60s, '70s and '80s, Dr. Don Egolf of the United States National Arboretum introduced selections from his hybridization program, and suddenly we were well stocked with glorious options. Others carried his work forward, and today we have scores of named varieties, and more arrive each year.

Garden Tip

Watering Tip 1: Learn to "read" your plants' symptoms of early drought. They may wilt, but some do not. Leaves may turn olive-drab or some other odd shade. Grass blades may roll or fold. Water at first signs of drought.

Eldorado Parkway, McKinney

Planting List for July

- Fall vegetables. Tomatoes and pumpkins by early July in North Texas and mid-July in South Texas. Peppers follow by two weeks. See August for rest of fall planting dates.

- Nursery stock. Trees, shrubs and groundcovers. Water new plants by hand every day or two during the rest of the summer and fall. Lawn irrigation alone will not be enough.

- Crape myrtles. Buy in full bloom so you'll get the exact colors you want. Plant types that match the space you have for them, so that you won't have to prune them to keep them in bounds.

- Lawngrasses. Bermuda, St. Augustine, zoysia and buffalograss. Water new plantings twice a day for short intervals to keep soil surface moist until the grass establishes good roots, usually in two to three weeks.

- Heat-tolerant annuals. Choose plants that have been acclimated to hot, sunny conditions at the nursery. Moss rose, hybrid purslane, trailing lantana, purple fountaingrass, firebush and copper plant.

Pruning Tasks of July

- Blackberries. Remove past spring's fruiting canes if you have not done so already. To encourage compact growth, tip-prune new shoots that are developing.

- Spring perennials. Remove dead foliage and spent flower and seed stalks.

- Annuals. Remove dead or dying plants and replace with other species. Pinch growing tips from lanky annual and perennial plants, including basil, coleus, wax begonias, chrysanthemums and Mexican bush sage.

- Trees. Remove dead or damaged branches. Remove lower limbs that are casting excessive shade onto lawn. Oaks can be pruned now, since oak wilt is not active. Apply pruning sealant to cut surfaces on oaks.

- Lawns. Mow at recommended height. Allowing grass to grow taller does not improve its vigor. If you find you are exposing browned stem stubble each time you mow bermuda turf, raise the mower one notch now. Lower it again for scalping next February.

It's Time to Feed

- Lawn, landscape and garden plants. With frequent watering, nutrients will be depleted quickly. Use all-nitrogen fertilizer for clay soils and high-nitrogen food for sandy soils. Water deeply after applying.

- Patio pots, hanging baskets and other container plants. Apply water-soluble, high-nitrogen fertilizer weekly. Supplement with a high-nitrogen, timed-release product.

- Iron deficiency. Symptoms include yellowed leaves with dark green veins, most prominent on newest growth (ends of branches). Use iron additive with sulfur soil-acidifier. Keep iron products off masonry and painted surfaces to avoid staining.

Crotons, vivid summer tropicals

FAQ

Q Why are my fruitless mulberry, cottonwood and catalpa trees dropping so many leaves?

A Large-leafed trees always produce more leaves in our cool, moist spring conditions than they are able to sustain during the heat of mid-summer. As soon as the humidity drops and temperatures climb into the 90s, you can expect these fast-growing trees to start turning yellow, oldest leaves (lowest points on the branches) first. It happens even if you water them properly. They just can't pull water through their systems fast enough to meet all of their needs. Assuming there are no other problems, your trees should be fine.

Visit Neil's FAQ pages at www.neilsperry.com

Garden Tip

Seeking a "tropical look" around a pool or patio? Bright colors help, to be sure, but so will varied textures. Use large-leafed plants, then contrast them with smaller-leafed types for interest.

Pink tropical hibiscus

Garden Tip

Everyone worries about slowing the cold blasts of north winds in winter, but remember that you want just the opposite in the summer. Plant shrubs for privacy, but don't stop the flow of southerly breezes. Remove lower branches to channel airflow down and across the pool and patio.

Lindheimer muhly grass heads

Timely Troubleshooting

- Chinch bugs in St. Augustine. Black insects are BB-sized, and they have irregular white diamonds on their backs. They're most active at the interface of the dying grass, and you'll see them only in hot, sunny locations. Grass will be wilted, but it won't respond to watering. Within days, it will become browned and even dead. Apply a labeled insecticide to eliminate them.

- Grasshoppers. Eliminate tall weeds that are providing breeding sites for the pests. Apply labeled insecticide in downward sweeping motion to coat them as they try to escape.

- Aphids. Small pear-shaped pests cluster in great numbers, secreting sticky honeydew residue on plants' leaves. Black sooty mold develops in the honeydew. Control aphids to prevent the mold. Most general-purpose contact and systemic insecticides will eliminate them.

- Leafrollers. Pests attack sweetgum, redbud, pyracantha, vinca groundcover, cannas and other plants. Larvae roll themselves up in cocoons made from stripped plant foliage. Best control is prevention. Apply systemic insecticide several weeks prior to expected appearance of the pests.

- Scale insects. Slow-mowing or immobile pests attack hollies, crape myrtles, euonymus, camellias and others. Apply systemic insecticide Imidacloprid to soil. Summer-weight horticultural oil sprayed onto foliage will also help.

- Cotton root rot. Soil-borne fungal disease that causes rapid death of established trees and shrubs. Hundreds of species are susceptible, notably apples and pears, also members of the cotton family. Plants die within days. There is no chemical control. Replant with resistant species.

- Gray leaf spot in St. Augustine. Fungal leaf spot that causes diamond-shaped gray/brown lesions on blades, runners. Avoid nitrogen mid-June until early September to reduce outbreaks. Apply labeled fungicide if necessary.

August

August gives us hope. Just a few more weeks until fall's wonderful weather. Fall crops to be planted. Fall flowers starting to set buds and bloom. It's a time to make plans for great gardening ahead.

Amaranthus and cosmos bask in summer sun on south wall of The Alamo.

Gold Star esperanza

Plant of the Month

Gold Star esperanza (*Tecoma stans*) came into the market in the '90s, and it's been a source of great hot-weather color ever since. It's a robust, leaning shrub that is perennial in South Texas and a tropical annual farther north. Its rich, buttery yellow bloom clusters are produced almost non-stop from spring until frost. As hummingbird plants go, this one's a magnet. Grow it in full or nearly full sun. Give it highly organic potting soil, and keep it moist at all times. The plant should survive South Texas winters, even if it suffers some leaf burn in extreme cold. In the northern two-thirds of Texas, however, it will either have to be brought into a greenhouse, or you'll need to start with a new plant the following spring.

FAQ

Q I think I've overwatered my plants. How can I tell if that's the problem?

A Of all the times that I've been asked this question, it has almost never turned out to be the case. Yet it seems like everyone assumes they have over-watered their plants. Almost always the plants have gotten too dry – the plants just weren't watered deeply and frequently. Often the plants have gotten too dry only one time. Other times, there have been injuries to the plants that kept them from taking up water properly. Occasionally, it's been because we tried a type of plant that couldn't handle Texas' heat.

Visit Neil's FAQ pages at
www.neilsperry.com

Planting List for August

• Warm-season lawngrasses. Planting St. Augustine, bermuda, zoysia and buffalograss early in month will give grass longest time to get established before winter. Water morning and evening daily for first two to three weeks.

• Trees, shrubs and groundcovers. Wrap plants to protect from drying wind on ride home. Plant immediately, and water deeply with hose every other day until mid-fall.

• Annuals for fall color. Marigolds, celosia, zinnias from 4-inch potted transplants that are in bud, but not yet in bloom. Also copper plants, purple fountaingrass and firebush.

• Perennials, as fall-flowering types come into nurseries. List includes chrysanthemums, fall asters, Mexican bush sage, Mexican mint marigold.

• Fall-flowering bulbs, including spider lilies (*Lycoris radiata*), naked lady lily (*Lycoris squamigera*), fall crocus (*Sternbergia lutea*) and oxblood lily (*Rhodofiala bifida*).

- Wildflowers. Sow seeds into gently tilled, low-fertility soil. Plant in full sun and where grass will not compete next spring. Use acid-treated bluebonnet seeds, available from wildflower seed sources, for most uniform germination.

- Fall vegetables. First week of month in North Texas and mid-month in South Texas: beans, cucumbers, squash, corn. Middle of month in North Texas and late in month in South Texas: broccoli, cabbage, cauliflower, Brussels sprouts. Late in month in North Texas and early September in South Texas: leafy and root vegetables such as lettuce, spinach, carrots, beets, radishes.

Pruning Tasks of August

- Annuals. Pinch lanky coleus, impatiens, begonias, geraniums and copper plants to encourage new, dense growth.

- Perennials. Remove dead and dying flower heads and seed stalks. Trim autumn sage by one-third to promote new fall growth and more flowers.

- Bush roses. Prune by one-third early in month to encourage flush of growth and fall blooms.

- Turf. Mow often (five-day intervals) and at recommended height. Raising the blade does not help with summer survival. Sharpen mower blade after every 30 hours of use or if grass blades appear frayed.

It's Time to Feed

- Lawn and landscape plants. Apply good-quality nitrogen fertilizer (half or more of the nitrogen in slow-release form) to clay soils and high-nitrogen (4-1-2 ratio) food to sandy soils. Wait until September to feed St. Augustine if gray leaf spot is a problem.

- Container plants, including patio pots and hanging baskets. Apply a diluted, water-soluble, high-nitrogen food weekly.

- Iron-deficient plants. Symptoms: yellowed leaves, dark green veins, most prominent on growth at ends of branches. Add combination iron/sulfur product. Iron is insoluble in alkaline soils, and sulfur helps lower the pH to keep iron soluble longer. Keep iron products off concrete and bricks to prevent staining.

Garden Tip

It's better to soak the soil deeply (and less frequently), to encourage deeper rooting. Sprinkler systems should never be set to run every day, even for short intervals. If water runs off when you let the sprinklers run longer, water in short and repeating cycles until you reach the desired amount.

August flowers of spider lilies

Garden Tip

Ever wish for a Summer Hardiness Zone map? There is one, but it's far less precise than the Cold Hardiness Zone Map. Plants gradually use up stored reserves in hot weather, as opposed to dying suddenly at one particular high temperature. Choose plants that are suited to your winter Zone, or one or two Zones to the north.

Cooling summer colors of moss rose

Pink pentas with purple fountaingrass

Garden Tip

Ways to get diagnostic help at the nursery: (1) Look for Texas Master Certified Nursery Professional. (2) Know what type of plant you have, or take generous sample in with you. (3) Know its growing conditions and your soil type (color, pH, sand or clay). (4) Know if there are other unrelated plants nearby affected in the same way. (5) Describe how long the problem has been going on and what you have seen.

Timely Troubleshooting

- Aphids. Look for telltale sticky drips on leaves of crape myrtles, red oaks, elms and other trees. Apply labeled insecticide. Without control, black sooty mold will begin to grow in honeydew the aphids exude.

- Chinch bugs. Watch for dry areas of St. Augustine turf, always in the sunniest, hottest parts of your yard. Grass doesn't perk up when you water it. Check the interface of dead and dying grass, looking for BB-sized black insects with irregular white diamonds on their wings. Apply labeled insecticide to eliminate them.

- Pecan pests. Hickory shuckworms and pecan weevils invade the shucks and nuts this month. Control with labeled insecticide applied early in month, repeated last week of month. You will need a power sprayer for good coverage.

- Gray leaf spot in St. Augustine. Grass will appear yellowed from a distance. Look for diamond-shaped, gray-brown lesions on the midribs and even runners. Apply turf fungicide if needed, but best long-term control is to avoid nitrogen fertilizers from mid-June through early September.

- Cotton root rot in trees and shrubs. Soil-borne fungus kills even mature plants almost overnight. There is no control for it. Prime candidates: apples, pears, roses, roses-of-Sharon, hibiscus, okra, silver maple, and to one degree or another, probably 80 percent of our other plant species. Hollies, crape myrtles, junipers, nandinas and oaks are highly resistant or almost immune.

- Nutsedge. Treatment time is running out, so don't delay. Nutsedge has triangular stems. (True grasses are all round-stemmed.) Apply Image or Sedgehammer early in month. Follow label directions.

Confetti lantana

September

In September we find that it's once again safe to come back outdoors in the midday sun. It's the beginning of the second season of gardening. Fact is, it's one of the best months in the entire Texas gardening year.

Fall crocus (Sternbergia) is an heirloom treasure of old Texas gardens.

Oxblood lily

Plant of the Month

Two lesser-known fall-flowering bulbs share the spotlight this month. Oxblood lilies (*Rhodofiala bifida*), also known as schoolhouse lilies, are small crimson perennials (8 to 10 inches tall) that flower about the time school resumes. Fall crocus (*Sternbergia lutea*, shown on previous page), similar to but not related to the true crocus of early spring, is far better adapted to Texas conditions. In fact, you're most likely to see them growing around old farmsteads and abandoned homes. Fall crocus grow to be several inches tall while flowering. Both of these bulbs are available online and from some local retail nurseries.

Garden Tip

Texas has very lax laws relating to soil amendments. Organic matter such as peat moss, compost, rotted manure and pine bark mulch works best. Also include expanded shale in clay soils. Avoid quack amendments that claim to "stimulate microbes" or "activate enzymes." Look for bona fide university research.

Hardy ageratum (Eupatorium) is a butterfly hot spot.

Planting List for September

- Trees and shrubs. Fall is prime time for planting, since it allows maximum months for roots to establish before the summer heat returns. Have a plan drawn to scale for the best final outcome.

- Spring-flowering perennials. Dig and divide daylilies, iris, Shasta daisies, violets, oxalis, hardy amaryllis and other spring bloomers late in month. Discard or share extra plants to avoid overcrowding.

- Naturalizing spring bulbs. Reblooming jonquils, species tulips, grape hyacinths and other heirloom perennials can be dug and divided early in month.

- Wildflowers. Sow seed into lightly tilled bare ground that is not shared with grasses. Acid-scarified bluebonnet seeds perform far better than untreated seeds.

- Cool-season color. Pinks, snapdragons and ornamental cabbage and kale late in month. Wait into early to mid-October to plant pansies. Planting while weather is too warm results in lanky plants.

- Turfgrasses. St. Augustine, bermuda, zoysia and buffalograss by mid-month to allow grass time to establish good roots before winter. Keep soil consistently moist for first two to three weeks.

- Cool-season grasses. If you wish, overseed established warm-season turf with ryegrass this month. "Perennial" rye is a better choice than annual rye (finer texture, more easily maintained). Like the annual form it, too, will die with late spring's warm weather. Fescue can be planted for permanent lawns in the Panhandle. If you have fescue, you should overseed established lawns at half the recommended rate each September to keep the stand strong.

Pruning Tasks of September

- Lawn. Mow frequently. Cut at the recommended height for type of grass to keep it low and dense, able to crowd out most weeds.
- Perennials. Deadhead beds to remove browned leaves and flower stalks. Continue through fall.
- Native and established trees and shrubs you intend to transplant in winter. Root-pruning encourages root growth in what will become the soil ball when plant is moved.
- Wisterias. Root-prune to stop vegetative growth and encourage flower bud formation. The cut should be 15 to 18 inches out from the trunk all the way around the plant. Cut only lateral roots and to a depth of 10 or 12 inches.

It's Time to Feed

- Lawns and landscape trees and shrubs. For clay soils, apply all-nitrogen fertilizer to prepare plants for fall, winter. For sandy soils, apply high-nitrogen food (4-1-2 ratio).
- Fall-flowering annuals. Apply all-nitrogen or high-nitrogen fertilizer to keep plants vigorous and blooming. Water-soluble food is best for pots and hanging baskets.
- Iron-deficient plants. Last call to treat plants that have yellowed leaves and dark green veins, most prominent on newest growth. Apply iron/sulfur combination. Keep it off surfaces that could be stained as the iron oxidizes.

Garden Tip

When we have our first break from summer's hot weather, many gardeners stop watering their plants. However, it can be really dry in most parts of Texas in fall. Don't assume that leaf drop you're seeing now is due to an early autumn. Keep the hose out!

Soapberry fruit cluster

Timely Troubleshooting

- Nutsedge. Final treatment must be made by middle of month.

- Winter weeds. Apply pre-emergent herbicide very early in month to stop germination of annual grassy weeds (annual bluegrass, ryegrass, etc.) and broadleafed weeds (clover, dandelions, henbit, etc.)

- Fire ants. Apply one of the long-term baits for 12-month control. Use individual mound treatments in populated areas of landscape.

- Webworms in pecans, walnuts, mulberries, persimmons and others. Use pole pruner to remove webs as soon as they're visible. They will be grapefruit-sized initially. If you wait a week or more, they'll have engulfed several feet of branches. Spraying at any stage is very difficult.

- Pests on patio plants. If you see scale, mealybugs, spider mites or other pests on tropical plants that you intend to bring indoors in a few weeks, control them while the plants are still outside. Your local nursery can identify them and help you find the best control.

- St. Augustine for gray leaf spot. This summer disease may still be present in lawn early in month. If you see diamond-shaped lesions on blades and runners, wait until mid-month to fertilize. This disease accelerates in summertime presence of nitrogen, so it's best not to apply fertilizers to St. Augustine mid-June through early September.

- St. Augustine for brown patch. This fall fungal disease causes grass to turn yellow, then tan in rounded patches 18 to 24 inches in diameter. Affected blades pull loose very easily from runners. Water only in morning, and apply labeled fungicide.

Morning glories prepare all summer for a lovely fall show.

Gardening Calendar
October

Enjoy what is probably the finest gardening weather of the entire year as you implement the changes you dreamed about all summer. Help spread the word: "Fall is for planting!"

Native American beautyberry brings dazzle to fall gardens.

Fall aster cluster

Plant of the Month

Fall aster (*Symphyotrichum oblongifolium*, formerly *Aster oblongifolius*) gets the nod this month. After all, it's been a stalwart survivor in old Texas gardens for decades. In fact, there was a time in the '60s and '70s when you couldn't find it in nurseries. About the only way to have one was to beg one. Now, it's widely grown, sold and planted. Its blue blooms in the fall are a wonderful complement to all the traditional reds, rusts, oranges and yellows. It grows to be 24 inches tall, but you're best off tip-pinching its growing shoots in May to force it to branch and stay more compact. Grow it in full or part sun, and cut it back near the ground after the first frost.

Planting List for October

- Cool-season grasses from seed. Ryegrass is commonly used for temporary winter cover. "Perennial" rye (not truly perennial here) is easier to maintain than annual rye. Fescue, also sown from seed, is used as a lawngrass in cooler parts of far North Texas and the Panhandle.

- Trees and shrubs. New plants will have many months to develop strong roots before summer. Wait until spring, however, to set out plants known to be winter-tender in your area, and limit the numbers you plant, so that an extreme winter won't ruin your gardens.

- Spring perennials. Dig and divide violets, phlox, iris, daylilies, Shasta daisies, coneflowers, gloriosa daisies, hardy amaryllis, Byzantine glads, hostas, peonies and other spring perennials early in month.

- Bulbs. Daffodils, summer snowflakes and grape hyacinths can be planted as soon as you buy them. Tulips and Dutch hyacinths, by comparison, should be "chilled" at 45 degrees for a minimum of 45 days in the refrigerator. Wait until mid-December to plant chilled bulbs.

- Winter annuals. Small to mid-sized varieties of pansies for the best landscape show. Complement them with snapdragons, pinks and ornamental cabbage and kale.

- Cuttings. Take cuttings of valuable annuals and tropical favorites this month while they're still active and vigorous. They will root best in loose, highly organic potting soil (not water).

- Elbon cereal rye in nematode-infested soils. The rye traps the microscopic, soil-borne worms in its root system. While it won't eliminate them, it does reduce their population significantly.

Pruning Tasks of October

- Trees. Remove damaged or dead branches. Cable trees that might be subject to winter limb loss in wind or ice storms. Remove surface roots that threaten slabs, driveways, sidewalks or patios. If you need help, hire a certified arborist.

- Shrubs. Limit trimming to clean-up, touch-up work. Save major reshaping for February, just before spring growth begins.

- Perennials. Remove dead leaves and stem stubble. Keep garden tidy as plants wind down for season.

- Lawn. Continue mowing until first frost stops all growth. Use mowing to remove fallen leaves. Bag and collect the clippings for use in compost or as mulch.

- Tropical plants. If you intend to move patio pots indoors as nights cool, reshape plants now.

It's Time to Feed

- Lawns. Apply quality turf fertilizer to warm-season grasses (bermuda, St. Augustine) very early in month. This would also apply to warm-season turf that has been overseeded with ryegrass. Feed fescue with high-nitrogen fertilizer middle of month.

- Pansies, ornamental cabbage and kale, pinks and snapdragons. Apply water-soluble high-nitrogen food to help plants establish quickly. Add granular high-nitrogen lawn and landscape fertilizer for sustained feeding through the fall and winter.

Bring tender tropicals into protection for winter before danger of frost.

Garden Tip

Poinsettias and Christmas cacti are photoperiodic. They prepare to bloom as nights lengthen. Beginning October 1, give them 14 hours of total and uninterrupted darkness each night, with 10 hours of bright light each day.

Chrysanthemum Milano Orange

Watch for early frosts in North Texas. Killing frosts can form on leaf surfaces at temperatures in the high 30s, particularly on calm, clear nights. That can happen as early as late October in North Texas. Have a lightweight frost cloth on hand to protect plants.

Firebush flowers

Garden Tip

Keep your line trimmer away from your trees' trunks. "Girdle" them, and you'll kill them. I tip my trimmer to taper the grass down to bare ground 4 or 5 inches away from the trunk. It looks manicured that way, plus it keeps the line away from the bark.

- Perennials. Apply high-nitrogen lawn and landscape fertilizer at half recommended rate immediately after digging and replanting spring-flowering perennials. Follow with a thorough watering.

- Compost. Include 1 cup of your favorite lawn fertilizer (no weedkiller included) per cubic yard of compost as you place the fresh organic matter into the pile.

Timely Troubleshooting

- Brown patch in St. Augustine. Watch for 18- to 24-inch yellowed patches that quickly turn brown. Affected areas may merge into irregular shapes. Surrounding grass remains green. Affected blades pull loose easily from runners, and you can see the decayed leaf blades where they attach to runners. Water only in morning, and apply a labeled fungicide.

- Potted tropicals for insect pests. Houseplants that are coming indoors for the winter must be free of scales, mealybugs, whiteflies and other pests. It's easier to treat the pests while the plants are still outdoors. Check drain holes of pots for ants and roaches. (Sinking the pots into a tub of water for an hour will eliminate those pests.)

- Household insects moving indoors for winter. Check weatherstripping and replace where needed. Apply perimeter insecticide around foundation and doors. Be prepared with labeled household insecticides.

- Trees and shrubs for insects and diseases. Most pest problems won't show up this late in season. Those that do probably do not justify spraying to eliminate, since many plants will soon lose their leaves anyway.

- Weeds and grasses where you want to plant new gardens in spring. Apply glyphosate herbicide to kill existing vegetation without contaminating the soil.

Fruit on old planting of standard nandina

November

Things are changing quickly. First frost is likely to happen this month in most parts of Texas. Use the pleasant fall days to complete landscaping projects and to prepare for late-winter and early-spring plantings.

Adapted maple species have outstanding fall color in Texas. (Caddo maple shown)

Ginkgo's fall color at Sperry house

Plant of the Month

If I could have only one tree for fall color in Texas, it might be a ginkgo (*Ginkgo biloba* 'Autumn Gold'). It's a compact shade tree for us, growing to 40 feet tall and wide in East Texas, somewhat smaller farther west. It has an interesting vase-form branching structure and fan-shaped leaf blades that look like fused pine needles. Fact is, this is a cone-bearing deciduous tree with broad leaves. All of that is botanically curious, but the fall color is what is horticulturally stellar. No tree that we grow has any better yellow fall foliage. Be sure you get a grafted male (fruitless) selection. The rotting cones aren't a pleasant experience.

FAQ

Q What has caused rows of holes in the trunks of my pecan and live oak trees?

A Those are the work of sapsuckers or woodpeckers. Damage is minimal, and the birds do not suggest the presence of any particular insect problem. In many cases, they come back to feed on sap that flows from the wounds. Unless they are repeatedly attacking small trunks – of tree-form hollies, for example – there is no call to action. In severe cases you could apply tree wrap or a sticky material such as Tree Tanglefoot to discourage them.

Visit Neil's FAQ pages at www.neilsperry.com

Planting List for November

- Ryegrass for winter cover. Last call to plant for temporary cover. Sow as early in month as possible. Perennial rye germinates better in November's cooler weather.

- Winter annuals. North Texas: pansies and violas, pinks, snapdragons, ornamental cabbage and kale. Along Gulf Coast and in protected areas in South Texas, include sweet alyssum, English daisies, petunias, hardy cyclamen and stocks.

- Perennials. Complete dividing and replanting early in month. Set into well-prepared garden soil. Water immediately after replanting, and apply a water-soluble fertilizer to get plants off to quick start.

- Daffodils and grape hyacinths, as soon as you buy them. Chill Dutch hyacinth and tulip bulbs at 45 degrees in refrigerator until mid- to late December to ensure normal bloom.

- Nursery stock. Trees and shrubs establish well when planted this month. Hand-water deeply after planting, and weekly during dry spells in winter.

Pruning Tasks of November

- Trees. Identify and remove dead or damaged branches before trees lose all of their leaves. If hiring, use certified arborist.

- Mistletoe. Remove as soon as it becomes visible. It is parasitic. There is no effective consumer spray product. Remove small clumps with pole pruner. Clip entire twig to get rid of clump, roots and all.

- Lawn. Mow until first freeze sends grass into dormancy. Use shredded leaves as mulch or in compost.

- Perennials. Remove all dead foliage and flower and seed stalks. Trim near the ground after first freeze. Mulch to reduce winter weed growth.

- Annuals. Remove stubble after first freeze. Mulch bed to keep weeds out over winter.

- Patio pots and hanging baskets. Trim before bringing into greenhouse or indoors. They will require bright light. The garage is inadequate, and artificial lighting would be insufficient.

It's Time to Feed

- Fescue, ryegrass. Apply high-quality, high-nitrogen fertilizer. Fertilize early in month, and water deeply after you feed.

- Pansies and other winter color. Apply high-nitrogen, water-soluble food every two or three weeks. Lawn-type nitrogen fertilizer is also useful in beds.

- Houseplants. Monthly feedings with high-nitrogen, water-soluble product will suffice until spring brings brighter conditions.

- Compost pile. Mix 1 cup of high-nitrogen fertilizer per cubic yard of compost. Turn pile with spading fork to keep it aerated and working actively.

Flameleaf sumac

Garden Tip

There are five things you can do to speed up the compost pile. (1) Shred all organic matter before putting it into the pile. (2) Keep it warm by exposing it to sun all winter. (3) Keep it moist, watering it when you have to. (4) Supply it with nitrogen (1 cup of a lawn fertilizer per cubic yard of compost). (5) Turn it monthly to keep it aerated.

Chalk maple's fall colors

Garden Tip

Rabbits are a real problem in urban landscapes – with no perfect solution. They're quite fond of pansies, cabbage and other winter annuals. Sometimes it helps to have a patch of overseeded winter rye to draw them away. Repellents don't work very well/very long. Planting in large pots, above their reach, sometimes is the best option.

Silver Dust dusty miller

Garden Tip

Wonder which pruning tool to use? Bypass shears give the cleanest cut (up to 1/4 inch). Anvil-type shears cut like an axe. They're sturdier, for twigs up to 1/2 inch. Use lopping shears for 1/2- to 3/4-inch cuts, or to 1 inch with better types. Use a small pruning saw for branches 1 to 2 inches, and a bow saw for 2 to 3 inches. A long-handled pruner will let you reach into trees.

Pinks

Timely Troubleshooting

- New garden plots. Eliminate grass and weeds with glyphosate-only herbicide. Spray before first freeze to get spaces ready for rototilling later this fall or in spring.

- Broadleafed weeds, including henbit, dandelions and clover. If you see them later this month, apply a broadleafed weedkiller spray containing 2,4-D to eliminate them. It will be safe on your lawn, and it will gradually kill out the undesirables. Left unsprayed now, the weeds will be large and unsightly by the next time you can spray (February).

- Brown patch in St. Augustine. Grass will show 18- to 24-inch patches that turn yellow, then brown within two to three days. Blades are rotted where they attach to runners, so they pull loose easily from runners. Apply labeled fungicide, and do not water in evenings. The disease spreads most rapidly in cool, moist conditions.

- Leaf curl of peaches; bacterial stem canker of plums. Prevent or lessen these diseases with application of copper-based fungicide late in month, once trees are completely bare.

- Caladiums. If you intend to save caladium tubers, dig them as soon as their tops have fallen over. Remove loose soil, but do not attempt to wash them clean. Let them air-dry on newspaper in the garage for a week. Dust them with sulfur fungicide, then layer them in dry sawdust or perlite. Don't let them touch one another, and put them in single layers only. Keep them dry and at 60 degrees over the winter. That's more likely to be in a cool room in your house than it is in a cold garage. Or, as many decide after one try at saving them, simply start with new plants or tubers in spring.

- Night of first freeze. When temperatures are finally forecast to drop near freezing, bring all tender tropicals indoors. Cover vegetables such as tomatoes, peppers, melons and cucumbers that would be damaged by frost. Use a lightweight frost cloth, and secure it to the soil to trap radiant heat from the ground. Disconnect hoses from faucets, and drain all hose-end sprinklers. If you have a greenhouse with a gas heater, be sure the pilot light and ventilation system are functioning properly after the summer. Have back-up heating source on standby.

December

The garden at rest: this can be a peacefully beautiful time. It's a month to appreciate the diversity of the seasons – deciduous plants contrasted against evergreens. It's also the time to tidy everything up before winter weather rolls in.

Camellia Chansonette

Plant of the Month

Hollies! We simply have to have hollies! Almost any local nursery can show you 15 or 20 different varieties ranging in mature height and width from 2 to 20 feet. Some are prickly, but some are not. Some bear fruit, but some do not. Most are evergreen, but a couple are not. They're suited to sun, part sun and shade. No plant group brings more variety and dependability to our Texas landscapes, but be sure you have the right type for your needs. A few selections require highly acidic soils and shouldn't be grown where soils are alkaline. Others grow well from border to border. Discuss your holly needs with your local Texas Certified Nursery Professional.

Yaupon holly berries in winter

Garden Tip

Brighten winter gardens with fruit-producing plants. Most reliable hollies include (shortest to largest) dwarf Burford, willowleaf, Nellie R. Stevens, female yaupons and Warren's Red possumhaws. Other winter fruit producers: leatherleaf mahonias, pyracanthas, and standard and compact nandinas.

"Hardy" cyclamen

Planting List for December

- Pansies, pinks, snapdragons, ornamental cabbage and kale and other winter annuals for use in beds and patio containers. South Texas gardeners can also include sweet alyssum, "hardy" cyclamen and stocks, among others.

- Spring-flowering bulbs. Daffodils, grape hyacinths and summer snowflakes, anytime during month. Tulips and Dutch hyacinths you have been chilling in the refrigerator, in mid- to late December.

- Fruit and pecan trees, grapes and berry vines from local retail nurseries or from Texas mail order sources. Best varieties for specific areas sell out quickly, so make your selections as early as possible.

- Living Christmas trees. Buy a type that has a reasonable chance of surviving in your climate, also that will fit the space you have available for it. Junipers and Arizona cypress are suited to most of Texas. Deodar cedar does well in South and Southeast Texas. Pyramidal hollies are another option. Plants should not be kept indoors more than seven to 10 days. Eldarica pines and Leyland cypress often fail during periods of heat, drought and waterlogged soils, so they are not good options.

- Landscape plants. Take advantage of breaks of nice weather to finish your plantings. Include plants that will offer colorful winter foliage, including many of the "blue" junipers, mahonias, nandinas, fringe flower, and purple wintercreeper euonymus groundcover.

Pruning Tasks of December

- Trees. Remove dead or damaged branches, also branches that are too low. Have branches that could break in wind or ice storms cabled for added support. Certified arborists are your best sources of dependable help.

- Tree roots. Remove roots that are threatening to lift concrete surfaces. Install a root barrier fabric 18 inches into the ground to stop the problem from recurring.

- Shrubs. If you want to reduce the height or width of shrubs, do so in winter. Use hand pruners for a more natural look.

- Crape myrtles. There is never justification to "top" a crape myrtle. It destroys the plant's natural shape, and it delays blooming by five or six weeks. If your plant is too tall or too wide, remove or relocate it, and replace it with something smaller.

- Mistletoe. This parasitic plant attacks cedar elms, hackberries and many of our other landscape and native trees. Cut it out at first sighting. It will usually get its start on small twigs, in which case a long-handled pole pruner will quickly remove it, twig and all.

- Grapes. Remove 80 to 85 percent of twiggy cane growth each winter. That ensures fewer, but larger, clusters of higher-quality berries. Prune to maintain the two or four scaffold branches along your supports.

- Fruit trees. Peaches and plums will require the most pruning. Remove vertical shoots as you maintain strong bowl-shaped form, 10 to 12 feet tall and 15 to 18 feet wide. Little or no pruning will be required for pecans, pears, pomegranates, figs and persimmons, except to remove dead or damaged branches. Remove "watersprouts" (vertical shoots) in apple trees.

FAQ

Q How often should I water during the winter?

A There is no good answer to this question due to the many variables that come into play (plant species, temperature, rainfall and other precipitation, wind, soil type, drainage, etc.). Learn to "read" your garden's soil. When it begins to change to a lighter color, and when it pulls away from your house foundation and tree trunks slightly, it's probably time. If it's been a couple of weeks since you've irrigated or had rain, you may want to water. Unless you have a "smart" controller, it's best to leave the sprinkler system in the "Manual" mode over the winter.

Visit Neil's FAQ pages at www.neilsperry.com

Pyracantha berries

Anytime you're dealing with a valuable shade tree, it's certainly worth the investment of hiring a certified arborist. Arborists "read" trees for a living, and they know how best to help you, your trees and your house all exist in the same space.

Primulas

Garden Tip

The tropical amaryllis you get at Christmas should be left in its pot in the northern half of Texas. Keep yours moist and actively growing from now through early September. Lay the plant, pot and all, on its side September 1 and let it dry and wither. October 1, repot it into fresh potting soil and resume watering. It should bloom again by Christmas. In warmer parts of Texas, you can plant the bulb into a well-prepared garden bed receiving morning sun and afternoon shade.

It's Time to Feed

- Compost pile. Incorporate 1 cup of high-nitrogen plant food per cubic yard of compost once or twice annually. Nitrogen, along with moisture and solar warmth, speeds activity of the microorganisms. Turn pile to blend it in completely.

- Pansies and other winter annuals. Apply water-soluble, high-nitrogen fertilizer each time that you water, to keep plants growing actively during warm spells.

- Newly planted trees and shrubs. Apply liquid root stimulator. Repeat monthly for first year if plants were balled-and-burlapped or bare-rooted.

- Tropicals indoors. Feed only monthly during darker days of winter. Growth produced under indoor conditions is likely to be lanky and unattractive.

Timely Troubleshooting

- Broadleafed weeds (clover, dandelions, chickweed and henbit) in lawn. Apply broadleafed weedkiller (2,4-D product) on a warm afternoon (above 70 degrees) early in month.

- Scale insects on hollies, euonymus, fruit or shade trees, camellias, crape myrtles, among others. Apply a horticultural ("dormant") oil spray.

- Houseplant pests. Spider mites, whiteflies and scale insects such as mealybugs will appear on plants indoors. Watch closely, and apply a labeled insecticide as needed. Spray outdoors or in garage, but only at temperatures of 45 degrees or warmer.

- Freezing weather. Disconnect hoses from faucets, and drain sprinklers. Cover vulnerable plants with lightweight frost cloth to gain a few degrees of protection. If cold will be extreme, move plants into garage until temperatures moderate.

Eastern redcedar cones

Trees

There's not a Texan among us who doesn't relish the shade of a big tree in the summer. But as with any other investment, we must make our selections carefully and nurture them patiently.

Soapberries line a rural Texas drive in the fall.

Young Chinese pistachio will provide shade for its surroundings for decades.

Mature, high-quality trees can be worth thousands of dollars in energy savings and property appreciation.

Flowering peach in spring

S*hade trees are the most critical element in fine landscape design. They're the most permanent parts of our gardens, and they add value to our lives and to our homes. It makes sense that we should choose our trees wisely and position them carefully.*

Whether you're planting new trees or trying to save native trees from the bulldozer, you'll have no trouble justifying their presence in your life.

What will your trees do for you?

If you're going to buy a new piece of furniture, you'll probably know what use it will have in your home before you ever go shopping. You need to have that same mindset when you head out to the tree yard. Your choices in trees should be determined by how the trees will add to the overall look and function of your landscape, probably depending on one or more of the following:

Trees in the landscape...

- provide shade,
- cool and purify their surroundings,
- offer seasonal changes of flowers, foliage and fruit, as well as winter bark character,
- reduce runoff and erosion,
- provide structure and framework to the garden designs,
- allow us to accent and highlight special places like entries and patios, and
- bring life and beauty to their surroundings.

Selecting and Planting a Tree

Nurseries today offer their trees three different ways. Each has its own advantages and drawbacks, and you'll want to consider them as you make your purchases.

- **Container-grown trees** have all of their roots intact, so they reestablish more quickly in their new homes. We're now able to find even very large trees that have been grown or at least "finished" in containers. These can be planted at any time of the year. However, you must always remember that the soil mixes that growers use in these pots will be chosen partially for light weight (to reduce shipping costs). That means that these trees can dry out quickly, so hand-watering will be required for the first year or two.

- **Balled-and-burlapped trees** have been dug from the nursery, from nature, or from one spot in a landscape to be moved to some other location. There is some root loss associated with the digging, so these trees typically do not start growing actively for the first one to three years. If you want a natural-looking clump-form shade tree, this is the way to get it. The actual digging is done during the winter dormant season, but the trees are often held in the nursery for several months. These "cured" trees will have started to produce new roots by the time you buy them.

- **Bare-rooted trees** suffer the most root loss during digging, so they have the highest mortality rate. Only young saplings are typically transplanted this way, most commonly fruit and pecan trees. Planting these is a process for mid-winter only.

Choosing the best tree at the nursery

Once you've decided which tree species best meets your needs, the next step is to choose the healthiest possible specimen from your local nursery.

- Unless you're looking for an unusually shaped tree, your new purchase should have a symmetrical form in keeping with its species.

- Look for a full complement of leaves. They should be of typical size and color for the species. Trees that have sparse, tiny or off-color leaves are much more likely to fail.

- The trunk should be straight and without signs of injury or sunscald.

- The root ball, whether balled-and-burlapped or confined to a container, should be proportionate in size to the canopy of the tree. Plants that have recently been repotted and plants that are root-bound may present unnecessary challenges.

Texas container nursery

Balled-and-burlapped redbuds have been trained for straight trunks. They have been dug and are ready to be delivered to retail nurseries.

Containerized trees have been dug, put into wire baskets for sale, transport and planting at any season.

Bur oak's planting site was carefully selected.

Picking the best spot for your tree

You may not consciously realize it, but just a few feet can make a huge difference in the impact a tree will have on its surroundings. In general terms, plant your new tree

- where it will provide shade from the summer sun,

- where it will provide a prominent visual frame at the side of your landscape,

- amply far from your house and from other trees (15 or 20 feet for one-story houses, 20 to 30 feet from two-story, 25 to 35 feet from other trees), so that it will never cause problems,

- in a random location, that is, not in line with the corners of your house, your fence, your neighbors' trees, the middle of the yard. It's usually best to follow the 60:40 ratio – plant your tree 40 or 60 percent of the way from the curb to the house and 40 or 60 percent from the front walk to the property line.

Planting your new tree

Home gardeners can usually manage to move trees that are as large as 2 or 2-1/2 inches in trunk diameter. Planting falls into a few easy steps:

- Carry the new tree by its root ball, not by its trunk.

- Measure the height and width of the soil ball, and dig the planting hole to match. It's fine to dig the hole slightly wider than necessary, but do not dig it any deeper than needed.

- Set the tree on firm soil and at the same depth at which it has been growing in the nursery or in its pot. Only in extremely wet settings where there is a very high water table should you plant the tree above the surrounding grade, and even then only by 1 to 2 inches. For almost all sites, plant at exactly the same depth as the tree has been growing.

- Use the shovel or hoe handle to tamp the soil firmly back into the hole around the tree's root ball.

- When you have the hole about halfway filled, water slowly and deeply to settle the soil and remove any pockets of air that might dry out the roots.

FAQ

Q When can new trees be planted?

A Landscape contractors plant trees 12 months a year. You'll find the best selections in the spring, but the truth is that fall (mid-September through November) is the best time to plant. That allows the longest possible time for the tree to establish new roots before summer's heat returns. Summer plantings are very vulnerable to getting too dry.

Visit Neil's FAQ pages at www.neilsperry.com

If you have a tree you'd like to dig and move, do so in the winter dormant season.

Transplanting redbud

Garden Tip

If it's during the growing season, your new tree will have leaves. Never allow them to be exposed to highway winds. No matter how slowly you drive, you'll still cause the leaves to become wind-burned. Have the nursery help you secure an old sheet, a scrap of old nursery shade fabric, or some other material tightly around the tree's canopy.

- Fill the rest of the way to bring soil even with the adjacent surface, and water again. If the freshly packed soil settles later, continue to add enough soil to bring it back to the original grade.

- Use the excess soil to create a doughnut-shaped berm around the hole. That berm will allow you to water deeply without losing any to runoff.

- Trim the top of the tree to its desirable form. Remove broken and dead branches and basal sprouts in the process.

- Wrap the trunks of red oaks, chinquapin oaks and Chinese pistachios, among others, to protect them from sunscald and borer invasion.

- Stake and guy the trunk of the tree to keep it completely plumb. Stakes should be stout and firmly anchored. Three stakes equally spaced south, northeast and northwest of the trunk will work best. Put cables above the mid-point of the trunk, and pad the trunk to protect the cables from rubbing. Remove the cables before they begin to girdle the trunk.

- Apply a high-phosphate liquid root-stimulator solution to the root ball. Repeat monthly for the first year for balled-and-burlapped trees. Container-grown trees can be fed with regular tree fertilizer after one or two months.

New red oak has been carefully planted and staked. Trunk wrap is only thing missing.

Red oak's drip line is obvious via midday shadow patterns.

Garden Tip

Don't overplant your landscape with too many trees. One healthy tree of a desirable species could be worth, just as an example, $2,500 in the resale value of your property, but 10 crowded trees could actually decrease the perceived value.

FAQ

Q Is "deep-root" watering a good idea?

A If by "deep" you mean deeper than 12 inches, the answer would be no. Most of the critical "feeder" roots aren't that deep. Root-watering rods should not be inserted more than a very few inches into the ground. Soaker hoses laid on top of the ground will do a much more efficient job of watering your tree's root system uniformly.

Care of Established Shade Trees

Since they represent such major assets in the property value of your house, it makes sense to care for your shade trees regularly.

Learn the term "drip line"

If you picture a tree as a living umbrella, its drip line is that area around its perimeter where water would be shed in a rainstorm. Or you could think of it as the area within the tree's shadow when the sun is directly overhead.

Most of any tree's roots will be within that drip line, and the most critical young "feeder" roots will be in the doughnut-shaped space at its very edge. If you concentrate applications of water and fertilizer anywhere, that is the place to do so.

Watering shade trees

This topic generates many questions. However, the overriding comment is that trees are pretty resilient if they were good species and healthy specimens to start with, and if they've been in your landscape for several-to-many years – long enough to establish good root systems.

How often to water

There are so many variables that it's difficult to assign any frequency to this question. Things like species, temperature, wind, humidity, rainfall, soil type, years the tree has been in the same location, and surrounding vegetation all enter the picture. However, a couple of facts come to mind:

- Trees compete very efficiently with grass and other landscape plants for available soil moisture. If you're keeping those other plants watered properly, your trees should be just fine.

- But if your tree is out in the open, away from other landscaping, and if it hasn't received any water for two or three weeks in the summer, you probably need to lay drip irrigation hoses around its drip line and water it slowly and deeply for several hours.

Proper fertilization

Like all of your plants, trees will benefit from proper fertilization. The guidelines are simple and straightforward:

- The Texas A&M Soil Testing Laboratory provides accurate analyses of garden soils 12 months a year. Find details and instructions online. Soil tests you have done for your turfgrass will suffice for trees that share the same soil.

- Texas soil tests almost always show the need for a high-nitrogen or all-nitrogen fertilizer. Lawn fertilizers, since they match these descriptions, can meet both needs.

- Never apply a weed-and-feed product beneath or near trees' root systems.

- Apply 1 pound of granular fertilizer per inch of trunk diameter unless instructed otherwise.

- Broadcast surface applications are entirely adequate. Using fertilizer spikes or punching holes and filling them with fertilizer puts too much material in one spot and none just a few inches away. Root-feeding rods bypass most of the active roots.

- Apply fertilizer near the outer drip line, where the "feeder" roots are most active.

- Fertilize in anticipation of new growth, that is, in late March. Repeat in late May, and feed a third time in early September. (Those coincide with times you are apt to fertilize your lawn.)

- Supplemental feedings may be in order, notably zinc for pecan trees (see Fruit chapter) and iron and sulfur for trees that are showing iron chlorosis.

Special Help for New Trees

Container-grown trees will have all of their roots intact at the time they are planted. However, those roots will initially all be in the original lightweight soil mix. You must hand-water new trees every day or two for their first couple of summers in your landscape. Sprinkler irrigation alone will not be sufficient!

FAQ

Q My tree is leaning. Can I stake it and cable it to get it straight?

A It is critical that your young tree be planted plumb, and that it be braced to stay that way until its new roots become firmly established (one to three years, depending on the size of the tree at planting and its subsequent health and vigor).

If the tree leans later and you merely push or pull it into a vertical angle and secure it, even for years, it will reassume its prior angle as soon as you release the supports. You must dig and reset trees that are not growing vertically.

Deodar cedar, like all trees, requires regular feedings.

SPECIAL PRECAUTIONS FOR IRON CHLOROSIS IN ALKALINE SOILS

Serious iron deficiency on sweetgum growing in alkaline soil

Bradford pears develop iron chlorosis in alkaline soils.

Before you try to correct iron deficiency in a shade tree, have the tree identified by a Texas Master Certified Nursery Professional. If it is a species that requires acidic soils and you live where soils are alkaline, you should seriously consider replacing it at once.

It is virtually impossible to sustain water oaks, willow oaks, pin oaks, dogwoods, slash and loblolly pines, sweetgums, cherry laurels and even bald cypresses, among others, in soils that are highly alkaline – especially if those soils are shallow and rocky, and most especially if the water used to irrigate them is also highly alkaline. You may succeed for a few years, but the needs will eventually become so great that you will give up. Almost everyone tries. Almost no one succeeds. It's better to cut your losses and replace the tree early on.

(Note that this suggestion is directed at large and mid-sized trees with extensive root systems. You may be able to create suitable planting beds for acid-loving shrubs and small trees.)

FAQ

Q Should I buy a guarantee with my new tree?

A Perhaps yes, perhaps no. If you buy your tree from a reputable nursery, and if you're careful to choose a healthy, vigorous specimen, you will probably be fine. If it's a large tree, however, that you'll be having the nursery or landscape contractor deliver and plant for you, it will probably come with a guarantee, hopefully one that's good for 12 months or longer.

Severe iron deficiency seen on pin oak (left), compared to Shumard red oak (right).

Pruning Your Trees

Sooner or later, every tree that you grow will need to be visited by pruning tools. In many cases, these are tasks you can perform yourself. In others, it will be work better left to the pros.

Why we prune...

Before you make your first cut, you need to determine the purpose of your pruning. Here are a few of the possible reasons:

- to compensate for roots lost during transplanting,
- to direct growth of young plants,
- to remove dead, damaged or rubbing branches,
- to remove erratic branching that ruins a plant's symmetry,
- to maintain a formal shape,
- to allow more sunlight to reach turf and other plants beneath,
- to remove roots that have become threats to foundations or hazards in walking,
- and to improve visibility and safety.

Tree-pruning tools

You probably won't have much use for small hand tools in pruning your shade trees. However, you'll certainly want to have a sturdy pruning saw, a bow saw, a long-handled pole pruner and perhaps even a chain saw.

Arborists work high in very large pecan tree's canopy.

FAQ

Q When should I prune my shade trees?

A Most pruning can be done at any time of the year. However, winter is the best time for most species. You can more easily see the branches that need to be removed while the trees are bare. Pruning of oaks is the one exception. To reduce the chance of oak wilt invasion, prune in winter or mid-summer and definitely not during the spring.

If lower limbs become a hazard during the growing season, or if they begin to cast excessive shade on the lawn, remove them on an as-needed basis.

Large limb has been removed from pecan tree to prevent damage to roof. Note small thickness of branch collar left in place. For fastest healing, no sealant was applied.

Yaupon holly is healing well from branch removal.

Garden Tip

Do not prune simply to reduce a tree's height or width. That tree is genetically predestined to grow to a specific size. If it's too large for the space you have for it, you should transplant it to more spacious surroundings or remove it entirely.

Site of branch removal on pecan has healed and has become unnoticeable.

Removing the lowest branches

Don't rush to remove lower branches from a young tree as it establishes and starts to grow. Those bottom branches, if left in place, will help the trunk grow thicker faster. It's best never to remove branches more than one-third of the way from the ground to the top of the tree. So, as an example, if the tree is 12 feet tall, you could consider removing lower branches up to 4 feet from the ground.

As the tree grows taller, be careful not to remove too many lower limbs. Once you take them away, the tree will never produce other low branches to replace them. Rather than making a mistake, it's a good idea to have someone pull down gently on a branch in question, to see what impact its removal would have on the look of the tree. If in doubt, wait. There will always be another day to do the removal, but you can never put the limb back.

It's also important to note that some trees, including live oaks and southern magnolias, typically have low-hanging branches that return to the ground. Many people prefer to see them that way. Think their pruning through carefully. Take a look at what others have done to their own trees, and let that factor into your decisions. Improper pruning can ruin trees' shapes forever.

A WORD OF WARNING: Pruning large trees is hazardous. It's work that is usually better left to professionals who have the proper climbing gear, training and experience. Hire a certified arborist for anything more than simple removal of low branches.

Removing large limbs

If you decide to remove a large branch from one of your trees, do so in stages. Your goal will be to prevent the weight of the branch from stripping bark and trunk tissues as it falls. It is almost always helpful if you remove some of the branch extremities first. Begin by making certain you will be in a safe position as you proceed.

Step 1: Make an undercut into the bottom of the branch 12 to 15 inches away from the trunk. The cut should be one-fourth to one-third of the way into the limb. Do not cut far enough that the saw becomes bound.

Step 2: Move 3 or 4 inches farther out on the branch. Cut through the branch from the top. The weight of the branch will peel the bark back to your undercut.

Step 3: Remove the remaining 12 to 15 inches of the limb. This final cut should be made so that it leaves a portion of the branch collar (where the branch swells as it joins the trunk). That collar contains the tissue from which new bark grows across the cut surface.

If this sounds like something beyond your capabilities, call for the help of a certified arborist. Your local nurseryman will be able to help with a referral.

Protecting trees' bark

Taken in cross section, a tree's trunk consists of the bark on the outside, then the phloem (a cylinder of tissues that carries sugars and starches from the leaves down to the roots), the cambium (the cylindrical layer that produces new cells, phloem to the outside and xylem to the inside), and the xylem (the major central core of the tree, through which plants pull water and nutrients up to the leaves).

Bark protects all of these tissues. When bark is lost halfway or farther around the trunk, it's likely that the tree will be lost. There is no way to repair or replace lost bark.

We must be careful never to damage our trees' bark when mowing or trimming. We should never leash dogs to tree trunks, and if we ever use cables or nylon twine around trunks, we must remember to remove them before the trunk grows larger and is girdled by the restriction. If you cut completely through the bark at any one level, the tree will almost assuredly die back to that point (or past it).

Garden Tip

Pruning paint is normally not recommended. It slows the healing process of new bark forming across cut surfaces. However, in areas known to be infested with oak wilt fungus, all cuts made to oaks should be coated with a light application of pruning sealant.

Silver maple bark shields trunk.

Garden Tip

When faced with a cavity in a tree's trunk, it's usually better to leave the cavity open while the tree forms a roll of new bark across it. Voids of that sort are quite common within old trees' trunks. Filling the cavity with mortar adds no strength to the trunk, and it traps moisture, which in turn can lead to decay. If you're uncertain about how best to cope with a tree problem of this sort, have a certified arborist look at your tree.

Red oak roots prepare to do battle with concrete (extreme lower right).

Concerns About Roots

Since we seldom see them, roots operate in a world of their own. Our trees' very lives depend on them. But sometimes those roots can become our worst nightmares. How we cope with them determines how well we and our trees get along. Here are some facts and guidelines.

- Perhaps 90 percent of a tree's roots are in the top foot of soil. Taproots function primarily for support, not to seek out deep streams of underground water.

- Compare a tree's root system to the spokes of a wooden wagon wheel. When it becomes necessary to dig trenches for sprinklers or utilities, stay outside the drip line as much as you can. When you must trench inside the drip line, come in from the outside, cutting parallel to the major roots instead of across them. The few extra dollars you'll spend in additional pipe or wiring will be repaid in the ongoing health of your tree.

Roots of young bald cypress threaten to "girdle" and kill one another. One or more should be removed in fall or winter.

- Trees' roots, like their trunks, grow larger as they mature. It is absolutely normal for roots to grow to the point that they extend above the top of the soil. That is not the result of erosion, and you must not attempt to conceal them by adding soil.

- If a root becomes hazardous to pedestrian traffic, it may be possible to remove it. The time to do so is in early fall, so the tree has maximum time to compensate for its loss before the next summer. Determine the tree's diameter a foot above ground line, then compare the diameter of the root(s) to be removed. You should not remove roots totaling more than 20 percent of the diameter of the trunk in any one year. If you have any doubts or concerns, consult a certified arborist.

- Roots can cause structural damage to concrete slab foundations, walks, drives and patios. If that is happening, or if it appears likely to happen, remove the offending root or roots (see immediately above) and install a root barrier.

Perhaps a live oak was not the best choice for this parkway setting. Live oaks typically produce large surface roots that become part of their character.

Elm roots have obviously ruined walk.

Installing a root barrier

Locate all underground utilities before you begin digging. Your trench should be 18 inches deep and, ideally, as far from the trunk as possible. If you have a landscape bed, dig the trench just outside the bed edging. You can use heavy vinyl pond liner or any other impervious and relatively permanent material as your liner. The barrier should not be visible once the trench has been refilled. Roots will deflect sideways along it, much as they do when they hit the wall of a flowerpot. That should allow the tree and your concrete to coexist. Again, this is work best left to a certified arborist or veteran landscape contractor.

Handling grade changes

There are times when you simply must change the grade around an existing shade tree. You would almost assuredly want to bring a certified arborist aboard to help with the decisions.

Since the roots that are critical to a tree's survival are near the soil surface, you must never add more than an inch of soil over the entire root system of a tree. If construction or rainfall runoff patterns require you to do more, hire a certified arborist and landscape contractor to design and construct a well at the original grade. Build the side walls of the well as far from the trunk as possible, preferably near the drip line. If water will be trapped within the well, make provision to route it off-site, either by French drains or by grating and pipes taken to a lower elevation. This is technical work that is best left to the professionals.

Concrete pavers allow air and water to reach roots. They also allow paver removal and adjustment as needed to accommodate growing trunks and roots.

Cottonwood trees typically produce very large roots at soil surface.

Ornamental pears, live oaks and several other shade trees may send up sprouts. Since they are a part of the mother tree, you must not apply herbicides to eliminate them. Instead, remove them with either a long-handled axe or a sharpshooter nursery spade.

Shumard red oak was preserved by landscape contractor. He built a retaining wall and maintained original soil grade.

Insect gall from red oak

Woodpeckers and sapsuckers riddle trees' trunks.

FAQ

Q What caused the rows of holes in the trunk of my tree?

A Sapsuckers or woodpeckers (closely related birds). The holes do not indicate that insects are present, nor do they lead to any serious threat. Apply tree wrap or sticky substance such as Tree Tanglefoot to discourage the birds.

Pest Control for Shade Trees

Almost all of our shade trees are vulnerable to one form of insect or disease damage or another. Here are steps to diagnosing and solving problems that may arise:

- Identify the tree species accurately. Knowing that, you can narrow your searches significantly.

- A Texas Master Certified Nursery Professional will be able to identify the species for you, and he or she will probably also already be very familiar with issues that might befall it.

- Online searches using words like *Texas A&M, entomology, pathology, Aggie Horticulture* and the correct scientific name for the plant will put you into wonderfully detailed websites where you can often match photos and descriptions to your tree sample.

- Certified arborists can step in if you are unable to determine any of the above information or if you are unable to do any of the work that is called for.

- Remember that some "problems" are not especially threatening to a tree's survival and do not merit any attempt at control. Insect galls in oaks are a classic example.

- Assess the time of year and whether a treatment would allow ample time for new growth in the same season. For example, if you're seeing insects devouring foliage in the fall, it's probably not worth the cost and effort of spraying the tree.

- Systemic insecticides offer control of many types of insects on trees and shrubs. Several kinds can be applied to the root zone. The insecticide will be carried throughout the tree's canopy, where it will control the pests as they attempt to feed. These materials may be expensive for large shade trees, and you have to give several weeks of lead time for the transport from the roots to the leaves.

Insect galls on oaks, hackberries, cottonwoods, pecans and other trees

There are literally hundreds of species of insect galls that attack Texas shade trees. Here are a few common galls:

- Wooly oak gall on live oak. Causes clusters of pea-sized, creamy white and fuzzy balls on backs of leaves.

- Woody oak gall on live oak. Resembles brown wooden marbles, typically on small twigs and often in clusters.
- Shumard red oak gall. Puffy tennis-ball-sized galls on leaf petioles.
- Pecan phylloxera gall on pecan. Causes knots and deformed leaflets on pecan foliage in spring.
- Nipple gall on hackberry. Small, BB-sized warts covering leaf surfaces.
- Cottonwood gall. Bean-sized swellings on leaf petioles.

The thing these galls all have in common is that they are essentially only cosmetic. They do no long-term harm to the tree. The adult female stings the plant's leaf or stem tissue and lays her eggs. The growth around the larval enclosure is plant tissue that is produced in response to the sting.

The critical point is that there are no products that will prevent or eliminate galls, but that may not matter. Gall insect populations will be worse some years than others, and they don't do any major damage anyway.

Nipple gall on hackberry

Controlling tent caterpillars and webworms

Eastern tent caterpillars and fall webworms are larval insects that frequent pecans, walnuts, persimmons and several other shade trees. Their webs begin as small clusters of leaves gathered together, and within a few days the webs grow to be 2 to 4 feet in length, engulfing entire branches in the process. The caterpillars move about on the branches devouring foliage. Their webs serve as protection from birds, sprays and the elements. The pests are more unsightly than they are harmful to the long-term health of the trees.

Phylloxera galls appear on pecan leaves in late spring each year. They are of no major concern.

Most general-purpose insecticides will kill the larvae, but you will need power equipment to reach webs that are more than 12 or 15 feet in the air. You will have to add a surfactant to break the surface tension of the webs, so that the insecticide can penetrate the web and kill the caterpillars. Buy a surfactant at the nursery or hardware store, or include one drop of liquid dishwashing detergent with your insecticide.

It's much easier simply to nip the pests out with a long-handled pole pruner when you first see the small webs. At that point, they'll be confined to the tips of the branches, and it will be easy to clip them and let them fall to the ground. Gather them up and send them off with the trash.

Webworms devour pecan foliage.

Many trees shed bark in chunks. This pecan does so in spring as new growth begins. Sycamores, crape myrtles and birch do so all through the year.

FAQ

Q My tree's bark is coming off in sheets. What causes it, and can the tree be saved?

A Bark is actually dead tissue. That means that it cannot expand as the tree's trunk grows larger. Instead it pops loose and falls away.

All trees lose bark in this manner, but some are more dramatic about it than others. Crape myrtles, sycamores and paper birch trees all shed their bark in visible pieces. So will pecans and other shade trees, although they're not as obvious about it. If you can see new bark beginning to form beneath the peeling tissue, your tree is doing just fine. If you see discoloration or decay, you need to contact a certified arborist at once.

Mistletoe in your trees?

Keep a close eye out for this parasitic plant. It develops its roots into the wood of trees' trunks and branches, and it derives its water and nutrients from the host trees. While it may not actually kill the trees, it certainly weakens them, so you'll want to remove it the first winter that it's visible. Cedar elms and hackberries are two of its favorite hosts, but you're likely to see it in many other species as well.

Because mistletoe is tethered to the support tree with its roots growing into the tree's tissues, you can't use any type of herbicide to kill the mistletoe. Arborists have products that will kill mistletoe back to the branches, but it usually comes back within a few months.

It's usually best just to clip mistletoe out as it first shows up. It almost always germinates on small twigs and branches where birds have perched and wiped their beaks clean of its sticky seeds. If you clip out those twigs when you first see the mistletoe, you can do so without disfiguring the tree in any way. If you wait a few years, however, the mistletoe and the tree branch will both have grown much larger, and pruning may actually affect the symmetry of the tree.

In serious outbreaks, it may be best simply to clip mistletoe off where its stems emerge from the wood of the tree. Do that each winter and you will not only keep it in check, but you'll also keep it from producing its fruit.

Mistletoe is parasitic; should be removed.

Think You Want a Fast-Growing Tree?

Be careful what you wish! The terms *good* and *fast-growing* are mutually exclusive. Every fast-growing shade tree comes with at least one fatal flaw. The truth is, we have many high-quality shade trees that will grow almost as rapidly as these "trash" trees, yet live 10 times as long.

When you think that fast growth is the most important factor in your tree selection, consider these other attributes:

Purpleleaf plum is handsome, but short-lived (five to seven years).

- Great looks

- Site and soil adaptability

- Pest resistance

- Drought tolerance

- Strong branching

- Longevity

Which of those would you be willing to give up for fast growth?

Given regular irrigation and normal lawn fertilization, live oaks can grow 75 percent as quickly as the "fast-growing" shade trees, but they'll live 10 to 40 times longer – and with far fewer problems. Judging from the age of the neighborhood, this tree is probably less than 50 years old in this current location.

Ornamental pear in spring

Summer Chocolate mimosa

Mimosa in late spring

Chinese tallow in fall

Loquat in fruit in spring

Flowering peach in spring

Spring bloom of Peppermint flowering peach

Life Expectancy of Texas Trees

How long does a tree live on average? There's no way to be precise, so it's probably best to quote life expectancy in general ranges. Here are some guides. Keep in mind that the numbers assume the trees are in ideal growing conditions as to climate and soil types. And remember that these are only estimates. Some trees will surely live longer, but some will die very young.

Purpleleaf plum	5-7 years
Weeping willow	5-10 years
Globe willow	5-10 years
Flowering peach	10-15 years
Ornamental pear	10-20 years
Leyland cypress	10-20 years
Arizona ash	10-20 years
Honeylocust	10-20 years
Siberian elm	15-20 years
Silver poplar	15-20 years
Eldarica pine	15-20 years
River birch	15-20 years
Mimosa	15-20 years
Fruitless mulberry	15-25 years
Chinese tallow	15-25 years
American elm	20-40 years
Tulip poplar	20-40 years
Loquat	20-40 years
Silver maple	20-40 years
Catalpa	20-40 years
Chinese parasol tree	20-40 years
Green ash	20-40 years
Lacebark elm	20-40 years
Fruiting mulberry	25-50 years
Golden raintree	25-50 years

Deodar cedar	25-50 years
Box elder	25-50 years
Redbud	25-50 years
Arizona cypress	25-50 years
Common persimmon	25-50 years
Mexican plum	25-50 years
Sycamore	30-60 years
Hackberry	30-60 years
Cottonwood	30-60 years
Post oak	50-75 years
Mesquite	50-75 years
Slash pine	50-75 years
Loblolly pine	50-75 years
Dogwood	50-75 years
Red maple	50-75 years
Japanese maple	50-75 years
Eastern redcedar	50-100 years
Sweetgum	50-100 years
Yaupon holly	75-100 years
Possumhaw holly	75-100 years
Crape myrtle	75-100 years
Ginkgo	75-100 years
Chinese pistachio	75-100 years
Cedar elm	75-100 years
Bois d'arc	75-100 years
Lacey oak	100-150 years
Pecan	100-150 years
Bur oak	100-150 years
Chinquapin oak	100-150 years
Water oak	100-150 years
Shumard red oak	100-150 years
Southern magnolia	100-150 years
Bald cypress	100-200 years
Live oak	100-500 years

Golden raintree in late spring

Lacey oak

Ginkgo in fall

Yaupon holly in winter

Redbud in spring

Southern magnolia in late spring

Weeping mulberry

Redbuds in spring

Dogwood in spring

Best Large Shade Trees

Live oak

Shumard red oak

Bur oak

Chinquapin oak

Pecan

Cedar elm

Chinese pistachio

Southern magnolia

Water oak*

Willow oak*

Bald cypress*

> ** Acidic soils only*

Best Small Accent Trees

Yaupon holly

Warren's Red possumhaw holly

Crape myrtle

Weeping mulberry

Dogwood*

Japanese maple**

Mexican plum

Redbud

Golden raintree

Little Gem and Teddy Bear southern magnolias

> ** Acidic soil*
>
> *** Shade only*

Best Flowering Trees

Crape myrtle

Rusty blackhaw viburnum*

Dogwood **

Redbud

Golden raintree

Mexican plum

Saucer magnolia **

Southern magnolia

> ** Shade*
>
> *** Acidic soil*

Best Trees for Fall Color

Dogwood *
Crape myrtle
Japanese maple**
Shantung maple
Shumard red oak
Ginkgo
Chinese pistachio
Ornamental pear
Chinese tallow***

    Acidic soil
    ** *Shade only*
    *** *Highly invasive in wetlands*

Best Evergreen Trees

Yaupon holly
Loquat
Eastern redcedar juniper
Live oak
Southern magnolia

Best Trees with Attractive Bark

Crape myrtle
Sycamore
Mexican plum
Persimmon
Bois d'arc
Chinese parasol tree
Lacebark elm

Chinese pistachio in fall

Southern magnolia

Eastern redcedar juniper

Crape myrtle trunk

Japanese maple in fall

Crape myrtle in fall

Ginkgo fall foliage

Forest Pansy redbud

USDA Hardiness Zones

ZONE 6
ZONE 7
ZONE 8
ZONE 9

Find Texas
Hardiness Zones
information page 5.

Small Trees (30 ft. or shorter)

Plants in the chart that follows have been arranged alphabetically by their scientific names. In Overall Ratings (column at far right), the number 1 indicates the highest recommendation.

Best Zones In Texas 6 7 8 9	PLANT AND COMMENTS	SUN/SHADE	HEIGHT	WIDTH	DECIDUOUS/EVERGREEN	FLOWERS (showy)	FRUIT (notable)	INSECTS (of significance)	DISEASES (of significance)	SPECIAL SOILS REQUIRED	OVERALL RATING
▪▪▪▪	Mimosa (*Albizia julibrissin*) Attractive in bloom, but messy other times; iron deficiency in alkaline soils; cotton root rot, mimosa webworms	●	30 ft.	30 ft.	D	spr.	no	yes	yes	no	4
▪▪▪	Japanese maple (*Acer palmatum*) Many types; some red-leafed; fall color; leaves scorch when exposed to sun; eastern half of Texas	●	5-25 ft.	5-20 ft.	D	no	no	no	no	moist	1
▪▪▪	River birch (*Betula nigra*) Severe iron deficiency in alkaline soils; leaf scorch in dry soils	●	25 ft.	20 ft.	D	no	no	no	no	acidic	3
▪▪▪▪	Redbud (*Cercis canadensis*) Many varieties; pink, burgundy and white flowers, also green, burgundy or variegated foliage, all depending on variety	●●	25 ft.	25 ft.	D	spr.	no	no	no	no	2
▪▪▪	Desert willow (*Chilopsis linearis*) Pretty whitish, pink or orchid flowers; erratic growth form; resembles willow, but related to catalpa	●	20 ft.	20 ft.	D	sum.	no	no	no	no	2
▪▪▪▪	Dogwood (*Cornus florida*) White to rose-red floral bracts; red fall foliage	●●	20 ft.	20 ft.	D	spr.	no	no	no	acidic	1
▪▪	Loquat (*Eriobotrya japonica*) Handsome shrubby tree; inconspicuous fall flowers are highly fragrant; plum-like fruit, maturing in spring, may be lost in cold winters	●	25 ft.	25 ft.	E	no	spr.	no	yes	no	2
▪▪▪	Varnish tree or parasol tree (*Firmiana simplex*) Very large leaves; green trunks; dramatic, but somewhat messy	●	30 ft.	30 ft.	D	no	no	no	no	no	3
▪▪▪▪	Ginkgo (*Ginkgo biloba*) Bright golden fall foliage; choose grafted male (fruitless) tree; fine accent tree	●	30 ft.	30 ft.	D	no	no	no	no	no	1
▪▪▪	Possumhaw holly (*Ilex decidua* 'Warren's Red') Warren's Red is most common improved selection	●●	15 ft.	12 ft.	D	no	win.	no	no	no	1

Saucer magnolia, early spring

Eldarica pine screen

Retama in Lajitas

Small Trees CONTINUED

Best Zones In Texas* — 6 7 8 9

*See Zones Map page 84.

Plant and Comments	Sun/Shade	Height	Width	Deciduous/Evergreen	Flowers (showy)	Fruit (notable)	Insects (of significance)	Diseases (of significance)	Special Soils Required	Overall Rating
American holly (*Ilex opaca*) Adapted only to East Texas; large pyramidal plant with large red berries all winter; several good hybrids	●●	30 ft.	25 ft.	E	no	win.	no	no	acidic	1
Yaupon holly (*Ilex vomitoria*) Prune into tree-form; only female plants bear fruit	●●	15 ft.	15 ft.	E	no	win.	no	no	no	1
Southern golden raintree (*Koelreuteria bipinnata*) Bright yellow blooms; pink fruit	●	30 ft.	30 ft.	D	sum.	fall	no	no	no	2
Golden raintree (*Koelreuteria paniculata*) Bright yellow blooms; attractive fall colors many years	●	30 ft.	30 ft.	D	sum.	no	no	no	no	2
Crape myrtle (*Lagerstroemia indica* and *L. fauriei* hybrids) Prune to train as small tree; choose variety that will fit space you have available for it	●	20 ft.	15 ft.	D	sum.	no	yes	yes	no	1
Saucer magnolia (*Magnolia* x *soulangeana*) Shrubby tree; best suited to East Texas; late-winter flowers are pink, burgundy or creamy white	●●	25 ft.	20 ft.	D	spr.	no	no	no	acidic	2
Crabapple (*Malus* spp.) Cedar-apple rust and cotton root rot limit tree's effectiveness	●	25 ft.	25 ft.	D	spr.	fall	no	yes	no	3
Chinaberry (*Melia azedarach*) Extremely brittle trunks, branches; very dark green foliage; messy fruit	●	25 ft.	30 ft.	D	spr.	win.	no	yes	no	4
Retama, Jerusalemthorn, Palo Verde (*Parkinsonia aculeata*) Drought-tolerant; fine-textured light green foliage; bright yellow blooms followed by pods; thorns; casts very little shade	●	25 ft.	25 ft.	D	spr.	sum.	no	no	no	3
Eldarica pine (*Pinus eldarica*) Also called Afghan pine; tolerates alkaline soils; intolerant of wet soils	●	30 ft.	25 ft.	E	no	win.	no	yes	no	3
Japanese black pine (*Pinus thunbergii*) Tolerant of alkaline soils, intolerant of poorly drained soils	●	20 ft.	20 ft.	E	no	no	no	yes	no	3

Small Trees CONTINUED
(30 ft. or shorter)

Best Zones In Texas* — 6 7 8 9

*See Zones Map page 84.

Best Zones (6 7 8 9)	Plant and Comments	Sun/Shade	Height	Width	Deciduous/Evergreen	Flowers (showy)	Fruit (notable)	Insects (of significance)	Diseases (of significance)	Special Soils Required	Overall Rating
6 7 8 9	**Silver poplar** (*Populus alba*) — Produces annoying root sprouts; silver trunk, dark green leaves with silvery reverses; cotton root rot (*Note that this tree is sometimes erroneously called "silver maple."*)	sun	25 ft.	25 ft.	D	no	no	yes	yes	no	4
6 7 8 9	**Mesquite** (*Prosopis glandulosa*) — Fine-textured native tree that is rarely given much respect; fits into xeriphytic landscapes well; handsome growth character; casts limited shade, so grass can thrive beneath it; seldom found in nurseries and difficult to transplant	sun	25 ft.	30 ft.	D	no	yes	no	no	no	3
6 7 8 9	**Purpleleaf plum** (*Prunus cerasifera*) — Extremely short-lived; peach tree borers, cotton root rot; trees often lean and must remain staked; purple foliage of many types fades to purplish-green in summer	sun	20 ft.	20 ft.	D	spr.	no	yes	yes	no	4
6 7 8 9	**Flowering peach** (*Prunus persica*) — Showy flowers in red, white, pink or bicolored peppermint stripe; short life expectancy due to peach tree borers, but some plant it for spring accents, knowing it will be replaced	sun	20 ft.	20 ft.	D	spr.	no	yes	yes	no	3
6 7 8 9	**Flowering pears** (*Pyrus calleryana*) — Cotton root rot, fire blight, weak branching; many varieties (Bradford, Aristocrat and others)	sun	25 ft.	25 ft.	D	spr.	no	no	yes	no	3
8 9	**Chinese tallowtree** (*Sapium sebiferum*) — Handsome small accent tree; reliable and rich fall colors; must not be planted where it has become invasive (South Texas wetlands)	sun	30 ft.	30 ft.	D	no	win.	no	no	no	3
7 8 9	**Jujube** (*Zizyphus jujuba*) — Unusual small tree due to its branching structure; suckers freely, so somewhat invasive; glossy green foliage; fruit is pulpy and enjoyed by some	sun	30 ft.	15 ft.	D	no	fall	no	no	no	3

Golden raintree in spring

Honey mesquite

Crape myrtle in fall

Red maple fruit in spring

Hackberries in former fencerow

Caddo maple fall color

Large Trees (greater than 30 ft. tall)

Plants in the chart that follows have been arranged alphabetically by their scientific names. In Overall Ratings (column at far right), the number 1 indicates the highest recommendation.

Best Zones In Texas*

6 7 8 9

PLANT AND COMMENTS	SUN/SHADE	HEIGHT	WIDTH	DECIDUOUS/EVERGREEN	FLOWERS (showy)	FRUIT (notable)	INSECTS (of significance)	DISEASES (of significance)	SPECIAL SOILS REQUIRED	OVERALL RATING
Box elder (*Acer negundo*) Messy habit; iron chlorosis in alkaline soils	●	40 ft.	35 ft.	D	no	no	yes	yes	no	4
Red maple (*Acer rubrum*) Red fall color; improved varieties; cotton root rot in alkaline soils	●	40 ft.	35 ft.	D	no	spr.	no	yes	no	2
Silver maple (*Acer saccharinum*) Fast-growing; weak-wooded; iron deficiency in alkaline soils; cotton root rot	●	40 ft.	40 ft.	D	no	no	yes	yes	no	3
Shantung maple (Acer truncatum 'Shantung') A superior selection; widely adapted; outstanding fall color	●	40 ft.	35 ft.	D	no	no	no	no	no	1
Pecans (*Carya illinoinensis*) Plant recommended varieties; insects and diseases not of major concern when used as landscape trees	●	60 ft.	60 ft.	D	no	fall	no	no	no	1
Catalpa (*Catalpa bignonioides*) Huge leaves are messy in dry seasons; fruit pods litter lawn and landscape	●	45 ft.	45 ft.	D	spr.	no	yes	yes	no	4
Deodar cedar (*Cedrus deodara*) Iron deficiency in alkaline soils; hurt by unusually cold weather in North Texas	●	40 ft.	40 ft.	E	no	no	yes	no	no	2
Hackberry (*Celtis laevigata*) Brittle wood; mistletoe; not showy in landscape	●	35 ft.	40 ft.	D	no	no	yes	yes	no	4
Leyland cypress (*Cupressocyparis leylandii*) Attractive habit, but extreme disease problems	●	35 ft.	30 ft.	E	no	no	yes	yes	no	4
Arizona cypress (*Cupressus glabra*) Drought-tolerant; "blue" selections striking in landscape	●	40 ft.	40 ft.	E	no	no	yes	no	no	2
Italian cypress (*Cupressus sempervirens*) Extremely columnar; drought-tolerant; spider mites, bagworms	●	35 ft.	3-4 ft.	E	no	no	yes	no	no	3
Common persimmon (*Diospyros virginiana*) Leafrollers, webworms; attractive fall color; fruit attractive to wildlife	●	30 ft.	25 ft.	D	no	win.	yes	no	no	3

*See Zones Map page 84.

Large Trees CONTINUED
(greater than 30 ft. tall)

Best Zones In Texas* 6 7 8 9	PLANT AND COMMENTS *See Zones Map page 84.	SUN/SHADE	HEIGHT	WIDTH	DECIDUOUS/EVERGREEN	FLOWERS (showy)	FRUIT (notable)	INSECTS (of significance)	DISEASES (of significance)	SPECIAL SOILS REQUIRED	OVERALL RATING
▪ ▪ ▪ ▪	**Green ash** (*Fraxinus pennsylvanica*) Native to eastern half of state and one of the prettier ashes; ash wood borers	◐	40 ft.	30 ft.	D	no	no	yes	no	no	3
▪ ▪ ▪ ▪	**Arizona ash** (*Fraxinus velutina*) Highly susceptible to ash wood borers; short life expectancy	◐	35 ft.	30 ft.	D	no	no	yes	no	no	4
▪ ▪ ▪ ▪	**Honeylocust** (*Gleditsia triacanthos*) Short life expectancy in Texas; thornless selections are available; messy pods	◐	35 ft.	35 ft.	D	no	no	yes	no	no	4
▪ ▪ ▪ ▪	**Black walnut** (*Juglans nigra*) Not highly refined; webworms and other pests; fruit stains pavement	◐	40 ft.	40 ft.	D	no	no	yes	no	no	3
▪ ▪ ▪ ▪	**Eastern redcedar** (*Juniperus virginiana*) Native and well-adapted screening tree	◐	45 ft.	40 ft.	E	no	no	yes	no	no	1
▪ ▪ ▪ ▪	**Sweetgum** (*Liquidambar styraciflua*) Outstanding fall color; must have acidic soil	◐	50 ft.	35 ft.	D	no	no	yes	no	acidic	2
▪ ▪ ▪ ▪	**Tuliptree, tulip poplar** (*Liriodendron tulipifera*) Large-leafed tree; requires consistent moisture to avoid summer leaf drop; tulip-like flowers face upward, so are not highly visible	◐	40 ft.	35 ft.	D	spr.	no	no	no	no	3
▪ ▪ ▪ ▪	**Osage orange, bois d'arc** (*Maclura pomifera*) Rugged-looking native tree; large sticky green fruit resembling immature oranges; wood is extremely hard and difficult to cut	◐	40 ft.	35 ft.	D	no	fall	no	no	no	3
▪ ▪ ▪	**Southern magnolia** (*Magnolia grandiflora*) Several varieties (some dwarf, including popular Little Gem); large white blooms; needs deep soils	◐	60 ft.	40 ft.	E	spr.	no	no	no	acidic	1

Fruitless mulberry leaves

Juvenile foliage of mulberry seedling

Young green ash

Large Trees CONTINUED

*See Zones Map page 84.

Best Zones In Texas* 6 7 8 9	PLANT AND COMMENTS	SUN/SHADE	HEIGHT	WIDTH	DECIDUOUS/EVERGREEN	FLOWERS (showy)	FRUIT (notable)	INSECTS (of significance)	DISEASES (of significance)	SPECIAL SOILS REQUIRED	OVERALL RATING
▪▪▪▪	**White mulberry (Morus alba)** Durable and attractive tree; very messy habits, both from piles of unpleasant fruit near tree and flies they attract; leaf litter in summer and fall; weedy seedlings sprout abundantly	○	40 ft.	40 ft.	D	no	spr.	no	no	no	4
▪▪▪▪	**Fruitless mulberry (Morus alba 'Fruitless')** Large leaves drop from mid-summer on; surface roots; dense shade that makes growing turf difficult; fast growth, but subject to borer damage, cotton root rot	○	40 ft.	40 ft.	D	no	no	yes	yes	no	3
▪▪▪▪	**Red mulberry (Morus rubra)** Attractive and relatively durable shade tree; fruit is smelly and stains badly – attracts both birds and hoards of flies; weedy seedlings germinate freely throughout neighborhood	○	40 ft.	40 ft.	D	no	spr.	no	no	no	4
▪▪▪▪	**Slash pine (Pinus elliottii)** Severe and uncontrollable iron chlorosis develops in alkaline soils; several insect and disease challenges; one of best pines for East Texas landscapes	○	60 ft.	40 ft.	E	no	win.	yes	yes	acidic	2
▪▪▪▪	**Loblolly pine (Pinus taeda)** Severe and uncontrollable iron chlorosis develops in alkaline soils; several insect and disease challenges; native pine of most of East Texas Piney Woods	○	60 ft.	40 ft.	E	no	win.	yes	yes	acidic	2
▪▪▪▪	**Chinese pistachio (Pistacia chinensis)** Outstanding red fall color; wrap trunks of young trees to prevent sun damage to bark	○	50 ft.	45 ft.	D	no	win.	no	no	no	1
▪▪▪▪	**Sycamore, American planetree (Platanus occidentalis)** Handsome tree with attractive silver bark; large leaves are messy in late summer, fall; anthracnose and lace bugs common problems	○	60 ft.	50 ft.	D	no	no	yes	yes	no	4
▪▪▪▪	**Cottonwood (Populus deltoides)** Handsome, fast-growing tree; large leaves are messy from mid-summer into winter; large surface roots; cottonwood borers and cotton root rot; clouds of cottony seeds in spring choke HVAC equipment, germinate freely	○	60 ft.	45 ft.	D	no	yes	yes	yes	no	4

Shumard red oak in fall

Slash pine

Native cedar elm among bluebonnets

Best Zones In Texas* 6 7 8 9	PLANT AND COMMENTS *See Zones Map page 84.	SUN/SHADE	HEIGHT	WIDTH	DECIDUOUS/EVERGREEN	FLOWERS (showy)	FRUIT (notable)	INSECTS (of significance)	DISEASES (of significance)	SPECIAL SOILS REQUIRED	OVERALL RATING
	Bur oak (*Quercus macrocarpa*) Coarse texture; native and suited to variety of conditions		60 ft.	60 ft.	D	no	fall	no	no	no	1
	Chinquapin oak (*Quercus muhlenbergii*) Native; well-suited to variety of conditions		50 ft.	50 ft.	D	no	no	no	no	no	1
	Water oak (*Quercus nigra*) Native East Texas tree; severe iron chlorosis in alkaline soils		50 ft.	50 ft.	D	no	no	no	no	acidic	1
	Willow oak (*Quercus phellos*) Native East Texas tree; resembles water oak closely		50 ft.	50 ft.	D	no	no	no	no	acidic	1
	Shumard red oak (*Quercus shumardii*) Native to Central Texas; red fall color		50 ft.	50 ft.	D	no	no	no	no	no	1
	Post oak (*Quercus stellata*) Native to neutral sandy loam soils of Central Texas, but not sold in nursery trade due to difficulty in transplanting; extremely intolerant of grade changes, high landscape maintenance, etc.		45 ft.	45 ft.	D	no	no	no	no	no	3
	Live oak (*Quercus virginiana*) Widely adapted to all of Texas; spreading habit		40 ft.	65 ft.	E	no	no	no	no	no	1
	Weeping willow (*Salix babylonica*) Extremely short-lived in landscapes; prefers water-side site; highly vulnerable to cottonwood borers, cotton root rot		35 ft.	35 ft.	D	no	no	yes	yes	no	4
	Corkscrew willow (*Salix matsudana* 'Tortuosa') Small accent tree; very short life expectancy due to cottonwood borers, cotton root rot		30 ft.	30 ft.	D	no	no	yes	yes	no	4
	Western soapberry (*Sapindus drummondii*) Handsome native tree; yellow fall color and amber fruit all winter; susceptible to borers		40 ft.	30 ft.	D	no	win.	yes	no	no	3
	Bald cypress (*Taxodium distichum*) Good for wet sites; iron deficiency in alkaline soils; root "knees" are objectionable		60 ft.	50 ft.	D	no	no	yes	no	acidic	2
	American elm (*Ulmus americana*) Attractive native tree; lace bugs, cotton root rot, perhaps Dutch elm disease eventually		60 ft.	60 ft.	D	no	no	yes	yes	no	3
	Cedar elm (*Ulmus crassifolia*) Fine-textured native; mildew and mistletoe can be problems		50 ft.	40 ft.	D	no	no	no	yes	no	1
	Lacebark elm (*Ulmus parvifolia*) Attractive trunks; tends to lean; cotton root rot; this is the plant correctly called "Chinese elm"		45 ft.	45 ft.	D	no	no	no	yes	no	2
	Siberian elm (*Ulmus pumila*) Fast-growing; subject to many serious diseases, insects; very poor landscape investment; this is the plant commonly incorrectly called "Chinese elm"		45 ft.	45 ft.	D	no	no	yes	yes	no	4

Shrubs

Ask a hundred gardeners what comes to mind when the topic turns
to landscaping, and *shrubs* will almost always be their first word.
Shrubs are the "bones" of our landscapes, and we use them
to paint the pictures of our gardening dreams.

Attractive variety of shrubs welcomes visitors to a McKinney garden.

Look back at the inventory lists of retail nurseries just 30 or 40 years ago. You'll find a fraction of the shrub varieties we have today. Part of the increase has come from breeding and selecting for plants that will stay smaller. Part of it has been to find types that are different in some special way (weeping, variegated, fragrant, pest-resistant, drought-tolerant, etc.). So for all of those reasons, we have wonderful choices available to us today.

Independent retail nurseries offer quality and service year 'round (Stuart Nursery, Weatherford).

Nicholson-Hardie Nursery (Dallas) in spring

Best Time to Plant Shrubs

Thanks to the fact that shrubs are almost always grown and sold in nursery pots now, we truly can plant whenever we feel like it. However, some months are better than others.

Spring: Nurseries have the greatest selections of shrub types in the spring selling season. It's also the best season to plant any species that you know is borderline in terms of winter hardiness in your area. Spring planting gives a new shrub the longest possible time to establish itself before the next exposure to cold.

Summer: Landscape contractors work 12 months a year, and you, too, can plant in the summer. It's a great time to choose your crape myrtles, for example, because you can buy them in bloom – to be sure of their color. But daily hand-watering will be required to keep first-year plants alive through the heat.

North Haven Gardens (Dallas) in summer

Fall: Most nurserymen will tell you that fall is the very best time to plant new shrubs (and trees). It gives them the longest possible time to establish their roots before the next summer drought rolls in.

Winter: If you are actually digging and relocating a shrub, it must be done while that plant is dormant. That means winter. And you can certainly plant container-grown shrubs in the winter. However, don't leave plants in pots sitting out in the cold after you bring them home – plant them immediately. Leaving their root systems exposed to a hard freeze will make new shrubs much more vulnerable to problems both before and after planting.

Shade shrubs are ready for new homes (North Haven Gardens in Dallas).

What Size Plant Should You Buy?

Except for large, almost architectural, balled-and-burlapped plants, most shrubs sold in garden centers today come in nursery pots. Pot sizes will vary from quarts and gallons to 3-, 5-, 7-, 10- and even 20-gallon containers.

Plants in smaller pots may cost less, but you'll be much more likely to plant them too near one another to prevent the bed from having an empty look. Those close plantings will soon lead to overcrowding.

The very large plants (20-gallons and larger) will give a nice impact beginning the day that they're planted, but they may run the costs up and beyond the budget.

The best compromise is usually to buy your main accent shrubs and trees in 7- and 10-gallon pots (larger if needed). Mid-sized shrubs, especially those that are forming the backbones of the design, can be planted out of 3- and 5-gallon containers. Smaller bordering shrubs work well from 1- and 2-gallon pots.

Find best selections and help in local independent retail nurseries.

Shrubs (boxwoods) are sold in a wide variety of pot sizes.

Spiral junipers and other specially trained plants should be bought already shaped. (Covington's Nursery, Rowlett)

Holly

...age sprouts red, then turns a glossy d...
abundance of showy red berries form...
...ms in fall and persist through winter...
...cellent textural variation. Great as a la...
...reen or specimen.

Bloom Time: Blooms mid- to late spri...
Height: 10-15' (3-4.6 m)
Space: 6-8' (1.8-2.4 m)
Hardy Zones: 5-9
Exposure: Sun or partial sun.

PLANTING INSTRUCTIONS:
- Dig hole. Loosen soil in bottom. Mi...
  planting mix half and half.
- **Remove plant from plastic or m...**
  If balled in burlap, cut top string c...
  remove burlap.
- If potted in fiber container, cut si...
  carefully in 2 or 3 places.
- Plant root ball so that its top is a...
  ...unding soil level. **Do not p...**
  ...ound r...

*Nursery tag gives good generic
information for each plant, but
verify details with local professional
nurseryman.*

Garden Tip

Nursery labels will almost always list a plant's Hardiness Zone from the U.S.D.A. winter low-temperature map, but it's still wise to ask your local independent nursery professional if a shrub you're about to buy is suited to the soil in your area and if it can survive the high temperatures of summer. Its ability to handle the cold doesn't guarantee that it will tolerate your other environmental conditions. Ask for localized advice.

Choosing the Right Shrubs for Your Design

Every good landscape begins with a plan. It should be drawn to scale, so that you'll be able to anticipate the eventual relationships of the plants to one another. As you develop that plan, select shrubs that will be the best possible matches for all of your goals.

Factors to consider

Save yourself huge headaches later. Take these several factors into consideration when choosing each one of your shrubs.

Botanical considerations:
- The plant's mature height and width if left unpruned
- The plant's needs for full sunlight, shade or something between
- Any special soil requirements, especially drainage and pH (acidity/ alkalinity)
- The plant's ability to survive normal winter weather in your area
- The variety's vulnerability to insects and diseases.

Design issues:
- The plant's growth form (rounded, spreading, oval, weeping, etc.)
- The plant's texture (leaf size, stem arrangement, etc.)
- Evergreen or deciduous
- Flowers and bloom season/length
- Foliar color, including variegation and seasonal changes.

Many factors were considered in designing this McKinney garden: heights of plants, growth forms (primarily rounded to complement fence angles), evergreen selections, and more.

Best Flowering Shrubs

(In general sequence of bloom, beginning in late winter)

- Camellias
- Mahonias
- Flowering quince
- Forsythia
- Azaleas
- Indian hawthorns
- Spiraeas (bridal wreath and others)
- Texas mountain laurel
- Oakleaf and other hydrangeas
- Oleanders
- Crape myrtles
- Texas sage (ceniza)
- Vitex
- Roses-of-Sharon

(Not all of the plants in this list will be equally suited to all parts of Texas. Your local professional nurseryman will be your best source of specific advice.)

Forsythia greets spring.

Hydrangea blooms in May.

Texas sage (ceniza) flowers following summer, fall rains.

CAN THE OLD SHRUBS BE SAVED?

One of the most difficult decisions a gardener has to make is in removing shrubs that have outlived their usefulness. It's not a task to be taken lightly, but once the decision is made, you may be surprised at how refreshing it is to have made the change.

It's time for new shrubs when:

- you're tired of pruning to maintain them at a manageable size.

- you're pruning into stem stubble each time that you trim them.

- the old shrubs have lost most of their vigor.

- the plants are badly misshapen due to overcrowding.

- trees now cast too much shade for the type of shrub that you're growing.

- you're doing a renovation to the rest of the landscape and the old shrubs aren't worth transplanting.

BEFORE

This 35-year-old Willowleaf holly had served through several landscape transformations, always emerging as the privacy plant that screened one part of this landscape from another.

AFTER

With selective removal of its lower branches, and with entire removal of the dwarf Chinese hollies that had become terribly misshapen at its base, the Willowleaf holly has taken a new position of prominence, this time as a small, multi-trunked accent tree that flanks the path from one garden "room" to another.

Planting Shrubs into Beds

Your shrubs will be more easily maintained and your landscape will look more coherent if you plant all of your shrubs into defined beds.

Shrubs and metal edging define curved lines of beds.

- Identify the bed outline by laying a supple garden hose in the configuration you'd like the bed to take. Use long, sweeping curves for the most natural look. The bed width should be in proportion to the size of the house and the types of shrubs you'll be planting.

- If planting during the growing season, kill existing turf and weeds within the new bed with a glyphosate-only herbicide (won't contaminate the soil). If you're working the bed during the winter, you'll have to dig and remove existing vegetation manually.

- Give the herbicide 10 to 12 days to do its job, then rototill to a depth of 6 or 8 inches.

- Incorporate organic matter into the front several feet of the bed – where you intend to plant annuals, groundcovers, low shrubs and other plants with small root systems. Mix in a total of 4 or 5 inches of compost, peat moss, rotted manure and pine bark mulch by rototilling it all into the top foot of soil. By rototilling along the front edge of the bed, you'll be able to keep the organic materials right where they'll be needed.

Angled boxwood border marks boundaries of plantings.

Rounded shrub bed with stone edging establishes look of this McKinney landscape.

Shrubs

All plants are within beds in this McKinney landscape. Best soil preparation is reserved for smaller types with more limited root systems.

- Large shrub varieties you choose to anchor the backs and corners of your landscaping beds, by comparison, should be able to withstand your native soil. It would be difficult to amend soils enough to satisfy their long-term needs – their root systems are simply too large.

- Rototill the bed again, then rake the soil surface to a smooth grade that drains away from the house. Be sure your planting soils do not cover weep holes in masonry walls.

- Remove each plant from its container carefully. Plant each one at the same depth at which it has been growing in its container. Water the bed carefully, then rake additional soil where settling occurs.

- Mulch the new bed to discourage weed germination and growth. Organic mulches such as compost or finely ground pine bark work well and give a very attractive finished look.

- Apply a high-nitrogen fertilizer to get the new bed up and growing. Follow the feeding with a thorough soaking.

Hydrangeas respond to special soil preparation.

Azaleas benefit from highly organic planting beds. (Columbus, Texas)

Garden Tip

If you are concerned that a bed might stay overly wet, rake the soil to an elevation 4 or 5 inches above the surrounding grade, so that rainfall and runoff will be redirected away from the bed. To correct more serious drainage problems, you may want to have drain grates installed in low spots within the lawn. They would allow water to flow into 4-inch PVC pipes, so that it could be carried to a lower elevation as it exits your property. Landscape contractors and drainage specialists will have still other means of getting excess water out of the way.

A dozen types of hollies, oakleaf hydrangeas, mahonias, aucubas and shade groundcovers grow in author's shaded backyard.

FAQ

Q Some of the shrubs that I'm planting were balled-and-burlapped. Should I remove the burlap when I plant them?

A No. You should remove any type of cord, cable, wire or plastic ties that hold it in place around the shrubs' stems, and you can fold it back away from the stems, but do not attempt to remove it. It will decay at the same time that the roots begin to grow through it.

Visit Neil's FAQ pages at www.neilsperry.com

QUICK LISTS
Best Shrubs for Shade

Hollies
Hydrangeas
Viburnums
Aucubas
Mahonias
Sweet olive
Fatsia
Cleyera

Oakleaf hydrangeas thrive, bloom in shade.

(Not all of the plants in this list will be equally suited to all parts of Texas. Your local professional nurseryman will be your best source of specific advice.)

Best Low Border Shrubs

Boxwood
Dwarf yaupon holly
Carissa holly
Dwarf Burford holly
Wheeler's Dwarf pittosporum

Japanese boxwood is most popular low border shrub. Nellie R. Stevens hollies provide privacy screen.

Note that giant liriope, aspidistra and rosemary, while technically not shrubs, are often used in low landscape borders.

Designing for Natural Clusters and Sweeps

As you finalize your landscape plan and its beds, there are several simple guidelines to a great-looking outcome.

- Your garden will be more relaxed and inviting if you avoid long, straight rows of plants. That presumes, of course, that you're not planning a formally trimmed and sculpted design.

- Think of your landscape as having "rooms." Just as you would decorate the inside of your home for continuity room by room, do the same with your landscape. Confine the number of species you use to six or seven for any given part of your plantings.

- Provide continuity by repeating one or two varieties through the entire garden. They become the warp threads around which you weave the entire living tapestry.

- Dark green is the default color, and the farther you depart from it, the more dramatic the visual effect on your landscape will be. Gray- and red-leafed shrubs and those that are brightly variegated can be really flashy. Unless you're prepared to look out on gardens that keep you permanently at attention, use them sparingly and primarily for accents.

- Measure the bed carefully, and flag each planting spot to determine how many plants of each variety you will need to buy. Know each type's mature spread, and allow for that growth.

Shade plants are arranged in small clusters.

Texas sage plants are viewed as one mass.

Sweet viburnum in gentle sweep also provides privacy.

Shrubs planted in groupings

Gentle sweep of lightly trained waxleaf ligustrums looks at home with natural stone path.

Unusually tall Nellie R. Stevens holly

Ilex cornuta *varieties (l to r) Carissa, Needlepoint (Willowleaf), Dwarf Burford, Burford, Dwarf Chinese*

Native possumhaw holly

Multi-trunked mature male yaupon holly

QUICK LIST
Best Hollies

(Listed in order of decreasing height)

Warren's Red possumhaw
Yaupon
Nellie R. Stevens
Oakland
Mary Nell
Burford
Willowleaf
Dwarf Burford
Dwarf Chinese
Carissa
Dwarf yaupon

Weeping yaupon holly in winter

(Clockwise from lower left) Young Carissa holly plants, large Nellie R. Stevens holly, tree-form yaupon holly in distance through arch, Needlepoint holly and dwarf Chinese holly

Mature clump of native possumhaw holly brightens drab winter day.

American beautyberry in fall

Leatherleaf mahonia fruit in spring

Nandina fruit in winter

Nellie R. Stevens holly fruit in winter

Best Fruiting Shrubs

(In general sequence of fruit production and ripening, beginning in early spring)

- Leatherleaf mahonia (late winter and spring)
- Oregon grape mahonia (spring into summer)
- Pomegranate (late summer, fall)
- American beautyberry (fall)
- Pyracanthas (late fall through winter)
- Dwarf Burford holly (late fall through winter)
- Burford holly (late fall through winter)
- Willowleaf holly (late fall through winter)
- Nellie R. Stevens holly (late fall through winter)
- Yaupon holly (late fall through winter)
- Warren's Red possumhaw holly (late fall through winter)
- Nandinas (late fall through winter)
- Chinese photinia (late fall through winter)

(Not all of the plants in this list will be equally suited to all parts of Texas. Your local professional nurseryman will be your best source of specific advice.)

Elaeagnus trained as tall privacy hedge

FAQ

Q Is bamboo a good privacy screening plant?

A No. It is a terrible option. So much so that cities are beginning to forbid the planting of common golden bamboo. It is a strong-growing grass that is almost impossible to contain and extremely difficult to eliminate. While there are some species of bamboo that do not spread aggressively, they are primarily tropical in nature and are generally suited only to warmer parts of South Texas.

When Privacy Matters

As urban properties have grown smaller and smaller, our needs for privacy have increased. We usually think first of fences, but when they become wearisome (and they always do), we start looking into the best shrubs for the purpose.

QUICK LIST
Best Shrubs for Screens

(Listed in order of decreasing height)

American holly *
Chinese photinia (not redtip)
Sweet viburnum **
Cherry laurel *
Nellie R. Stevens holly
Yaupon holly
Savannah holly *
Texas mountain laurel **
Oakland holly
False Japanese yew **
Mary Nell holly
Oleander **
Willowleaf holly
Burford holly
Waxleaf ligustrum **
Green pittosporum **
Pampasgrass **
Glossy abelia
Elaeagnus
Primrose jasmine **
Italian jasmine
Sea Green juniper

   * *East Texas acidic soils only*
   ** *Can be damaged by cold in northern half of Texas*

(Not all of the plants in this list will be equally suited to all parts of Texas. Your local professional nurseryman will be your best source of specific advice.)

Shrub beds benefit from early-morning watering.

Care of Shrubs

Well-designed shrub beds should thrive in your landscape for 20, 30 or 40 years and longer. But that longevity will demand your constant attention to your plants' needs. The responsibilities are basic, but they're critical. Here are your guidelines.

Watering

Learn to recognize the early warning symptoms of drought. Many plants, of course, will wilt. But don't wait to see hollies or junipers (among others) wilt. They will begin to change leaf color to a dull olive drab, and when you see that, you will have waited almost too long. You'll have only hours to soak them enough to save them.

If you can see or feel the soil in which shrubs are planted, that's usually your best indicator of when they're getting too dry. You'll see it lighten in color, and you'll see small cracks start to develop. Stoop over – the soil will be dry to the touch.

You want to encourage deep root growth with shrubs. That means that you should soak the soil to 8 to 12 inches, then let it begin to dry out before you water again. That will encourage the roots to grow deeper into the soil as they seek the moisture.

Drip irrigation can work well with shrub plantings, but it's best if you install it at the time of planting, so the root systems will grow into soil that is being kept moist. Know the emitters' output, and place several emitters around each shrub. Run the watering cycle long enough to ensure deep soakings.

Garden Tip

If you have new shrubs that have been planted within the past six or eight months, and if the plants have turned completely brown, that's almost always a sign that you let them get too dry at least once. Insects and diseases typically don't overtake a plant that quickly, and rarely will they develop over the entire plant simultaneously. Drought will impact the entire plant, and it will do so rapidly.

Slow soaking of newly planted shrub

Oakleaf hydrangea requires moist soils.

Evergreen hollies and low groundcover; Miscanthus 'Cabaret' ornamental grass in back

Flowering quince blooming in early spring

Vitex flowering in May

Fertilizing

Nitrogen promotes stem and leaf growth in all plants, shrubs included, so it's going to be the element of greatest need. The fact is, you can apply a high-quality, all-nitrogen lawn fertilizer to your shrubs with great results. Be sure, of course, that it does not contain a weedkiller.

Timing of feedings

Apply that all-nitrogen fertilizer in anticipation of growth – that is, ahead of bursts of growth by several weeks. Here are a few general guidelines.

- **Evergreen shrubs**: early spring (early March), just as new growth is beginning; late spring (late May, early June) as a supplement before summer; and early fall, to promote fall growth and get plants ready for winter.

- **Spring-flowering shrubs**: immediately after spring bloom, again two months later (late May or early June). Most of these plants can be fed a third time in early September. Included in this list: camellias, flowering quince, forsythia, spiraea, oakleaf hydrangea, oleanders, gardenias and others.

  Note regarding reblooming azaleas: Spring feedings remain the same as for other spring-flowering shrubs, but you might want to change the early fall feeding to a complete-and-balanced analysis (all three components in comparatively equal percentages).

- **Summer-flowering shrubs**: early March as growth begins; mid- to late May, before flowering begins; again in early September. Apply the all-nitrogen food each time. These plants flower on new growth. Included: vitex, crape myrtles and althaeas (roses-of-Sharon).

Summer, early fall flowers of crape myrtles

Summer blooms of rose-of-Sharon Ardens

Pruning

Ideally, you will have chosen plants whose mature sizes fit the surroundings you have for them, so that pruning will be reserved primarily for shaping their errant growth and not for "cutting them back."

If your goal is to maintain natural forms to each of your plants, try never to use hedge shears and gasoline or electric hedge trimmers. Hand shears and loppers will allow you to remove one branch at a time while you maintain an open and natural look. That type of pruning can be done in any month of the year.

Special note on pruning nandinas

Nandinas grow differently than most other shrubs. They do not develop branches. Instead, they send up multiple new shoots from the ground, so any cut that you make should be almost flush with the soil. You can do this stem removal most easily with lopping shears, and it can be done at any season.

The best way to keep nandinas full and compact clear to the soil is to remove the tallest canes (one-third to one-half of the total number of canes) to the ground in early February. Vigorous new shoots will be produced around the remaining canes. Repeat annually and your nandinas will always be attractive.

Hand shears, lopping shears and pruning saw may be used to trim shrubs.

Garden Tip

Major pruning of shrubs is always best saved for mid- to late winter. That's the time to do corrective reshaping of plants like junipers, ligustrums, hollies, Indian hawthorns and others. It may mean that spring-flowering shrubs won't bloom that upcoming spring (you would be removing most of their flower buds), but it's the only good time to do any major trimming.

FAQ

Q How far back can I prune my shrubs, and when should I do so?

A If it's the first time that you've trimmed them, you can probably remove as much as one-fourth to one-third of the top growth from most shrubs. It's best to do so with lopping shears and hand shears instead of hedge trimmers. That makes it easier for you to leave some green growth in place as you trim. It also allows you to reach into the plants to remove dead stubble. Late winter is the time to do this. If you find that you have to repeat this process often, consider moving the plants to more spacious surroundings (also a winter task).

Arapaho is true red, tall variety.

Acoma blooms white on arching branches.

Best Crape Myrtle Varieties for Texas

(Recommended by The Crape Myrtle Trails of McKinney as being reliable and low-maintenance shrubs for Texas landscapes.)

Dwarf: 3 to 5 ft. tall
Intermediate: 5 to 10 ft. tall
Medium: 10 to 20 ft. tall
Tall: More than 20 ft. tall

Reds
Dwarf: Cherry Dazzle
Intermediate: Cheyenne, Tonto
Medium: Centennial Spirit, Country Red, Dynamite, William Toovey
Tall: Arapaho, Red Rocket

Pinks
Dwarf: Pokomoke
Intermediate: Hopi, Pecos
Medium: Osage, Pink Velour, Seminole, Tuskegee
Tall: Biloxi, Choctaw, Potomac, Tuscarora

Unusual mix of heirloom crape myrtles in historic Chestnut Square, McKinney

Old planting of unnamed dwarf varieties

Lavenders

Dwarf: none recommended

Intermediate: none recommended

Medium: Apalachee, Lipan, Yuma

Tall: Muskogee

Purples

Dwarf: Centennial, Velma's Royal Delight

Intermediate: Zuni

Medium: Catawba, Powhatan

Tall: Twilight

Whites

Dwarf: none recommended

Intermediate: Acoma (arching), White Chocolate

Medium: none recommended

Tall: Fantasy, Glendora White, Kiowa, Natchez, Townhouse

Arching habit of Acoma is quite unusual.

Cinnamon-colored bark of Lagerstroemia fauriei trunk

NEW HOME FOR AN OLD CRAPE MYRTLE

1. Plant overtaken by neighboring trees

2. Roots cut and soil ball secured for move

3. Watering plant, tamping soil in new home

4. Berm of soil formed, soil soaked

Mix of crape myrtles in nursery

Merciless topping has no defense.

FAQ

Q What pruning *is* acceptable for my crape myrtles?

A There are three situations where pruning crape myrtles is a good idea:

- To remove damaged or dead branches at any season.

- To remove low side branches as well as extra trunks if you are trying to convert a shrubby crape myrtle into a tree-form plant. This can be done at any time, but it's easiest to see the branching patterns in the winter dormant season.

- To remove errant branches that extend beyond the plant's desired canopy. Do so by cutting them flush with another branch. Never leave stubs when pruning crape myrtles.

Pruning crape myrtles

There has never been an acceptable reason for "topping" crape myrtles. It's bad business – the quickest possible way to ruin the beauty of a handsome shrub or small tree forever. In fact, what some Texans do to their lovely crape myrtles is downright barbaric.

Debunking the myths

- Topping does not improve flower production of crape myrtles. In fact, it delays it by six to eight weeks. Plants that have been topped commonly have only one bloom cycle per summer. Plants that are allowed to grow naturally can have four or five.

- Topping does not keep a crape myrtle short. "Height" is a genetically pre-determined factor, variety-by-variety. If you feel compelled to prune a crape myrtle to keep it shorter, you have the wrong variety. You should either transplant it to more spacious surroundings or take it out entirely, but don't top it!

Glorious trunks of Crape Myrtle Allée in winter (Dallas Arboretum)

RESTORING A CRAPE MYRTLE THAT WAS PREVIOUSLY TOPPED

It's virtually impossible to reshape a crape myrtle that has gnarly nubs of old trunks and branches, even if you're patient. The scars will always be there. But here is a quick way to get a handsome plant back into your life.

- Cut the plant back to within 1 inch of the soil. It will have all of its root system, but no top growth to support, so it will produce scores of vigorous new shoots.

- Let 12 or 15 of the straightest stems develop for one year. They will probably be 3 to 5 feet tall at the end of one season.

- Before new growth begins the second spring, prune to leave the straightest seven or nine stems.

- As those stems begin to turn woody and gain strength, you can gradually thin their numbers down to three or five final trunks. (Odd numbers are visually more restful.)

- As the new trunks begin to send out young branches, you can begin to "limb the plant up" into the tree-form crape myrtle you wanted originally.

The entire process won't take more than two or three years, and you'll have a glorious new plant in the process.

These plants were never officially "topped," but they froze to the ground one winter, and the results were just about the same. The regrowth from their roots was retrained tree-form, and this is how they looked less than 30 months later.

Crape Myrtles: A Texas Tradition

Many cities across Texas feature crape myrtles in their public landscapes. The photos you see to the right and above are from McKinney (officially designated as "America's Crape Myrtle City"), where The Crape Myrtle Trails of McKinney Foundation has partnered with the city and with private developers. The organization has worked with the city to develop The World Collection Park showcasing all of the known varieties in existence at the time of the park's opening.

Blend of colors, Chestnut Square, McKinney

July 4 in McKinney

Catawba crape myrtles, McKinney

Purple Plateau in The World Collection Park, McKinney

Pindo palms' feathery texture

Prominent trunk of Florida sabal

Bismarckia palm lovely, but unable to withstand any freezing weather.

Palms Across Texas

When you're striving for a tropical look in your landscape, palms spring to mind instantly. And lucky for most of us, there are palms that have outstanding chances of surviving winters in much of the Lone Star State. But you do have to be careful, because there also are palms that have no business ever being planted outdoors where it will freeze – and that includes most of Texas.

Choosing and Caring for Your Palms

Consider these factors before you go shopping:

- How tall and wide will the palm grow? You can't really prune a palm, so you must choose one that will grow no larger than the space you have available for it.

- Do I want "feather" or "fan?" That's referring, of course, to each plant's leaf type. Some have their leaflets arranged like a feather, with one central midrib. Other types have the leaves in the form of the palm and fingers of your wide-open hand (fan). Feather types are generally much finer-textured. Fan types are coarser, making a much bolder statement.

- How cold-hardy must my plant be? This is the factor that trumps everything else. It makes no difference the plant's mature size or leaf type. If the variety won't make it through winters in your area, those other things will be of absolutely no concern. Consult the Zone Hardiness map to determine which Zone fits for your county. Buy only types that are reliably winter-hardy for your area.

Tropical look of a North Texas (McKinney) landscape

Choosing when to plant palms

We all want "the tropical look" from late spring through summer and into the fall. After all, that's when we're entertaining outdoors. Luckily, late spring and summer are the ideal times to buy and plant new palms into your garden. It's even the time that larger bare-rooted specimens are frequently moved. Unlike almost all other plant species, palms reestablish best when it's warm.

Picking the right spot

Palms do best in sandy or loamy soils that are well drained. They require full sun for symmetrical growth. If you're in a part of Texas where palms are a bit of a risk, or if you're trying a type that isn't quite as winter-hardy as it ought to be for your area, increase your odds of success by planting it on the south or east side of your house (protected from winter winds). Utilize fences, high house walls, alcoves and atriums that might catch and retain a bit of warmth, to better the chances of your palm's surviving.

Palm care and feeding

Apply nitrogen fertilizer (same that you're using on your lawn, as long as it's free of weedkiller additives) in spring and summer. Most palms grow rather slowly, so be patient. Keep the plants moist at all times. That's especially important during winter cold spells. Dry plants suffer more injury than plants that are properly hydrated. Trim to remove dead leaves from your palms. It's primarily a cosmetic thing, but it's important to the plants' contributions to your landscape.

Winter protection

Wrapping palm trunks in several layers of burlap will help with mid-winter protection, particularly if you're growing a type that is marginal for your area anyway. Pull the burlap around the trunk and secure it with duct tape to hold it in place. Some people also place small incandescent Christmas lights around the trunks for whatever tiny amount of warmth they might provide. If the palm is short enough that you can cover it entirely with a large piece of frost cloth that you secure to the ground, that would be even better. You'll gain 4 or 5 degrees of added protection and insulate the critical tip (the palm "heart"). Do not use plastic film to wrap or cover your palm. Think more along the lines of some way to insulate the trunk and growing tip.

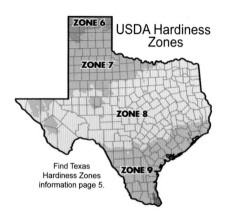

USDA Hardiness Zones

Find Texas Hardiness Zones information page 5.

Palms you consider must be of your county's Zone Hardiness number or a smaller number. Example: You determine from the map that you're in Zone 8. Zone 8 palms should be fine. Zone 7 palms will certainly be fine. Zone 9 palms would be a big risk.

Young Mediterranean fan palm

Older Mediterranean fan palm

Pindo palm

Common Palms for Texas Landscapes

Plants in the chart that follows have been arranged alphabetically by their scientific names. Please note that the sequence is not intended to represent rankings of any kind.

Best Zones In Texas 6 7 8 9	PLANT AND COMMENTS	HEIGHT*	WIDTH*
Fan types			
▨▨	Mediterranean (European) fan palm (*Chamaerops humilis*) Compact, so ideal for urban landscapes; very stout and multi-trunked habit; leaves range from bluish-green to grayish-green; outstanding and popular where temperatures stay above 10 F.	20 ft.	12 ft.
▨▨	Chinese fan palm (*Livistona chinensis*) Lush, dark green leaves 3 to 5 ft. long and wide; popular because widely adapted to sun/shade, variety of soils; very graceful form; can be used as understory palm in shade of taller trees	35 ft.	15 ft.
▨▨▨▨	Needle palm (*Rhapidophyllum hystrix*) Hardiest of all palms; grows slowly; forms dense clumps; sharp needle-like spines on leaf petioles, so keep away from areas with children and pets.	10 ft.	10 ft.
▨▨▨	Florida sabal or cabbage palmetto (*Sabal palmetto*) Single-trunked; adapted to variety of soils; quite winter-hardy and useful in a variety of landscaping situations; stout habit; salt- and drought-tolerant	35 ft.	15 ft.
▨▨▨	Texas sabal (*Sabal texana* or *S. mexicana*) Native palm to Southeast Texas and northward almost to DFW; most cold-hardy of all palms; taller in South Texas, but can be used as large tropical-looking shrub in North Texas; survives temperatures several degrees below zero without damage	35 ft.	20 ft.
▨▨▨	Windmill palm (*Trachycarpus fortunei*) Compact habit makes it very suitable for pool, patio and urban landscape use; very cold-hardy; leaves are silvery-green; leaf petioles have small teeth along edges; commonly used and deservedly so; dwarf form (to 6 ft.) available	20 ft.	10 ft.
▨▨▨	California fan palm (*Washingtonia filifera*) Single-trunk plant; grows slowly and remains compact for years; large, dark green leaves; an iconic palm for Texas landscaping – easily found and easily grown, unless temperatures fall to extremes	50 ft.	18 ft.
▨▨	Mexican fan palm (*Washingtonia robusta*) Single-trunk palm; thin trunks to 1 ft. in diameter, yet very tall; leaves grow to 5 ft. long and 4 ft. wide; very commonly used along Texas Gulf Coast; tolerant of marine salts, variety of soils	60 ft.	15 ft.
Feather types			
▨▨▨	Pindo palm (*Butia capitata*) Blue-gray leaves; characteristic graceful, arching and fountain-like growth; slow-growing; suited to wide variety of soil types, including clays	20 ft.	15 ft.
▨	Pygmy date palm (*Phoenix roebelenii*) Often multi-trunk, small palm; shiny green leaves; popular in South Texas, but best in pots so it can be moved into protection; warning: can be damaged or lost at temperatures below 30 F	8 ft.	6 ft.
▨	Queen palm (*Syagrus romanzoffiana*) Graceful appearance; adapted to variety of soils; orange flowers are attractive all summer; warning: very sensitive to cold – damaged at 25 F and killed at 20 F	50 ft.	20 ft.

* Maximum heights and widths in perfect growing conditions

Sago – the "Pretender" Palm

They're called sago *palms*, but sago palms are really cycads (*Cycas revoluta*). They're prehistoric plants, yet they're still present today in thousands of Texas landscapes. So, even though sago palms are not related to true palms at all, this is a great place to include them.

Sago palms are frequently used in South Texas landscapes, where they can grow to be 4 or 5 feet tall and wide. They grow wonderfully in morning sun with a bit of protection from the hottest mid-afternoon sun in mid-summer. Give them moist, well-draining soils and nitrogen fertilizer in spring and summer.

Note that the "wingspan" of sago palms' long leaves can reach well beyond the original planting site. Their leaf tips are rather sharp, so be sure you have ample room before you plant them alongside a pool, walk or patio.

Check cycads' Hardiness Zone!

Do a little research, and you'll find sago palms listed as hardy in Zones 9 and 10, and only marginally hardy in the southern half of Zone 8.

North Texas gardeners, notably in DFW, have included sago palms in their landscapes, too. Whether those people realize it or not, that's being done at great risk. Sago palms are not reliably winter-hardy in the northern half of Texas. Consumers see them in restaurant and hotel patio landscapes, then they encounter them in national cash-and-carry stores (where there is no professional nurseryman to offer appropriate cautions), and they are shocked to find some winter soon thereafter that they've planted a sub-tropical plant that should never have been sold for that purpose.

Exotic foliage, growth habit of sub-tropical sago palms

If you're in a colder region, however, you can still grow sago palms. Just do so in large patio pots. Put them on plant dollies so you can easily roll them into the garage when it drops below freezing. The plants will grow very large, and you may eventually decide they're not worth it, but as long as you have the patience, they have the time – remember: they're prehistoric.

Bagworm spray after young larvae are detected

Extreme outbreak of euonymus scale

Garden Tip

Keep a log of all the types of plants that you're growing. Do a little research online and in references, also by asking your nurseryman if your plants are prone to any specific pest problems. Know what those problems look like and when they occur. Keep a close eye on the plants at those times, and intervene at once when you must.

Insect and Disease Control in Shrubs

If you choose your shrubs carefully and tend them regularly, insect and disease problems should be minimal. Still, occasional problems will crop up. Here are several of the most common insects and diseases – most of them impacting more than one species – along with suggestions of how best to deal with them.

Bagworms: Junipers and other conifers are their host plants. Larvae begin feeding in late spring and continue for several weeks into early summer, devouring needles in the process. Larvae are easily controlled by most organic and inorganic pesticides if the spray is applied while they are young (small) and still feeding actively. Once they sequester themselves within their bags and attach the bags to the twigs, they are through for the year. Moths will emerge from the cocoons the following spring and start the process over again. Plants that have been stripped of foliage often do not recover.

Scale insects: These slow-moving, even immobile, pests come in several different forms. Most form white, tan or brown crusts or shell-like formations on twigs and leaves. Common host shrubs: euonymus, photinias, crape myrtles, camellias and hollies. Systemic insecticides applied to the soil in late spring will usually prevent rapid build-ups. Horticultural oils applied during winter will help with many types. Systemic insecticide sprays applied during the growing season will reduce numbers somewhat.

Grasshoppers: Populations of these assertive eaters will vary from one year to the next. They attack a wide variety of plants, and populations usually run their course within several weeks. Contact insecticides provide fairly good control, but spray in a downward motion, so you'll coat the insects as they try to fly away. Baits offer some help. Keep tall grass and weeds trimmed, as they harbor the pests.

Caterpillars: These are most common in spring, as the various insects begin their annual life cycles, but there are many species that appear in summer and fall. Begin by identifying the type of caterpillar involved (and its adult form). Some caterpillars do little damage, but then pupate into beautiful adult moths and butterflies, so you probably wouldn't want to harm them. If you determine that it's a damaging type, apply a contact or systemic insecticide, organic or inorganic, to control most types of caterpillars. If they are loopers (form horseshoe-shaped loops in their bodies as they move), you will need to apply *Bacillus thuringiensis* biological worm control.

Aphids: These are communal pests that colonize very rapidly on tops and bottoms of leaves of shrubs (and other plants). They will always be pear-shaped, and most types are smaller than BBs. Colors will vary from white to black, green, yellow, rust and brown, depending on the species. They often leave a sticky residue ("honeydew") on leaves and stems. A black sooty mold will grow in the honeydew substrate. General-purpose insecticides eliminate aphids fairly easily.

Lace bugs: Several types of shrubs are frequented by these elusive pests, including boxwoods, azaleas, loropetalums and Texas sage. At first, leaves will be stippled with tiny tan spots. As populations build, leaves will turn tan all over and you'll see waxy black globs (excrement) on the backs of the leaves. Sticky honeydew residue will also begin to appear. The insects are BB-sized, but they have clear wings and are hard to spot. You may go years without seeing the actual insects, even though their damage is evident. For the record, you'll see their damage on Boston ivy, sycamores and bur oaks as well.

Spider mites: Of all garden pests, these are the smallest, and they may be the most damaging. They attack a wide host of landscape and garden plants, leaving foliage stippled tan, then almost white, then browned and lifeless. You can see the tiny mites if you thump a suspect leaf or small twig over a sheet of white paper. They'll be the nearly microscopic dark specks that start to move almost immediately. They're common on annuals and vegetables, and you'll see them occasionally on shrubs. Most notable host shrubs are the junipers. These pests will turn affected branches to a dull shade of green. Do the thumping to identify them, and if you do find them, treat at once. Their damage can soon become irreversible. Note that most spider mite damage shows up when the weather turns really warm, but the mites that attack junipers get an early start, often appearing in late winter.

Entomosporium fungal leaf spot: It began by ravaging redtip photinias, but now it has also taken a heavy toll on redtip's close relative, Indian hawthorn. It begins as small maroon "freckles" spotted all over the leaves. With redtips, the next phase is branches that begin to turn pale green, even white. As they weaken, those branches begin to die, until sections of the plant are lost. Eventually, the entire plant dies away. With Indian hawthorns, the leaf-spotting phase is soon followed by severe leaf drop, until the plants are virtually bare. Unfortunately, there is no fungicide that offers much help with this disease. It is best not to plant new redtip photinias and to be guarded in the numbers of Indian hawthorns that you use.

Aphids congregating on crape myrtle leaves

FAQ

Q How can I control the black mold on leaves of my shrubs (and trees)?

A That is a fungus known as sooty mold, and it grows in the sticky honeydew left behind by scale insects, aphids and lace bugs, among others. Control the insect pest to prevent the mold. The mold is harmless, and it will be shed with old leaves and bark.

Maroon spots on redtip photinia leaves are early signs of the fatal Entomosporium fungus.

Garden Tip

If you are growing species of shrubs that are known to be winter-tender in periods of extreme cold in your area, use frost cloth or other porous, lightweight fabric (not plastic) to give them short-term protection. Drape the wrap over the tops of the plants, and secure it to the soil. It will trap warmth from the soil and radiate it up and around the plants overnight, making as much as 4 to 8 degrees of difference beneath the cover. It will also keep the cold winds from making direct contact with the foliage. Leave the frost cloth in place until temperatures climb above freezing. If snow or ice is forecast along with extreme cold, use stakes to keep the cover held up, so that the weight of the moisture won't break the plants. Keeping shrub beds watered properly will also lessen the chances of freeze damage.

Frost cloth is secured in place to protect tender shrubs from a spell of extremely cold winter weather. It stops the bitter wind, and it provides several degrees of warmth that will be radiated from the covered soil.

Powdery mildew: Its name derives from the fact that it looks like a dusting of flour on leaves and new twigs. Within the world of shrubs, the plants most commonly impacted by this common fungus are some varieties (especially older types) of crape myrtles, euonymus and old-fashioned Chinese photinia. Powdery mildew is most prevalent in spring, and it will cause puckering and discoloration of new growth, but it rarely does serious damage. Many fungicides are labeled for its control. Keeping shrub foliage dry as much as you're able will also help.

Cotton root rot: It's also called "Texas root rot," because it's a notorious threat in the Blackland Prairie soils where cotton used to be king. Its signature is that it kills plants almost overnight. They may appear healthy and thriving one week and browned and crisp the next. It attacks perhaps 80 percent of the plant species we grow in our landscapes, but some are much more susceptible than others. Most vulnerable: roses-of-Sharon, ligustrums, cherry laurels, forsythias and oakleaf hydrangeas. It's best to replant infected areas with resistant species like junipers, hollies, nandinas and crape myrtles.

Powdery mildew on crape myrtle (late spring)

Carissa holly (left) and dwarf
Chinese holly

Indian hawthorn and boxwood at
top, variegated abelia in middle, and
Japanese barberry at bottom

USDA Hardiness
Zones

ZONE 6
ZONE 7
ZONE 8
ZONE 9

Find Texas
Hardiness Zones
information page 5.

Small Shrubs (up to 4 ft. tall and wide)

Plants in the chart that follows have been arranged alphabetically by their scientific names. In Overall Ratings (column at far right), the number 1 indicates the highest recommendation.

Best Zones In Texas 6 7 8 9	PLANT AND COMMENTS	SUN/SHADE	HEIGHT	WIDTH	DECIDUOUS/EVERGREEN	FLOWERS (showy)	FRUIT (colorful)	INSECTS (of significance)	DISEASES (of significance)	SPECIAL SOILS REQUIRED	OVERALL RATING
▪▪▪	Japanese barberry (*Berberis thunbergii*) Several varieties; brilliant spring foliage; intolerant of reflective hot sun; semi-evergreen	●●	2 ft.	2 ft.	D/E	no	no	no	no	no	2
▪▪▪▪	Japanese boxwood (*Buxus microphylla japonica*) May bronze in winter (choose selections that do not); nematodes; lace bugs	●●	2 ft.	2 ft.	E	no	no	yes	yes	no	2
▪▪▪▪	Golden euonymus (*Euonymus japonicus* 'Aureo-marginatus') Bright variegation catches shoppers' eyes, but a poor choice for Texas landscapes; euonymus scale (life-threatening); powdery mildew; leaves scorch and brown in hot, sunny exposures; Silver Queen euonymus is variegated white – faces same issues	●●	4 ft.	4 ft.	E	no	no	yes	yes	no	3
▪▪▪	Hydrangea (*Hydrangea macrophylla*) Popular East Texas flowering shrub; floral bracts are blue in acidic soils and pink in alkaline; severe iron deficiency in alkaline soils; bed preparation similar to that for azaleas; do not allow to wilt badly; many varieties, some blooming repeatedly	●	4 ft.	4 ft.	D	spr.	no	no	no	acidic	2
▪▪▪▪	Carissa holly (*Ilex cornuta* 'Carissa') Bold texture; good replacement for Indian hawthorns when needed; not suited to hottest reflective western exposures	●●●	3 ft.	3 ft.	E	no	no	no	no	no	1
▪▪▪▪	Dwarf Burford holly (*Ilex cornuta* 'Dwarf Burford') Dense; heavy berry producer; a favorite low border and hedge shrub	●●●	4 ft.	3 ft.	E	no	win.	no	no	no	1
▪▪▪▪	Dwarf Chinese holly (*Ilex cornuta* 'Rotunda') Prickly leaves; good at controlling pedestrian flow; dependable low grower	●●●	3 ft.	3 ft.	E	no	no	no	no	no	1

Best Zones In Texas* 6 7 8 9	PLANT AND COMMENTS *See Zones Map page 117.	SUN/SHADE (Sun / Partial Sun / Shade)	HEIGHT	WIDTH	DECIDUOUS/EVERGREEN	FLOWERS (showy)	FRUIT (colorful)	INSECTS (of significance)	DISEASES (of significance)	SPECIAL SOILS REQUIRED	OVERALL RATING
	Heller's Japanese holly (*Ilex crenata* 'Helleri') — Resembles dwarf yaupon, but not as adapted to variety of soils; deep green spineless foliage; fine texture; East Texas only	Sun / Partial / Shade	3 ft.	3 ft.	E	no	no	no	no	acidic	2
	Dwarf yaupon holly (*Ilex vomitoria* 'Nana') — No spines; tolerant of shearing; often used for low borders; fine texture	Sun / Partial / Shade	3 ft.	3 ft.	E	no	no	no	no	no	1
	Dwarf junipers (*Juniperus* spp.) — Many varieties; bagworms and spider mites are main pests	Sun	2-4 ft.	2-4 ft.	E	no	no	yes	no	no	1
	Dwarf crape myrtles (*Lagerstroemia indica*) — Many varieties; use in front of dark green evergreens for best show	Sun	2-4 ft.	2-4 ft.	D	sum.	no	no	yes	no	1
	Oregon grape mahonia (*Mahonia aquifolium*) — Holly-like foliage on upright stalks; must have afternoon shade	Partial / Shade	4 ft.	3 ft.	E	win.	spr.	no	no	no	1
	Compact nandina (*Nandina domestica* 'Compacta') — Multi-colored winter foliage; one of best nandinas; easily divided for new beds	Sun / Partial	3 ft.	3 ft.	E	no	win.	no	no	no	1

Anthony Waterer spiraea

Compact nandina

Dwarf crape myrtles

Mix of Indian hawthorn varieties, colors

Wheeler's Dwarf pittosporum

Snow and Hinodegiri red azaleas.

Small Shrubs CONTINUED

Best Zones In Texas* 6 7 8 9 — PLANT AND COMMENTS *See Zones Map page 117.	SUN/SHADE (SUN / PARTIAL SUN / SHADE)	HEIGHT	WIDTH	DECIDUOUS/EVERGREEN	FLOWERS (showy)	FRUIT (colorful)	INSECTS (of significance)	DISEASES (of significance)	SPECIAL SOILS REQUIRED	OVERALL RATING
Gulf Stream nandina (*Nandina domestica* 'Gulf Stream') Maroon winter foliage; tallest canes must be pruned to ground each winter to keep plants compact	●●	3 ft.	3 ft.	E	no	no	no	no	no	1
Moonbay nandina (*Nandina domestica* 'Moonbay') Cherry-red winter foliage; tallest canes must be pruned to ground each winter to keep plants compact	●●	3 ft.	2-1/2 ft.	E	no	no	no	no	no	1
Nana nandina (*Nandina domestica* 'Nana Purpurea') Red winter foliage; requires perfect drainage; can show iron deficiency	●●	2 ft.	2 ft.	E	no	no	no	no	no	2
Wheeler's dwarf pittosporum (*Pittosporum tobira* 'Wheeler's Dwarf') Glossy dark green; variegated form also sold; often planted too far north of its zone of adaptability	●●	2 ft.	2 ft.	E	no	no	no	no	no	2
Indian hawthorn (*Raphiolepsis indica*) Blooms most years; many varieties; Entomosporium fungal leaf spot	●	3 ft.	3 ft.	E	spr.	fall	no	yes	no	2
Azalea (*Rhododendron* spp.) Many varieties; new selections bloom repeatedly through year; lace bugs	●	3-4 ft.	3-4 ft.	E	spr.	no	yes	no	acidic	1
Anthony Waterer spiraea (*Spiraea* x *bumalda* 'Anthony Waterer') Magenta flowers; will show iron deficiency in alkaline soils	●	2 ft.	2 ft.	D	spr.	no	no	no	acidic	1

Medium Shrubs (4 to 8 ft. tall and wide)

Plants in the chart that follows have been arranged alphabetically by their scientific names. In Overall Ratings (column at far right), the number 1 indicates the highest recommendation.

Best Zones In Texas*

6 7 8 9   PLANT AND COMMENTS   **See Zones Map page 117.*

Plant and Comments	Sun/Shade	Height	Width	Deciduous/Evergreen	Flowers (showy)	Fruit (colorful)	Insects (of significance)	Diseases (of significance)	Special Soils Required	Overall Rating
Glossy abelia (*Abelia grandiflora*) Arching branches; white bell-shaped flowers produced continuously; dwarf, pink-flowering and variegated selections are also sold	sun/partial	6 ft.	6-8 ft.	E	spr./sum.	no	no	no	no	1
Gold Dust aucuba (*Aucuba japonica*) Highly variegated; dwarf forms available; turns black when exposed to sunlight	shade	5 ft.	4 ft.	E	no	no	no	no	no	2
American beautyberry (*Callicarpa americana*) Native woodland plant of East and South Central Texas; large leaves resemble those of mulberries (not related); iridescent purple fruit borne in fall in clusters along stems; fruit persists several weeks until devoured by birds; great small, slow-growing shrub to use among shade perennials such as ferns	shade	6 ft.	6 ft.	D	no	fall	no	no	moist	2
Flowering quince (*Chaenomeles japonica*) Among showiest of late-winter/early-spring flowering shrubs; blooms brilliant red, pink, white, apricot and others; outstanding new varieties available; use toward back of landscape, since unattractive when not flowering	sun	5 ft.	5 ft.	D	win.	no	no	no	no	2
Elaeagnus (*Elaeagnus pungens*) Gray foliage; fragrant fall flowers are inconspicuous	sun	6 ft.	8 ft.	E	no	no	no	no	no	1
Japanese fatsia (*Fatsia japonica*) Huge star-shaped leaves; bold tropical look	shade	5 ft.	5 ft.	E	no	no	no	no	no	2
Forsythia (*Forsythia intermedia*) Brilliant yellow spring flowers; several varieties	sun	6 ft.	6 ft.	D	spr.	no	no	no	no	2
Gardenia (*Gardenia jasminoides*) Dwarf form less winter-hardy; all highly fragrant; whiteflies; iron deficiency	partial/shade	5 ft.	5 ft.	E	spr.	no	yes	no	acidic	2

Flowering quince bloom

Gardenia flower

American beautyberry with fruit

Glossy abelia blooms in summer, fall

Variegated shrubs in nursery

Italian jasmine flowers in spring

Medium Shrubs CONTINUED

Best Zones In Texas* 6 7 8 9	PLANT AND COMMENTS *See Zones Map page 117.	SUN/SHADE SUN PARTIAL SUN SHADE	HEIGHT	WIDTH	DECIDUOUS/EVERGREEN	FLOWERS (showy)	FRUIT (colorful)	INSECTS (of significance)	DISEASES (of significance)	SPECIAL SOILS REQUIRED	OVERAL RATING
▦▦▦▦	Burford holly (*Ilex cornuta* 'Burfordii') Large red berries; dense and rather stiff habit; not to be confused with dwarf Burford holly	○●●	7 ft.	7 ft.	E	no	win.	no	no	no	1
▦▦▦	Willowleaf holly (*Ilex cornuta* 'Willowleaf') Large red berries dependably produced; outstanding mid-sized screen; also called "Needlepoint" holly	○●●	7 ft.	7 ft.	E	no	win.	no	no	no	1
▦▦▦	Little Red holly (*Ilex* x 'Little Red') Shortest of the "red holly" seedlings of Mary Nell holly	○●●	7 ft.	7 ft.	E	no	win.	no	no	no	1
▦▦▦	Italian jasmine (*Jasminum humile*) Arching branches; deepest green foliage; under-used	○●	5 ft.	6 ft.	E	win./spr.	no	no	no	no	1
▦▦	Primrose jasmine (*Jasminum primulinum*) Arching branches; double yellow blooms; medium-green foliage	○●	6 ft.	7 ft.	E	win./spr.	no	no	no	no	2
▦▦▦	Ceniza or Texas sage (*Leucophyllum frutescens*) Intolerant of poor drainage; lace bugs; blooms after summer, fall rains; white, lavender and purple selections available	○	5 ft.	5 ft.	E	sum./fall	no	yes	no	dry	2
▦▦▦▦	Variegated privet (*Ligustrum sinense* 'Varigatum') Brightly white-variegated shrub is inexpensive and fast-growing; tempting, but short productive life in landscape; unstable selection, since strong-growing green branches sprout out and must be removed by hand; green privet fruits very heavily and is ultimately invasive of native areas – should never be planted	○●	6 ft.	6 ft.	E	spr.	no	yes	no	no	4

Medium Shrubs CONTINUED
(4 to 8 ft. tall and wide)

*See Zones Map page 117.

Best Zones In Texas* (6 7 8 9) / PLANT AND COMMENTS	SUN/SHADE	HEIGHT	WIDTH	DECIDUOUS/EVERGREEN	FLOWERS (showy)	FRUIT (colorful)	INSECTS (of significance)	DISEASES (of significance)	SPECIAL SOILS REQUIRED	OVERALL RATING
Fringe flower (*Loropetalum chinense*) Many varieties, most with purple foliage; some dwarf forms are also sold; lace bugs; iron deficiency shortens productive life expectancy in alkaline soils; confirm mature height, as some varieties outgrow space available	●	4-8 ft.	4-8 ft.	D	win./spr.	no	yes	no	acidic	2
Leatherleaf mahonia (*Mahonia bealei*) Striking blue-gray spiny foliage; steel-blue fruit in showy clusters; dramatic habit; several cultivars, including 'Soft Caress' are available	●	5 ft.	4 ft.	E	win.	spr.	no	no	no	1
Standard nandina (*Nandina domestica*) Original species; outstanding winter color from foliage and showy berries; prune tallest canes to ground each winter to keep plants compact	◐●	5 ft.	4 ft.	E	no	win.	no	no	no	1
Bridal wreath (*Spiraea* spp.) Arching branches covered with blooms in spring; many varieties; most white-flowering, some lavender-purple	◐●	5 ft.	5 ft.	D	spr.	no	no	no	no	2
Cleyera (*Ternstroemia gymnanthera*) Requires perfect drainage; glossy foliage; new growth coppery-red	●	5 ft.	5 ft.	E	no	no	no	no	no	2
Spring Bouquet viburnum (*Viburnum tinus* 'Spring Bouquet') Popular small-leafed viburnum that bears pink blooms; tolerates morning sun, but also good in shade; often sold north of where it is reliably winter-hardy	●●	5 ft.	5 ft.	E	spr.	no	no	no	no	1
Weigela (*Weigela florida*) Colorful blooms mid-spring; not commonly used	◐	6 ft.	6 ft.	D	spr.	no	no	no	no	2

Nandina and Indian hawthorn in early spring

Leatherleaf mahonia in bloom in winter

Loropetalum in bloom in early spring

Large Shrubs (More than 8 feet tall and wide)

Plants in the chart that follows have been arranged alphabetically by their scientific names. In Overall Ratings (column at far right), the number 1 indicates the highest recommendation.

Best Zones In Texas* — 6 7 8 9

*See Zones Map page 117.

Plant and Comments	Sun/Shade	Height	Width	Deciduous/Evergreen	Flowers (showy)	Fruit (colorful)	Insects (of significance)	Diseases (of significance)	Special Soils Required	Overall Rating
Camellia (*Camellia japonica* and *C. sasanqua*) — Many varieties; Japonica camellias are shorter and bloom during mid-winter, when danger of freeze damage to buds is greater; Sasanqua camellia plants are generally larger and bloom in November and December, before worst of cold weather; Sasanqua blooms are usually smaller than those of Japonica camellias	Partial Sun	8 ft.	8 ft.	E	win.	no	yes	no	acidic	2
Burning bush euonymus (*Euonymus alatus*) — Stunning red fall foliage; corky ridges show on stems when bare in winter	Sun	7 ft.	7 ft.	D	no	no	no	no	no	2
Rose-of-Sharon (*Hibiscus syriacus*) — Many varieties; white, pink, lavender and rose-colored single or double flowers; will abort up to half of buds if weather suddenly turns hot; cotton root rot	Sun	12 ft.	12 ft.	D	sum.	no	no	yes	no	2
Oakleaf hydrangea (*Hydrangea quercifolia*) — Bold textured; woody shrub; large white floral heads; crimson fall color; peeling bark; highly outstanding flowering shrub for shade	Partial Sun, Shade	6 ft.	8 ft.	D	spr.	no	no	no	no	1
Sky Pencil holly (*Ilex crenata* 'Sky Pencil') — Dramatic growth form; branches tend to splay out and may have to be tied in place; East Texas only due to need for acidic soils	Sun, Partial Sun, Shade	10 ft.	4 ft.	E	no	no	no	no	acidic	3
Warren's Red possumhaw holly (*Ilex decidua* 'Warren's Red') — Outstanding red berries borne on bare stems; native types are usually orange-red	Sun, Partial Sun, Shade	12 ft.	12 ft.	D	no	win.	no	no	no	1

Camellia Winter's Joy in late fall

Oakleaf hydrangea fall color in November

Weeping yaupon holly fruit in winter

Bold but harmless foliage of Mary Nell holly

Large Shrubs CONTINUED
(More than 8 feet tall and wide)

Best Zones In Texas* 6 7 8 9	PLANT AND COMMENTS *See Zones Map page 117.	SUN/SHADE	HEIGHT	WIDTH	DECIDUOUS/EVERGREEN	FLOWERS (showy)	FRUIT (colorful)	INSECTS (of significance)	DISEASES (of significance)	SPECIAL SOILS REQUIRED	OVERALL RATING
▦▦▦	**American holly** (*Ilex opaca*) Native to East Texas; requires acidic soils; lovely, very large shrub or small landscape tree; better with some shade in afternoon	●●●	30 ft.	25 ft.	E	no	win.	no	no	acidic	1
▦▦▦▦	**Yaupon holly** (*Ilex vomitoria*) Several varieties; berries are small, but produced liberally; male plants will produce pollen, but no berries	●●●	15 ft.	15 ft.	E	no	win.	no	no	no	1
▦▦▦▦	**Weeping yaupon holly** (*Ilex vomitoria* 'Pendula') Visually heavy; extremely dramatic weeping habit, so use strategically; multitudes of winter berries	●●●	15 ft.	15 ft.	E	no	win.	no	no	no	1
▦▦▦▦	**Will Fleming yaupon holly** (*Ilex vomitoria* 'Will Fleming') Columnar form of yaupon holly; better adapted to alkaline soils than similar Sky Pencil, but still difficult to utilize effectively due to dramatic habit; branches tend to splay out, requiring tying	●●●	10 ft.	2 ft.	E	no	win.	no	no	no	2
▦▦▦	**Cardinal holly** (*Ilex* x 'Cardinal') Medium texture in appearance; another "red holly" developed from Mary Nell holly	●●●	12 ft.	8 ft.	E	no	win.	no	no	no	1
▦▦▦	**East Palatka holly** (*Ilex* x *attenuata* 'East Palatka') Lovely tree-form holly; *Ilex opaca* hybrid; East Texas only due to need for acidic soil	●●	20 ft.	16 ft.	E	no	win.	no	no	acidic	2
▦▦▦	**Festive holly** (*Ilex* x 'Festive') One of the fine "red holly" hybrid selections from Mary Nell holly	●●●	12 ft.	8 ft.	E	no	win.	no	no	no	1

Large Shrubs CONTINUED

Best Zones In Texas* (6 7 8 9)	Plant and Comments	SUN/SHADE	HEIGHT	WIDTH	DECIDUOUS/EVERGREEN	FLOWERS (showy)	FRUIT (colorful)	INSECTS (of significance)	DISEASES (of significance)	SPECIAL SOILS REQUIRED	OVERALL RATING
▩▩▩▩	**Foster holly** (*Ilex* x 'Foster') Good holly for East Texas due to need for acidic soil; formal habit	○◐●	20 ft.	16 ft.	E	no	win.	no	no	acidic	1
▩▩▩▩	**Liberty holly** (*Ilex* x 'Liberty') Another of the "red holly" hybrids chosen from seedlings of Mary Nell holly.	○◐●	12 ft.	8 ft.	E	no	win.	no	no	no	1
▩▩▩▩	**Mary Nell holly** (*Ilex* x 'Mary Nell') Large leaves; bold texture; popular screening holly	○◐●	10 ft.	8 ft.	E	no	no	no	no	no	1
▩▩▩▩	**Nellie R. Stevens holly** (*Ilex* x 'Nellie R. Stevens') Perhaps our best large screen; deep green foliage; very large red berries produced once plant becomes well established	○◐●	16 ft.	12 ft.	E	no	win.	no	no	no	1
▩▩▩▩	**Oakland holly** (*Ilex* x 'Oakland') One of our finest screening shrubs for sun or shade; outstanding relatively new type	○◐●	12 ft.	8 ft.	E	no	win.	no	no	no	1
▩▩▩▩	**Oakleaf holly** (*Ilex* x 'Oakleaf') Very similar in appearance to Oakland holly	○◐●	12 ft.	8 ft.	E	no	win.	no	no	no	1
▩▩▩▩	**Patriot holly** (*Ilex* x 'Patriot') Seedling selection of Mary Nell holly, known as one of the "red hollies"	○◐●	12 ft.	8 ft.	E	no	win.	no	no	no	1
▩▩▩▩	**Robin holly** (*Ilex* x 'Robin') One of tallest of the "red holly" hybrids from Mary Nell holly seedlings	○◐●	15 ft.	10 ft.	E	no	win.	no	no	no	1
▩▩▩▩	**Savannah holly** (*Ilex* x 'Savannah') Outstanding shrub for East Texas and other areas with acidic soils	○◐●	20	16	E	no	win.	no	no	acidic	1

*See Zones Map page 117.

Oakland holly leaves

Evergreen shrubs against fall foliage (author's yard)

Nellie R. Stevens holly

Large Shrubs CONTINUED
(More than 8 feet tall and wide)

Best Zones In Texas* 6 7 8 9	PLANT AND COMMENTS *See Zones Map page 117.	SUN/SHADE	HEIGHT	WIDTH	DECIDUOUS/EVERGREEN	FLOWERS (showy)	FRUIT (colorful)	INSECTS (of significance)	DISEASES (of significance)	SPECIAL SOILS REQUIRED	OVERAL RATING
■ ■ ■ ■	**Junipers** (*Juniperus* spp.) Many varieties and growth forms; bagworms and spider mites; heat-proof if kept moist	○	8-20 ft.	4-15 ft.	E	no	no	yes	yes	no	2
■ ■ ■ ■	**Crape myrtles** (*Lagerstroemia indica* and *L. fauriei* hybrids) Many varieties and sizes – see list of Best Varieties for Texas, page 106.	○	10-30 ft.	10-25 ft.	D	sum.	no	yes	yes	no	1
■ ■ ■	**Waxleaf ligustrum** (*Ligustrum japonicum*) Good; glossy foliage; once was over-used	○●	10 ft.	10 ft.	E	spr.	no	no	no	no	2
■ ■	**Japanese ligustrum** (*Ligustrum lucidum*) Tallest screening shrub; fruit is carried by birds to extent that plant has become very invasive	○●	18 ft.	18 ft.	E	spr.	win.	no	no	no	3
■ ■ ■	**Southern wax myrtle** (*Myrica cerifera*) Light green foliage; branches tend to die without warning; short productive life expectancy in landscape	○●	10 ft.	10 ft.	E	no	win.	no	no	no	3
■ ■ ■	**Oleander** (*Nerium oleander*) Beautiful blooms once plants are established; drought-tolerant; note that plant parts are poisonous	○	8-20 ft.	8-20 ft.	E	spr./sum.	no	no	no	no	2
■ ■ ■	**Sweet olive** (*Osmanthus fragrans*) Deep evergreen foliage on slow, upright shrub; flowers not conspicuous, but deliciously fragrant; needs acidic bed preparation	●●	10 ft.	8 ft.	E	fall	no	no	no	acidic	2

Waxleaf ligustrum in spring

Oleander in late spring

Assorted upright junipers at nursery

Ornamental (non-fruiting) pomegranate

Mock orange in spring

Chinese photinia fruit in winter

Large Shrubs CONTINUED

Best Zones In Texas* 6 7 8 9 / PLANT AND COMMENTS *See Zones Map page 117.*	SUN/SHADE	HEIGHT	WIDTH	DECIDUOUS/EVERGREEN	FLOWERS (showy)	FRUIT (colorful)	INSECTS (of significance)	DISEASES (of significance)	SPECIAL SOILS REQUIRED	OVERAL RATING
Mock orange (*Philadelphus coronarius*) Lovely loose upright shrub is covered with dogwood-like white blossoms each spring; tolerates some morning sun, but protect from hot summer sun; keep moist	●	10 ft.	8 ft.	D	spr.	no	no	no	no	2
Redtip photinia (*Photinia fraseri*) Should not be planted because highly impacted by fatal Entomosporium fungal disease; brilliant new growth in late winter	○	18 ft.	15 ft.	E	spr.	no	yes	yes	no	4
Chinese photinia (*Photinia serrulata*) Old-fashioned screening shrub that is seldom seen in nurseries; well-adapted and apparently not highly susceptible to Entomosporium fungal leaf spot	○	15 ft.	15 ft.	E	spr.	win.	yes	yes	no	2
Pittosporum (*Pittosporum tobira*) Green variety is larger than variegated type at maturity	●●	6-12 ft.	6-12 ft.	E	no	no	no	no	no	2
Japanese yew (*Podocarpus macrophyllus*) Graceful upright shrub; handsome landscape plant; requires moist soils that drain well	●●	12 ft.	8 ft.	E	no	no	no	no	no	2
Carolina cherry laurel (*Prunus caroliniana*) Large old-fashioned screen; borers; cotton root rot; compact varieties available	●●	15 ft.	15 ft.	E	no	win.	yes	yes	acidic	2
Flowering pomegranate (*Punica granatum*) No edible fruit on the several varieties of double-flowering ornamental pomegranates; yellow fall foliage	○	10 ft.	8 ft.	D	spr.	sum.	no	no	no	1

Large Shrubs CONTINUED
(More than 8 feet tall and wide)

Best Zones In Texas* 6 7 8 9	PLANT AND COMMENTS *See Zones Map page 117.	SUN/SHADE	HEIGHT	WIDTH	DECIDUOUS/EVERGREEN	FLOWERS (showy)	FRUIT (colorful)	INSECTS (of significance)	DISEASES (of significance)	SPECIAL SOILS REQUIRED	OVERALL RATING
■ ■ ■ ■	**Pyracantha (Pyracantha coccinea)** Orange-fruiting types more winter-hardy than reds; very thorny; lace bugs; leaf rollers; fire blight; cotton root rot	◔	10 ft.	10 ft.	E	spr.	win.	yes	yes	no	3
■ ■ ■	**Texas mountain laurel (Sophora secundiflora)** Highly fragrant lavender flowers; glossy deep green foliage; genista caterpillars	◔	10 ft.	10 ft.	E	spr.	no	yes	no	dry	2
■ ■	**Sweet viburnum (Viburnum odoratissimum)** Very large, extremely glossy leaves; bold texture	●	15 ft.	12 ft.	E	spr.	no	no	no	no	1
■ ■	**Eastern cranberrybush viburnum (Viburnum opulus)** Showy white floral bracts; outstanding flowering shrub for shade	●	10 ft.	8 ft.	D	spr.	no	no	no	no	1
■ ■ ■ ■	**Rusty blackhaw viburnum (Viburnum rufidulum)** Large shrub or small tree native east of I-35; protect from afternoon summer sun; glossy foliage is bright green in spring, deep lustrous green in summer and brilliant red in fall; fine understory plant beneath tall trees	◐ ●	15 ft.	12 ft.	D	spr.	fall	no	no	no	1
■ ■ ■	**Vitex (Vitex agnus-castus)** Old favorite that has become highly popular again; lavender blooms; also called "chaste tree" and "Texas lilac" (although it is not related to true lilacs and does not have their fragrance)	◔	15 ft.	15 ft.	D	spr.	no	no	no	no	1

Texas mountain laurel in spring

Rusty blackhaw viburnum in fall

Vitex in May

Vines

The more compact our landscapes become, the more useful vines are to us. To a large extent, vines are two-dimensional plants that provide many of the benefits of trees and shrubs without taking up valuable horizontal space in their surroundings.

Vining English ivy used to provide garden "wall"

White wisteria covers arbor.

Fig ivy clings to wall.

Star jasmine climbs trellis.

*T*hey cling and they tumble. They twist and they twine. They're vines, and they may be the most overlooked group of landscaping plants in Texas gardens. Surely you have room for one or two in your plantings.

We Use Vines to

- Provide overhead shade
- Cool exposed walls
- Soften fences and walls visually
- Provide seasonal color
- Absorb neighborhood noises
- Block strong winds

Yellow and orange trumpetcreepers soften fence.

Crossvine

Hall's honeysuckle

English ivy

Choosing the Best Vine

Not all vines are equally well suited to the various landscaping needs. Several factors should be considered:

- How much sunlight will the vine receive?
- Do you want an annual (seasonal) or a perennial (permanent) vine?
- How large a space do you want the vine to fill?
- Is the support adequate for the size and weight of the vine?

POISON IVY

Leaves of three, let it be! The old adage makes reference to the three-parted leaf that distinguishes poison ivy. It's commonly found vining up the trunks of Texas trees, but you'll also encounter it in waist-high thickets where it has no support but its own stems. Most gardeners run into it when they're

Poison ivy fall color

pulling weeds and working in beds – small seedlings (always with the three leaflets) that come up among the other plants.

The photo shows fall color of poison ivy. It's deep green all summer, and its stems are bare every winter. But all parts of the plant have the oil that causes the serious allergy, so learn to recognize the plant in all seasons.

Your nurseryman will have herbicides that will eliminate poison ivy. Be precise – do not apply them where they would make contact with desirable plants. If poison ivy is climbing a tree trunk, carefully cut its stalk with an axe or saw, but do not let the oils or sawdust make contact with your skin. Leave it attached to the tree to die. It will eventually fall to the ground. Wear long sleeves, long pants and gloves, and shower as soon as you're finished.

FAQ

Q Will English or Boston ivy growing on my bricks hurt the mortar – or the house in general?

A Usually no. They will use the wall surface only for support as their small root-like appendages stick tightly to it. However, there are two places where you might have concern: (1) If the surface is light-colored, the vine might trap dust and debris behind its leaves and stems, possibly causing discoloration, and (2) If the vine grows beyond the masonry and onto wood trim, window screens or siding, it might be difficult to remove its roots without damaging the house.

Visit Neil's FAQ pages at www.neilsperry.com

Sweet autumn clematis

Purple wisteria twines over fence.

Hall's honeysuckle twines.

Lady Banksia rose leans against fence.

How Vines Climb

You must know how a vine is going to attach itself before you can make the best plant selection. Here are the ways vines ascend:

- By twining around their supports. Carolina jessamine, trumpetcreeper and morning glories are common examples.

- With specialized roots functioning as suction cups. Boston ivy and English ivy adhere to solid walls in this way.

- With tendrils that reach out and attach to rails, wires and other branches. Grapes and crossvine are examples.

- Simply by leaning against posts, fences and walls. This is the way climbing roses ascend. In most cases, they must be tied and trained to their supports.

Carolina jessamine twines up rail fence.

Boston ivy clings to brick.

Madame Galen trumpetcreeper

Getting a Vine Started

Once you have selected the best vine for your needs and made the subsequent purchase, you're ready to plant.

- Most vines are sold in 1- to 5-gallon pots growing on nursery stakes. Leave the support in place while you carefully slip the plant out of its pot.

- Set it as close to its new support as possible, and plant it at the same depth at which it has been growing in the container.

- Tilt the plant slightly, so that the stake or trellis on which it has been growing from the nursery leans against the permanent support. The old stake will gradually decay and fall away.

- Fill the hole with topsoil, and water the plant deeply.

- Begin applying a high-nitrogen fertilizer soon after planting and repeat every six to eight weeks.

- Keep the vine's root system moist at all times.

- Start training it to its support immediately, and remove any errant growth.

Ivy climbing pecan trunk

FAQ

Q Will English ivy climbing up a tree harm the tree?

A Vines draw no moisture or nutrition from the trees that support them. There are two ways a vine could cause harm to its support tree: (1) If it formed a shading canopy over the top of the tree (as kudzu and wild grapes will do), or (2) If it grew out onto the horizontal branches, and if it were an evergreen vine, and if an ice storm coated the leaves of the vine, adding weight to the tree branch, it might cause the limb to break. Without the vine, odds of limb breakage are much reduced.

Coral vine (Queen's wreath)

A Word About Espaliers

These vine-like plants are "imposters." They're really trees and shrubs that have been trained to grow flat against walls. They may require a bit more maintenance when grown this way, but the results can be quite attractive.

The quickest way to get an attractive espalier is to buy one pre-trained from a nursery. It will have been grown on a wooden trellis. Its extra cost can be justified by the year or two you'll save in the initial training.

You must have an idea of the form you want your espalier to take as it matures. Whether it's a geometric or freeform design, it must fill out from the ground up. Since new growth occurs at the tips of the branches, you must finish each lower layer before you move up to the next.

Secure the branches to a strong and permanent support. Wrought iron forms work very well, or you can use masonry anchors and wires.

Remove all shoots that start to grow out from the wall, and do so every two or three weeks during the growing season so that their removal won't leave gaps in the greenery.

Apple espalier

English ivy is trained as espalier on shaded north wall.

Tropical Vines for Summer

Because most parts of Texas experience freezing weather in winter, these will also be annual vines in most of our state. However, they, too, bring their own special elegance to our gardens. We have several nice choices.

Bougainvillea

Mandevilla

Passion vine

USDA Hardiness Zones

ZONE 6
ZONE 7
ZONE 8
ZONE 9

Find Texas Hardiness Zones information page 5.

Tropical Vines (Frost-tender perennials)

Plants in the chart that follows have been arranged alphabetically by their scientific names. In Overall Ratings (column at far right), the number 1 indicates the highest recommendation.

Best Zones In Texas 6 7 8 9 / PLANT AND COMMENTS	SUN/SHADE (Sun / Partial Sun / Shade)	HEIGHT	WIDTH	DECIDUOUS/EVERGREEN	FLOWERS (showy)	FRUIT (colorful)	INSECTS (of significance)	DISEASES (of significance)	SPECIAL SOILS REQUIRED	OVERAL RATING
Queen's wreath, coral vine (*Antigonon leptopus*) Twining, sprawling habit; panicles of pink flowers late summer, fall; dies to ground in winter	Sun	40 ft.	50 ft.	D	sum./fall	no	no	no	no	1
Bougainvillea (*Bougainvillea* spp.) * Leaning and gently twining; showy bracts in red, pink, white, purple, orange; blooming slows in summer	Sun/Partial Sun	12 ft.	12 ft.	E	sum./fall	no	no	no	no	2
Dipladenia, Chilean jasmine (*Mandevilla laxa*) * Twining, dark green foliage; very compact growth; single red, white, pink flowers	Partial Sun	6 ft.	4 ft.	E	sum./fall	no	no	no	no	1
Mandevilla (*Mandevilla splendens*) * Twining; large single pink flowers	Partial Sun	8 ft.	6 ft.	E	sum./fall	no	no	no	no	1
Passionvine (*Passiflora alatocaerulea*) * Twining and tendrils; species hardy to Zone 9, but others tropical; flowers white, pink, purple and red	Sun/Partial Sun	10 ft.	10 ft.	D	sum./fall	no	no	no	no	1
Stephanotis (*Stephanotis floribunda*) * Fragrant; plant very early in spring	Sun/Partial Sun	5 ft.	3 ft.	E	spr.-fall	no	yes	no	no	2

* Tropical perennial vines can be used for seasonal color outdoors beyond their adapted regions, but they will not survive freezing temperatures. If grown in pots, they can be overwintered in a greenhouse.

Woody Perennial Vines

When the subject turns to "landscaping vines," most people are thinking of these plants. These are the vines that we use over fences and patio covers. These are the vines we encourage to climb up our walls. These are the vines that are as permanent as our trees and shrubs are. They are backbones of fine landscaping.

Coral honeysuckle

Woody Perennial Vines

Plants in the chart that follows have been arranged alphabetically by their scientific names. In Overall Ratings (column at far right), the number 1 indicates the highest recommendation.

Best Zones In Texas* 6 7 8 9	Plant and Comments *See Zones Map page 135.	Sun/Shade	Height	Width	Deciduous/Evergreen	Flowers (showy)	Fruit (colorful)	Insects (of significance)	Diseases (of significance)	Special Soils Required	Overall Rating
■ ▢ ▢ ▢	Crossvine (*Bignonia capreolata*) — Twining and tendrils; tubular flowers of coral, rose and yellow; may show iron deficiency	◐ ●	20 ft.	20 ft.	D	spr.	no	no	no	no	2
■ ▢ ▢ ▢	Madame Galen trumpetcreeper (*Campsis radicans* 'Madame Galen') — Twining; large tubular orange blooms (red and yellow forms also sold); grow this and other improved forms – native species wildly invasive	◐	15 ft.	30 ft.	D	sum.	no	no	no	no	1
▢ ▢ ▢	Evergreen clematis (*Clematis armandii*) — Twining; creamy white blooms; stunning foliage	◐ ●	15 ft.	10 ft.	E	spr.	no	no	no	no	1
■ ▢ ▢	Sweet autumn clematis (*Clematis paniculata*) — Twining stems are covered with quarter-sized white blooms early fall; dies to ground or should be trimmed heavily over winter	● ●	15 ft.	15 ft.	D	fall	no	no	no	no	1
▢	Climbing fig, fig ivy (*Ficus pumila*) — Densely adhering, compact growth; popular in topiary; foliage may burn in winter	◐ ●	20 ft.	20 ft.	E	no	no	no	no	no	1
▢ ▢	Carolina jessamine (*Gelsemium sempervirens*) — Twining stems, glossy foliage; tubular yellow blooms in early spring are highly fragrant. One of our few compact, evergreen vines for shade	◐ ◐ ●	15 ft.	15 ft.	E	spr.	no	no	no	no	1
■ ▢ ▢ ▢	English ivy (*Hedera helix*) — Climbs by adhering; used to soften impact of shaded walls; requires perfect drainage	●	20 ft.	20 ft.	E	no	no	no	yes	no	2
■ ▢ ▢ ▢	Hall's honeysuckle (*Lonicera japonica* 'Halliana') — Twining; requires training to prevent ragged appearance; due to prolific seed production considered "invasive"	◐	15 ft.	15 ft.	E	spr.	no	no	no	no	3

Virginia creeper fall color

Virginia creeper summer foliage

Carolina jessamine

Woody Perennial Vines CONTINUED

Best Zones In Texas* — 6 7 8 9
*See Zones Map page 135.

Plant and Comments	Sun/Shade	Height	Width	Deciduous/Evergreen	Flowers (showy)	Fruit (colorful)	Insects (of significance)	Diseases (of significance)	Special Soils Required	Overall Rating
Coral honeysuckle (*Lonicera sempervirens*) — Twining; growth may become stemmy; powdery mildew	Sun/Partial Sun	10 ft.	8 ft.	E	spr.	no	no	yes	no	3
Evergreen wisteria (*Millettia reticulata*) — Twining; purple summer flower panicles resemble true wisteria but less showy; cold-tender	Sun/Partial Sun	10 ft.	10 ft.	E	sum.	no	no	no	no	2
Virginia creeper (*Parthenocissus quinquefolia*) — Clings, some twining; rank native vine; bright fall colors; requires large wall	Sun/Partial Sun	40 ft.	40 ft.	D	no	no	no	no	no	3
Boston ivy (*Parthenocissus tricuspidata*) — Clinging stems cover walls densely; beautiful fall color; lace bugs	Sun/Partial Sun	40 ft.	40 ft.	D	no	no	yes	no	no	1
Climbing roses (*Rosa* spp.) — Leaning growth requires support; Earth-Kind® types are most dependable	Sun	20 ft.	20 ft.	E	spr./fall	no	yes	yes	yes	1
Confederate star jasmine (*Trachelospermum jasminoides*) — Twining; very fragrant white pinwheel-form flowers; winter-tender northern half of Texas	Sun/Partial Sun	15 ft.	15 ft.	E	spr.	no	no	no	no	1
Grapes (*Vitis* spp.) — Twining and tendrils; strong vines for shading large areas; fruit may be messy on pavement. (See Fruit chapter for information on cultivated grapes for consumption.)	Sun	25 ft.	25 ft.	D	no	fall	no	no	no	3
Wisteria (*Wisteria sinensis*) — Twining; fragrant panicles of purple or white blooms in spring; iron deficiency in alkaline soils; often sold trained in tree-form	Sun	40 ft.	40 ft.	D	spr.	no	no	no	yes	2

Hyacinth bean

Black-eyed Susan

Morning glory

Annual Vines in the Landscape

Sometimes you want something temporary. Perhaps it's while you're waiting for shrubs to grow taller, or maybe you're just looking for a spot of color. Granted you'll have to replant these from seeds every year, but they're quick and they're handsome.

Annual Vines

Plants in the chart that follows have been arranged alphabetically by their scientific names. In Overall Ratings (column at far right), the number 1 indicates the highest recommendation.

Best Zones In Texas* 6 7 8 9	PLANT AND COMMENTS *See Zones Map page 135.	SUN/SHADE	HEIGHT	WIDTH	DECIDUOUS/EVERGREEN	FLOWERS (showy)	FRUIT (colorful)	INSECTS (of significance)	DISEASES (of significance)	SPECIAL SOILS REQUIRED	OVERALL RATING
■ ▦ ▦ ▦	Hyacinth bean (*Dolichos lablab*) Twining; maroon leaves, flowers, pods; showiest in fall	◐ ●	10 ft.	8 ft.	ann.	sum./fall	fall	no	no	no	1
■ ▦ ▦ ▦	Moonvine (*Ipomoea calantha*) Twining; white-flowering, night-blooming	◐ ●	10 ft.	8 ft.	ann.	sum./fall	no	no	no	no	1
■ ▦ ▦ ▦	Morning glory (*Ipomoea* spp.) Twining; blooms late summer and fall; blue, white, pink.	◐	8 ft.	8 ft.	ann.	sum./fall	no	no	no	no	1
■ ▦ ▦ ▦	Cypress vine, cardinal climber (*Ipomoea quamoclit*) Densely twining; finely textured leaves, small bright red flowers	◐ ●	8 ft.	8 ft.	ann.	sum./fall	no	no	no	no	1
■ ▦ ▦ ▦	Sweet pea (*Lathyrus odoratus*) Fragrant; plant very early spring	◐	8 ft.	4 ft.	ann.	spr.	no	no	yes	no	2
■ ▦ ▦ ▦	Clock vine, black-eyed Susan vine (*Thunbergia* spp.) Twining; small yellow or orange flowers, often with dark eyes	◐ ●	8 ft.	6 ft.	ann.	sum./fall	no	no	no	no	1

Groundcovers

You don't have to go back very far in Texas landscaping history to find life without groundcovers. It wasn't until the 1960s and '70s that they became commonplace, and now they're features of almost everyone's plantings.

Sedum, English ivy, ajuga and even one flowering clump of variegated liriope groundcovers thrive in this setting.

English ivy, liriope

*T*here are times when you just don't want (or can't grow) turfgrass in a particular part of your landscape. Still, you need something short, and flowers aren't really the solution. Well, gardener, that's when you need to call in the groundcovers. They're your perfect alternatives.

Groundcovers Fill Many Needs

- As transitions between low shrubs and turfgrass,

- To provide continuity through an entire landscaping bed made up of groupings of several types of shrubs,

- As water-conscious alternatives to expanses of turfgrass,

- In shaded areas, where there isn't enough sunlight for St. Augustine or fescue (less than four hours of direct sunlight daily),

- On slopes that would be difficult to mow and maintain, and

- In long, narrow areas where grass would be difficult to trim.

Garden Tip

It takes a groundcover two or three years to cover completely. Learn to recognize early symptoms of drying plants, and water immediately. Protect your investment! Just a few dollars' worth of water applied before it's too late can save hundreds of dollars, time and effort.

Bronze ajuga

English ivy varieties

Ajuga, English ivy

Mondograss solves problems of excessive shade where turfgrass cannot survive.

Getting Started with Groundcovers

- Eliminate all existing grass and weeds, either manually or by applying appropriate herbicide.

- Use rear-tine rototiller to work soil to depth of 8 to 10 inches.

- Incorporate 3 to 5 inches of organic matter (sphagnum peat moss, compost, pine bark mulch, etc.) by rototilling, again to 8 to 10 inches.

- Install edging around perimeter of bed.

- Rake bed to a gentle crown in the middle.

- Measure bed to determine number of plants to buy (see page 143).

- Set plants at same depth at which they have been growing in their pots. Firm the loose soil up around them.

- Water immediately and deeply.

- Apply high-nitrogen fertilizer to encourage vigorous growth.

- Pull weeds by hand until groundcover is thick enough to crowd them out.

Regular mondograss, dwarf mondograss

Lamium (dead nettle)

Asian jasmine bed

Removing winter damage to mondograss

Garden Tip

In case of damage done to Asian jasmine, mondograss or other groundcovers by extreme cold, trim away dead plant tissues before new growth begins in the spring. You may be able to run the lawnmower over the planting at its highest setting, or you may have to do the trimming with a gasoline or electric hedge trimmer. Try a small, inconspicuous area first to see if you like the results.

Buying the Plants

Groundcovers are sold in several pot sizes, from small transplants (3- and 4-inch pots) to quart- and gallon-sized containers.

Larger plants:

- Can be planted farther apart.

- Give a more immediate impact.

- Have deeper root systems, so they won't dry out as quickly while they're getting established.

- Are less likely to be hurt by cold weather if planting is done in the fall.

- Sometimes (with clump-type groundcovers) can be divided into quarters to lower cost of the planting.

Smaller plants:

- Are less expensive.

- Are more easily planted.

- Are less "clumpy" in their first year or two.

Variegated Asian jasmine

Purple Japanese honeysuckle

Confederate star jasmine

Purple wintercreeper in winter

Calculating how many plants to buy

Once you have measured the bed and figured the square feet involved, multiply that number times the plants-per-square-foot in this chart to determine the number of plants you should buy. It's wise to buy 15 percent more to fill the odd corners.

Spacing of Plants (inches)	Plants per Square Foot
8 by 8	2.25
10 by 10	1.44
12 by 12	1.00
15 by 15	.64
18 by 18	.44
20 by 20	.36
24 by 24	.25

Purple wintercreeper in spring

Purple wintercreeper in summer

Liriope in long, narrow bed

Tam juniper

Liriope blooms beautifully for four to six weeks each summer.

Care of New Groundcover Plantings

If planted in spring and at the recommended spacings, groundcovers typically cover in their first growing season. There are things you can do to speed that along, however.

- Water regularly, especially until the plants are established and growing actively. You may want to water by hand with a water breaker and wand.

- Keep the plants properly nourished. (Nitrogen stimulates new growth.) Apply a diluted, liquid high-nitrogen fertilizer each time that you water. Or, at a minimum, apply a high-quality lawn food (no herbicide included), using half the recommended rate at four- to six-week intervals.

- Pull or cultivate weeds by hand. There is no herbicide that can safely do this job for you. If you prepared the soil carefully initially, this won't be as bad as it might sound.

- Trim off upright shoots of trailing groundcovers or retrain them to fill empty spaces.

Care of Established Groundcover Plantings

- **Watering.** If you have a sprinkler system, groundcover and shrub beds should have their own stations (separate from turf) on the controller. If you're watering with hose-end sprinklers, be sure the entire bed is irrigated uniformly.

- **Fertilizing.** Apply a high-nitrogen granular lawn food (no weedkiller included) at six- to eight-week intervals. Hand-held spreaders are easiest. Wheeled spreaders can be used in most groundcovers. Scattering fertilizer by hand is the least precise way.

- **Trimming.** Maintain a neat edge to groundcover beds. Line trimmers can be used on some types, hand shears on others. Taper the cuts down toward the edges so you don't end up with a vertical cross-section of stubble. Use the line trimmer to keep the tops of trailing groundcovers even.

A 180-degree sprinkler head waters only groundcover.

Hand-held spreader makes feeding groundcover easier.

Vinca groundcover flower

Variegated vinca

Asian jasmine, wood fern, mondograss

Trimming groundcover

USDA Hardiness Zones

ZONE 6
ZONE 7
ZONE 8
ZONE 9

Find Texas Hardiness Zones information page 5.

Groundcovers

Plants in the chart that follows have been arranged alphabetically by their scientific names. In Overall Ratings (column at far right), the number 1 indicates the highest recommendation.

Best Zones In Texas 6 7 8 9	PLANT AND COMMENTS	SUN/SHADE	HEIGHT	WIDTH	DECIDUOUS/EVERGREEN	FLOWERS (showy)	FRUIT (colorful)	INSECTS (of significance)	DISEASES (of significance)	SPECIAL SOILS REQUIRED	OVERALL RATING
	Ajuga (*Ajuga reptans*) Many varieties; may die in patches; nematodes	shade	6 in.	6 in.	E	spr.	no	no	yes	no	3
	Purple wintercreeper (*Euonymus fortunei* 'Coloratus') Maroon foliage in winter; euonymus scale in rare instances	sun/partial	10 in.	spreads	E	no	no	yes	no	no	1
	English ivy (*Hedera helix*) Many varieties; requires good drainage; fungal leaf spot	shade	6 in.	spreads	E	no	no	no	yes	no	2
	Trailing junipers (*Juniperus* spp.) Tam one of best; spider mites; tolerate sun and heat	sun	4-18 in.	spreads	E	no	no	yes	no	no	1
	Lamium (*Lamium maculatum*) Several varieties; handsome markings	partial/shade	8 in.	18 in.	E	spr.	no	no	no	no	1
	Liriope (*Liriope muscari*) Great border or tall groundcover	partial/shade	15 in.	15 in.	E	sum.	win.	no	no	no	1
	Purple Japanese honeysuckle (*Lonicera japonica* 'Purpurea') Good for embankments; unruly in home landscapes	sun	18-24 in.	spreads	E	spr.	no	no	no	no	3
	Dwarf nandinas (*Nandina domestica* dwarf varieties) Harbour Dwarf, Flirt and others	partial/shade	20 in.	20 in.	E	no	no	no	no	no	1
	Mondograss (*Ophiopogon japonicus*) Outstanding shade groundcover; tree leaves easily removed	partial/shade	8 in.	6 in.	E	no	no	no	no	no	1
	Dwarf mondograss (*Ophiopogon japonicus* 'Nana') Slow-growing, so use in small spaces	partial/shade	3 in.	3-4 in.	E	no	no	no	no	no	1
	Asian jasmine (*Trachelospermum asiaticum*) Very popular; may brown in winter	sun/partial	6 in.	spreads	E	no	no	no	no	no	1
	Confederate star jasmine (*Trachelospermum jasminoides*) Highly fragrant white blooms; more often used as vine	sun/partial	15 in.	18 in.	E	spr.	no	no	no	no	1
	Vinca (*Vinca major*) Lovely in bloom in spring. Leafrollers ruin appearance by late summer. Variegated form also sold.	shade	10 in.	24 in.	E	spr.	no	yes	no	no	3

Lawns

Some of our fondest memories from childhood are of running barefoot across our lawns. We played on the grass. We went "camping" out there. We had special parties on our lawns, and our families sat and visited there. Some of us were even married there. That grass was cool on hot summer evenings, and it was soft during tag football scrimmages in the fall. We Texans loved our lawns – and we still do!

A healthy lawn is the beginning of a good landscape.

Thick stand of common bermuda

Dense St. Augustine turf

Weed-free St. Augustine lawn

Palisades zoysia's fine texture

*L*awns are the bindings of our surroundings. They're the visual element that ties things together. They're the foundations for our landscape designing, the surfaces upon which all of our creative dreaming comes true. It's hard to imagine a Texas without lawngrasses. What a stark and depressing place this would be.

Let's pledge to find ways to have terrific Texas turf, but concurrently, let's conserve money, time, effort and water in the process. It is possible, and this chapter will show you how.

Texas Turf Types

We have only a handful of choices in lawngrasses for Texas. Sadly, none of them would score an *A-plus* in the classroom, but we're getting closer and closer.

Common bermudagrass is the most popular lawngrass in the northern half of Texas. It's durable, inexpensive to plant from seed, and it tolerates heat, cold and drought. Hybrid varieties that resemble common bermuda can be grown from seed. They are said to be more drought-tolerant still. Common bermuda can also be planted from sod, plugs or by hydromulching. On the down side, bermuda invades groundcovers and flowerbeds, and it doesn't grow well in the shade.

Manicured dwarf hybrid bermuda lawn

St. Augustine is the prevalent lawngrass in South Texas. It's less common in North Central Texas, but many do grow it. Wherever it is, it's the dominant grass, crowding out all other turfgrasses. It's a brighter, more cheerful shade of green than bermuda from mid-summer on. Importantly, it's our most shade-tolerant turfgrass – all it needs is five or six hours of direct sunlight daily. But it's more prone to diseases and insects, and severe winters in North Texas can damage or kill it. St. Augustine is intolerant of drought and needs water, but most Texans actually overwater it. You'll see varieties such as Raleigh, Palmetto, Delmar and, well suited to South Texas, the less winter-hardy selection Floratam. Talk to your local sod vendor for specific recommendations for your needs.

Zoysias are becoming more prevalent in Texas landscapes. They are intermediate to bermuda and St. Augustine in terms of texture, shade tolerance and ability to withstand drought. There is a great deal of research on zoysias now, both in the sod industry and in agricultural universities, and we can look for many improvements in upcoming years. Two of the best varieties currently are Palisades and Jamur, but again, you should ask your local sod vendor for help in choosing the best type for your needs. Ask for specific addresses where you can see the grass a year or two after planting.

Dwarf hybrid bermudas provide the ultimate in a manicured lawn. After all, they were developed for golf greens and fairways. (Tifgreen 328 and Tifway 419 were developed decades ago, and are variety names familiar to consumers and turf specialists alike.) As with common bermuda, the dwarf varieties are pedestrian- and drought-tolerant, but they require special mowing equipment (reel mower) so you can maintain them at 1/4 to 3/4 inch (depending on variety). You'll also need to mow several times weekly. They're expensive to plant, and you must be very careful not to get common bermudagrass mixed in with them – there is no spray to eliminate it. Taking all of that into consideration, unless you have a small area that must be a showplace of a lawn, or unless you're willing to set yourself up for maximum lawn maintenance, these grasses are probably not your best choice.

Garden Tip

Beware of ads touting "The Miracle Grass – Zoysia." Very misleading ads from out-of-state sources have appeared each spring for decades. The ads make incredible claims about the vendors' particular varieties of zoysia, when in reality, what they're selling is almost always older, inferior selections. The plugs are expensive, and they usually arrive in poor condition. When planting new turf, buy Texas-grown sod from a local sod yard. Never send your money out of state to buy zoysia plugs.

Stepping stones trimmed into a lawn sound like a good plan at the outset, but keeping up with it can become overwhelming. This hand-chiseled look may be the ultimate example.

Centipede lawn

Fescue in shaded lawn in Addison

Buffalograss came into the Texas turf marketplace in the early 1990s. Many of us thought it would become a go-to lawngrass, but we were quickly disappointed to realize that common bermudagrass almost always invades and overtakes it. Several improved selections were offered, most notably Prairie and 609. They are equal to bermuda in their drought tolerance. They will not grow in the shade. They are typically mowed rather tall, and because of that, some gardeners may not find buffalograss to be a family-friendly turf for recreational activities. In all honesty, common bermudagrass is usually a better lawngrass alternative than buffalograss, since you're likely to end up with bermuda anyway.

Centipedegrass has been around for decades, but its use in Texas has been confined to East Texas due to its requirements of acidic soils (pH of 5 to 6) and 40 inches or more of annual rainfall. It is poorly suited to alkaline soils (where iron chlorosis develops) and arid conditions. It somewhat resembles St. Augustine. In fact, because it has low fertility needs, it is often called the "lazy man's grass" or "poor man's St. Augustine." Centipedegrass is best adapted to full sun, although it will tolerate some shade. It is intolerant of pedestrian traffic. It is best used along roadsides, in low-traffic parks and on commercial properties. It is propagated by sod, sprigs or seed.

Tall fescue is a cool-season grass. Where all of the grasses mentioned up to this point do all of their growing in the warm months, fescue is just the opposite. It starts growing in fall. It's green over the winter, and it slows down when the weather starts to get hot. It's best suited to parts of Texas with cooler evening temperatures in summer: Northwest Texas and the Panhandle. It does not produce runners, growing instead in clumps (hence its description as a "bunch" grass). Fescue is planted from seed sown at the rate of 4 to 8 pounds per 1,000 square feet in September, and it is overseeded at half the initial rate each successive September to keep the planting dense.

Fescue and bluegrass adapted in mountainous Fort Davis

Buffalograss turf

Ryegrass is used to overseed warm-season lawns, primarily bermudagrass turf, for the winter. Annual ryegrass seed is less expensive, but "perennial" rye is finer-textured, much easier to maintain and more attractive in the landscape. Both types are annual grasses in Texas, dying away with the first very warm days of May. Sow rye seed in early September at the rate of 4 to 8 pounds per 1,000 square feet. Water immediately after planting to settle the seed onto the soil, and water two or three times after that to get it established. Some cities discourage planting of ryegrass due to ongoing water curtailments, but if you sow it on your watering day, and if you take the chance that you will have supplemental rainfall thereafter, the ryegrass does not have to require any more water than your bermuda or St. Augustine turf. Those years that you have ample rainfall and are able to water occasionally, it will do well. Many of us are willing to take that chance when planting time comes in September. Fertilize it at half the recommended rate in late October and again in mid- or late February.

Do not overseed St. Augustine lawns in shaded settings. The rye may be slow to thin and die in late spring when it's in the shade, and that added competition can harm the St. Augustine turf as it tries to green up and start growing.

Garden Tip

Overseeding with ryegrass is primarily an aesthetic thing for people who prefer not to look at browned turf all winter. It can help with pedestrian wear on athletic fields and yards that must endure children or pets.

Commercial landscape of rarely mowed buffalograss

Ryegrass one week after September sowing

Perennial rye overseeding

Perennial rye is finer textured than annual rye.

Temporary cover from ryegrass

Baked enamel edging is boundary between grass and beds.

St. Augustine sod being delivered

Dormant bermuda sod in winter

Establishing New Turf

New lawns are planted from seed, sod, plugs, sprigs (runners) and by hydromulching. Here are some comparisons to help you decide.

Seed: used primarily for common bermuda, fescues and ryegrass; least expensive means of starting new turf.

Sod: frequently used for common bermuda; the primary way that dwarf hybrid bermudas, zoysias, St. Augustine and buffalograss hybrids are planted; expensive; quickest way to an established lawn; best means of avoiding erosion.

Plugs: can be used for all bermudas, St. Augustine, zoysias and buffalograss; can be bought as potted plugs or cut as 4- or 5-inch plugs from sod or from your existing lawn; labor-intensive to plant; intermediate in cost; will take one to several months to cover.

Sprigs: not commonly used, but a no-cost method by which homeowners can start St. Augustine from 6- to 8-inch runners taken from their own lawns; stems are inserted into slits made with sharpshooter spade and spaced 12 inches apart across lawn; several months to cover. (For the record: small sprigs from shredded sod are used in commercial hydromulching.)

Hydromulching: used for bermudas primarily, especially on slopes; seed or sprigs are combined with mulching material in a large tank and sprayed onto bare ground; intermediate in cost to seeding and sodding; comparatively quick way to have established turf.

Soil preparation prior to planting

Soil preparation for the planting of new grass is the same, regardless of the type of grass you'll be planting and regardless of which method you'll be using to plant it. Follow these several steps.

- Apply a glyphosate-only herbicide to kill existing grass and weeds. Allow the herbicide 10 to 15 days to do its job.

- Mow to remove all browned stubble.

- Rototill with a rear-tine tiller to 3 to 4 inches depth.

- Rake to remove stem stubble and root debris, also to establish a smooth grade that drains water away from your home and properly off your property.

Planting grass seed

If you're planting bermuda from seed, mix in equal amounts (by weight) of corn meal. Bermuda seed is very tiny, and the corn meal will allow you to cover the new planting area completely and uniformly before you run out of seed. Sow bermuda at the rate of 2 to 4 pounds of seed per 1,000 square feet. Use a hand-held spreader to distribute the seed.

If you're sowing ryegrass or fescue, apply it at the rate of 4 to 8 pounds per 1,000 square feet (2 to 4 pounds per 1,000 square feet if you're overseeding established fescue, to keep the stand dense). Seed of both of these grasses is fairly coarse, so distribution will be comparatively easy.

Whatever type of grass seed you're sowing, adjust your seeder very carefully before you fill it completely. Your goal should be to plant half of the seeds walking east and west, and the other half walking north and south. That will prevent missed spots.

If you have beds immediately adjacent to the areas being planted, have someone hold a large piece of cardboard at the edges of the beds. The cardboard will serve as a baffle, deflecting the seeds where they're not wanted.

Water the newly seeded lawn lightly to settle the seeds into the freshly tilled and raked soil. Do not allow the soil to dry out for the first couple of weeks. Recently germinated seedlings are especially vulnerable.

Well-maintained common bermuda turf

Hand-held spreader is useful in sowing seed for new lawns onto freshly tilled soil, also for overseeding or applying fertilizer.

Sod unloaded in shade ready for planting.

Common bermuda is easily started from sod.

Bermuda sod should have been leveled with topsoil or planted more carefully.

Planting new grass from sod

Buy good-quality sod from a reputable grower or dealer. If at all possible, meet the delivery truck at the sod yard, to be sure that the new grass is fresh. If you're having it delivered, ask that the grass arrive early in the morning while it's still fresh. Have them drop the pallets into a shaded spot. To avoid the grass overheating, do not leave the sod stacked for more than a few hours.

Plant the new sod carefully onto the freshly tilled soil. Avoid leaving footprints, either in the sod or the soil, as they'll be difficult to remove later. It may help to walk on small sheets of lightweight plywood.

Snug the pieces of sod together carefully, so that no cracks are left between the pieces. If you do find such voids, use loose topsoil to fill them before you water the new grass.

If it's hot when you're laying the sod, water the new grass within 30 minutes of planting. That may mean that someone is designated to use a water wand and breaker to irrigate soon after the grass has been planted. This will minimize setback and keep the grass green and vigorous.

You may want to smooth the new planting lightly with a lawn roller that you have filled partially with water. That will even out many of the little hills and valleys that otherwise might cause problems when you start mowing.

As soon as the new sod is all in place, run the sprinklers for 15 or 20 minutes to settle it all together. No fertilizer is needed at the time of planting.

Solid sodding of St. Augustine is best option for shade.

St. Augustine sod thrives in sun or part sun.

Post-planting care of new grass

Seeds will start germinating within the first seven to 10 days after planting. Sodded grass may appear worse after two or three days due to the shock of being dug, stacked, transported, and replanted, but it will bounce back after roots begin to grow into the tilled soil, usually within the first week.

It's better, for the first couple of weeks that the new turf is becoming established, to water more often, but to apply less water at each irrigation. You want to keep the surface of the soil constantly moist, but try not to let it become waterlogged. That's a fine line, so use your best judgment.

As the grass begins to develop roots into the soil (usually after a couple of weeks), gradually increase the length of each watering and decrease the frequency.

Start mowing your new lawn as soon as the grass is tall enough to mow at the recommended height. Allowing it to grow tall will weaken the new grass.

After you mow the lawn the second time, apply a high-quality lawn fertilizer (with no weedkiller added) at half the recommended rate. Wait one month, then fertilize again, but this time at the full recommended rate.

Properly functioning sprinkler system

"Smart" controllers on automated irrigation systems can be programmed to include soil types, plant types, sun/shade, slope, rainfall, wind, temperature, approved water days and other factors in determining when the water will come on. These controllers are typically not extremely expensive, and they frequently cut 30 to 40 percent of water consumption. You often save enough in water bills within just the first year or two to cover the costs of their purchase and installation. Many cities require they be included with new sprinkler systems.

Outdoor monitor for smart controller

Indoor smart controller is programmed and ready to activate.

Watering Turf

Water is critical to all life, lawngrasses included. However, many Texans water their lawns to excess. It's better for our water reserves, and it's better for our grasses if we learn to recognize signs of dry grass and wait until we see them before we turn on the sprinklers.

Turf experts suggest 1 inch of water per week in the summer, whether from irrigation or rainfall. In spring and fall, that would drop to 1 inch every couple of weeks, and in winter, only as needed, but probably only 1 or 2 inches per month.

To encourage deep root growth, water deeply when you irrigate, then wait until the grass is dry before you water again.

CRITICAL TIMING

Your grass is getting dry when…

- its blades fold or roll;

- it turns a drab, olive-green color; and

- you leave footprints in the blades when you walk across it.

SUGGESTIONS FOR AN EFFECTIVE, EFFICIENT SPRINKLER SYSTEM

You can save water and money with a well-designed irrigation system. Here are important steps to success.

- Use an experienced irrigation contractor.

- Ask for references and call those referrals.

- Use drip irrigation where it's practical.

- Ask for low-throw, low-volume heads.

- Familiarize yourself with how the controller works and how you can make adjustments in its "run" cycles as weather conditions and landscaping needs change.

Good habits in watering the lawn

Follow these several tips in watering turfgrass:

- Early morning irrigation is always better. Evening irrigation encourages spread of diseases. Winds are also lightest prior to sunrise and in the early hours of daylight.

- Use sprinklers that deliver water in large droplets. That minimizes blowing and loss to evaporation.

- Keep sprays low to the ground. Once again, you will reduce spray drift and water loss.

- When watering heavy clay soils, water at multiple intervals for shorter runs rather than for one longer period of time. That allows water time to soak into the soil with far less runoff.

- When only one part of your lawn is dry, don't feel that you have to run the automatic system in its entirety. You may be able to use a hose-end sprinkler to water that one spot.

Fertilizing the Grass

Tests from the Texas A&M Soil Testing Lab and other reputable labs have been telling us for years that most Texas soils have excessive levels of phosphorus (middle number of the three-number analysis). Their recommendations have called for use of high-nitrogen, or more commonly, all-nitrogen fertilizers.

Further research from Texas A&M has shown that we need to choose fertilizers that have half or more of their nitrogen in encapsulated or coated slow-release form. That ensures sustained feeding, and it also lessens the likelihood of accumulations of thatch. These high-quality fertilizers will cost more than the fast-release types like ammonium sulfate (21-0-0), but the results over a period of time will be measurably better.

Uniform, regular feeding is one of the keys to a dense lawn.

Garden Tip

After you have applied fertilizer to your lawn, carefully sweep up any granules that have spilled out onto paved surfaces to prevent both staining of the concrete and runoff into the storm sewers. Finish by watering to wash the granules off the leaves and into the soil, and once again, watch to be sure there is no runoff.

Touch-up watering as needed

FAQ

Q Are "weed-and-feed" products good?

A Trees and shrubs in your landscape share the soils with your lawn, so it's really important that you choose a product that will meet their needs, yet not cause damage to them in the process. While it's certainly acceptable to use herbicides, rarely will you need to apply them over the entire lawn, and often the timing of the weedkiller treatment will not coincide with timing for feeding. For both of those reasons, it's better to handle these processes independent of one another.

It's quite normal to see seed heads on bermuda and St. Augustine lawns, especially in early to mid-summer. That's the reproductive phase that every plant has. If it's been a while since the lawn received nitrogen fertilizer, feeding might help it swing back toward vegetative (leaf and stem) growth. Otherwise, just mow a bit more frequently until the seed heads finish their season.

FAQ

Q How can I know for sure when it's time to fertilize my lawn?

A That's a great question, because we Texans do tend to over-fertilize our lawns. The answer is "You'll learn what to look for." As you mow and maintain your lawn, you'll notice how the rate of leaf growth slows when the turf begins to run out of nutrients during the growing season. You may see a gentle shift from dark green leaf blade color to a lighter green or even pale green. When you see those things happening, check your garden log for the last time that you fed the grass. If it's been eight or 10 weeks or longer, it's time once again.

When should you fertilize?

Timing of lawn feedings will depend on where you live in the state and also on the type of grass that you're growing. Here are some guidelines, but they have been left rather general on purpose. Environmental factors such as unusually heavy rainfall or erratic temperatures can make adjustments necessary.

CRITICAL TIMING

Common bermudagrass needs a higher and more sustained level of nutrition than most of our other grasses. Fertilize it every eight or nine weeks starting in late March or early April and finishing for the season by late September or early October.

St. Augustine develops gray leaf spot when recent applications of high-nitrogen fertilizers coincide with the hottest part of mid-summer. Avoid fertilizing during that disease's prime season by feeding in early April, early June and early September.

Zoysias are a bit slower to green up in spring. Fertilize them in early April, mid-June and early September.

Dwarf hybrid bermudagrasses are mowed more frequently and they also have less extensive root systems than common bermuda, so you'll need to fertilize more often (six- or eight-week intervals) and less at each time (half the recommended rate). First feeding would be late March or early April, and final application would be late September or early October.

Buffalograss requires the least amount of fertilizer of our Texas lawngrasses. (Don't let that be a governing factor in choosing a type of turf, however.) One feeding in mid-May and a second in September should be sufficient.

Tall fescue varieties are cool-season grasses, which means that they do most of their growing in the cooler months. Fertilize in late September, late November and again in mid-February. Do not apply fertilizer during late spring and summer.

Ryegrass is a temporary cover. It's a cool-season grass. Fertilize it in late September, late November and again in mid-February. Since your permanent grass will be sharing the soil with the rye, feed at only half the recommended rate – enough to keep the rye sustained, but not enough to cause the warm-season grass to try to grow.

Organic fertilizers for lawns

Some gardeners prefer to use organic plant foods. In that case, your main consideration will still need to be with their analyses and the ratios of nitrogen, phosphorus and potassium. Organic fertilizers have low analyses, so you'll have to use more to get equal results. They're also slower at releasing nutrients for uptake by plants' roots, so it takes a period of time to build up the nutrient levels in the soil. You may want to supplement them with an occasional inorganic feeding until you get to the levels of fertility you want.

Garden Tip

When fertilizing your lawn, apply half of the granules (half the recommended rate) going east-and-west, followed by the other half going north-and-south. While it requires you to make an extra pass across the lawn, this will ensure more uniform feeding. No one wants to see alternating stripes of over- and under-fed grass.

WHETHER TO SCALP

Scalping is the term that describes setting your lawnmower blade down one or two notches in order to remove all of the winter-killed stubble as well as many of the cool-season weeds. By getting the browned blades out of the way, scalping allows the sun's rays to hit the soil, warming it sooner. That results in green turf two or three weeks earlier than you would have seen without the scalping.

However, scalping is still primarily aesthetic, and in that regard, it's pretty much optional. If you decide that you do want to scalp your lawn, it's best to do so in late February or early March in most of Texas, before your warm-season turfgrass begins to green up and start growing. Be forewarned that scalping is an especially dusty task. You must wear goggles and a top-quality respirator.

Clippings from scalping bermuda

The dried stubble removed during scalping can be put into compost or used as a mulch beneath shrubs and in the perennial garden. Do not send it to the landfill. It fills our landfills prematurely, and it's an extremely valuable source of organic matter for use in our own gardens.

Bermuda with attentive feeding

St. Augustine lawn awaiting September feeding

Well-nourished St. Augustine lawn

Letting grass grow taller than the recommended mowing height is not a good plan. Tall grass quickly becomes lanky and weak as the blades reach up toward light. Tall growth will not help conserve water in the summer, nor does it add any measure of protection against winter's cold. Generally speaking, you can mow your yard for years without varying the height.

Electric mower suitable for small lawns.

Gasoline mower made for years of service.

Well-manicured zoysia

Mowing for Best Results

Our common lawngrasses in Texas produce stolons. Those are the stems that spread across the soil's surface as the grass establishes and grows thicker. To encourage low and dense sod, you want to mow frequently and at the recommended height for the type of grass that you're growing.

Recommended mowing heights

Common bermudagrass: 1-1/4 to 1-1/2 inch

St. Augustine: 2 to 2-1/2 inches

Zoysias: 2 to 3 inches, depending on variety

Dwarf hybrid bermudas: 1/4- to 3/4-inch, depending on variety*

Buffalograss: 3 to 4 inches

Turf-type fescue: 3 to 4 inches

Ryegrass: 2 inches

  * *Most types require reel mower.*

Frequency of mowing

Many people mow their lawns (or have them mowed) every seven days during the prime part of the summer growing season. This suggestion probably won't meet with much favor, but the truth is, it's really much better for the grass if you mow it somewhat more often. That's especially important if you're mulching the clippings, in which case you might consider mowing every five days. This means a few extra mowings, but it's much quicker and easier to mow when the grass isn't overly tall.

Try never to remove more than one-third of the blade length from your lawngrass at any one mowing. On those occasions when you must trim more heavily – for example, following an extended period of rainfall – consider doing it in stages. Raise the mower one notch as you mow the first time, then drop it back down to the normal height and mow again a couple of days later.

Mulching grass clippings

Most new mowers are made to mulch clippings, so that they are left as small remnants on the lawn surface. That can reduce your need to feed. Those clippings are rich sources of nutrients that you originally applied as fertilizers. They also reintroduce organic matter back into the soil, and that will improve growing conditions for the grass as well. However, if you prefer the look of a lawn where clippings have been bagged, use them in the compost. Again, just don't send them to the landfill.

Keeping the blade sharp

Frayed blades of grass after you mow suggest a dull lawnmower blade. Sharpen the blade after every 30 hours of use (more often if you've been mowing through high weeds or if you've hit a hidden obstacle). Remove the same amount of metal from each side of the blade to keep it in balance.

Leveling the lawn

It may be possible, on a one-time basis, to roll your lawn to even out the high spots and valleys. Rent a lawn roller and fill it partially with sand or water. Your goal is to compress the soil slightly, not to compact it firmly. Do so after a heavy rain for best results. You can either push the roller manually or pull it behind a small garden tractor.

You can use brick sand (as used in mixing mortar) to fill low spots in your lawn, as long as they're not too deep or too wide. One inch deep and 8 or 10 inches wide are good limits to set. Sand is poor at retaining moisture and nutrients, so if you use too much of it, your grass won't have a uniform appearance. In cases of more extensive fills, it would be better to use topsoil taken from somewhere else in your garden. If you must bring in new sandy loam topsoil, be sure that it's free of noxious weeds like nutsedge.

From a different direction, many Texans have grown up with the idea of spreading sand, topsoil or compost across their lawns in the spring. That practice has been done not so much as a means of leveling the surface, but more in the expectation of invigorating the grass. Save the energy – it's not a good plan. It's not one that's practiced by the professionals.

City block of vigorous bermudagrass

Time to sharpen mower blade (frayed leaves)

Problem either with uneven soil or with wheel settings

Line trimmer for finishing touch on turf

St. Augustine starting to fail due to shade

Thatch

Thatch is the layer of undecomposed organic matter that can form between your lawn's runners and the soil's surface. It's the layer of "padding" between the lawn carpet and the soil floor, except that it doesn't help matters; it can create problems. (Note that "thatch" does not refer to the harmless browned stubble of leaf blades following the winter.)

Thatch layers form over a period of years. You'll gradually become aware that the grass doesn't appear to be vigorous. It remains dry after rains and irrigation, because the compressed layer of thatch sheds the water (as with thatch roofs). The grass develops a "hungry" appearance, because nutrients can't penetrate the thatch and enter the soil.

Conditions that favor formation of thatch

- Over-use of fast-release nitrogen encourages production of cell tissues that are slow to decay.

- Long clippings are not properly mulched as they are returned to the soil; rather than decaying, they compress and become compacted.

- Certain grasses are more prone to the development of thatch, including bermudas and zoysias.

Coping with thatch

- Mow frequently and at the recommended height.

- Remove clippings and use in compost, or use a mulching mower.

- Use high-quality fertilizer with half or more of the nitrogen in slow-release form.

- Use a core aerator to remove small plugs of thatch from the lawn. That will allow air, water and nitrogen to penetrate into the thatch, speeding up its decay. Core aerators can also be of value in loosening compacted soils, for example, where cars have been parked or children have played.

It is best not to use dethatching devices or tools that "comb" or "rake" the grass, since they often tear the runners of warm-season grasses loose in the process. They are of more value in northern lawns of bluegrass and other bunch grasses. And, those "aerating shoes" with spikes on the bottoms? Don't waste your time or money.

Selecting a Lawn Care Company

Many Texans opt to have professional landscape contractors and lawn care companies tend to their turfgrass. That can be a great labor-saver, but it also means that you'll be putting your trust in them to do the right things at the right times.

When choosing a lawn care team, look for those who are already in your neighborhood. Watch to see the level of care they give their other customers. Ask questions of your neighbors to see how well they're satisfied, and ask the company for references, then call those customers or drive by for a look.

Examine the company's service options. Many will do all of the work, from mowing, trimming and blowing to applications of insecticides, fungicides and fertilizers. Be sure that your contract gives details on what they'll be doing and when they'll be doing it. Hire them to do what you need, but not anything more. If you feel that they're proposing too many visits to your yard, or if they would be coming at unusual times (for example, mid-winter) to make applications you don't feel will be useful, tell them of your concerns and discuss everything before you sign up.

The garden calendar of monthly activities (pages 15 to 62) will give you details of lawn management tasks through the year. However, the timings that are listed will be rather specific – for the use of homeowners who are caring for only one lawn. Lawn care companies won't be able to be on every one of their customers' lawns on the same day, so don't expect them to follow these guidelines precisely. If you've hired a good company, you need to trust that they will get the job done for you, even if the timing varies somewhat from the dates you find in our calendar pages.

Buffalograss in Texas Hill Country

Rotary spreader for more uniform feeding

Meticulously tended common bermudagrass

Vigorous St. Augustine in fall

A Before you give up completely on lawngrass, at least consider if any lower branches of trees could be sacrificed. That would allow more sunlight to reach the grass early and late in the day. Sometimes it works, but often it doesn't. Don't allow your trees to be mangled by excessive pruning in the process if the outcome is just going to be frustrating anyway.

If grass just simply cannot grow there, your next alternative would be one of the several good shade-tolerant groundcovers such as regular mondograss, liriope, English ivy (perfect drainage required), and even a couple of our best sun groundcovers, Asian jasmine and purple wintercreeper euonymus. (See Groundcovers chapter for details.)

Deciphering the Turf Chart

This chart is designed to make choosing the best grass for your needs a bit easier. Here is a brief explanation of the star system opposite.

Attractiveness: Scale of 1 star (only modestly attractive) to 5 stars (superior good looks)

Durability: Scale of 1 (paths easily worn) to 5 (resilient to pedestrian traffic)

Ease of planting: Scale of 1 (slow and costly to get started) to 5 (quick and inexpensive to establish)

Drought tolerance: Scale of 1 (requires irrigation every three or four days) to 5 (survives Texas summers with irrigation only every couple of weeks)

Shade tolerance: Scale of 1 (requires full sunlight all day) to 5 (grows in total shade with no direct sunlight)

Insect resistance: Scale of 1 (ongoing and recurring issues with insects) to 5 (no potentially fatal insect pest problems)

Disease resistance: Scale of 1 (ongoing and recurring issues with diseases) to 5 (no potentially fatal disease problems)

Fertilizer requirements: Scale of 1 (requires minimal supplemental feeding) to 5 (requires frequent fertilization)

Dominance: Scale of 1 (easily invaded by most other turfgrasses) to 5 (crowds out all other turfgrasses).

St. Augustine thinning due to shade

Bermudagrass thriving in full sun

Texas Turf Types

PLANT AND COMMENTS	GRASS ATTRACTIVENESS	DURABILITY	EASE OF PLANTING	DROUGHT TOLERANCE	SHADE TOLERANCE	INSECT RESISTANCE	DISEASE RESISTANCE	FERTILIZER REQUIREMENTS	DOMINANCE
Common bermuda Most popular lawngrass in northern half of Texas; mowing height 1-1/4 to 1-1/2 inches; seed, sod, plugs, hydromulch	★★★★	★★★★★	★★★★★	★★★★	★★	★★★★	★★★★	★★★	★★★★
St. Augustine Most popular lawngrass for South Texas; varieties Raleigh, Delmar, Palmetto good for most of Texas and Floratam for South Texas; maintains crisp green appearance all summer, into fall; most shade-tolerant grass; prone to pests; mowing height 2 to 2-1/2 inches; sod, plugs or sprigs	★★★★	★★	★★★	★★	★★★★	★★	★★	★★	★★★★★
Zoysias Best varieties include Palisades and Jamur; intermediate in many respects to bermuda and St. Augustine; long dormant season each winter; mowing heights vary, but generally 2 to 2-1/2 inches; sod or plugs	★★★★	★★★	★	★★★	★★★	★★★★	★★★★	★★	★★★
Dwarf hybrid bermudas Ultimate in appearance when planted and properly cared for; high-maintenance; common varieties include Tifdwarf (318) and Tifway (419); mowing heights vary from 1/4- to 3/4-inch (shorter varieties require reel mower); sod, plugs, hydromulch	★★★★★	★★★★★	★	★★★	★★	★★★★	★★★★	★★★★	★★★★★
Buffalograss Native Texas grass; selections include Prairie and 609; quickly overtaken by common bermuda if it is present in vicinity (no control available); mowing height 3 inches; sod or plugs	★★★	★★★	★★	★★★★	★★	★★★★★	★★★★★	★	★★
Centipedegrass Coarse-textured grass; best in low-traffic, rather industrial settings; requires acidic East Texas soils and high rainfall; not a common lawngrass in Texas; medium-green leaf blade color; fertilize only in spring and fall; mowing height 1-1/2 to 2-1/2 inches inches; sod, sprigs or seed	★★	★★	★★★	★★	★★	★★★★	★★★★	★	★★★
Tall fescue Cool-season grass common in Northwest Texas; "bunch" grass (no runners); sown from seed in September; overseeded at half normal rate each September thereafter to keep planting solid; mow at 3 to 3-1/2 inches; do not use to overseed bermuda or St. Augustine	★★★★	★★	★★★★★	★	★★★★	★★★★★	★★★	★★	★★
Ryegrass* * Cool-season grass used for temporary turf in bare areas, also to overseed established bermuda or St. Augustine; annual rye is less expensive, but "perennial" rye is finer-textured, more attractive and easier to maintain; sow seed in early September; mow at 2 to 3 inches; both types die away naturally with warm weather in May; do not use to overseed St. Augustine in shady settings	★★★★★	★★	★★★★★	★★★★	★★★	★★★★	★★★★	★★	★★

FAQ

Q My St. Augustine has runners that arch over the lawn without rooting into the soil. Is this anything I need to worry about?

A No. You'll see this almost every summer, but it never develops into any kind of problem. Lift the runners up with your shoe just before you mow and then trim the loose runners off. The situation will probably run its course within a couple of weeks.

Garden Tip

Keep leaves off your lawn in fall. Left in place, they increase likelihood of fungal diseases such as brown patch. They also keep grass from going dormant with first freezes of fall. Strong north winds can then expose the tender grass to hard freezes in winter. At time of maximum leaf drop, collect leaves in mower bag and use them as mulch beneath shrubs and perennials, or put them into the compost pile.

Insect and Disease Pests

Here are the most common pest problems that befall Texas lawns. To get the most from these tips:

- Pay close attention to timing, because most of these problems are very seasonal. If one of them appears in your lawn, keep a log of when it showed up. It will probably come back about the same time in future years. Learn to watch for it ahead of time.

- Study symptoms carefully, because many problems will exhibit similar early warning signs. This may involve tugging on the blades, parting the grass with your fingers and even digging small amounts of soil in your search.

- Those symptoms you identify, combined with the timing, will almost always nail down the cause of the problem.

Common lawn problem-makers

(Listed in rough chronological order through the gardening year)

- **White grub worms**

  Grasses affected: any

  Timing: early spring, as grass should be greening up

  Symptoms: grass is dead and lifeless on top of soil; pulls loose easily (runners and all) like pieces of old carpet padding.

  Control: by the time damage is evident in the spring, the grubs have pupated and the insects are about to emerge as June beetles, so no treatment is needed in spring; prevent next generation by application of labeled turf insecticide one or two weeks after major June beetle flight (usually late May in South Texas, mid-June in Central and North Central Texas and early July in far North Texas); if you do not see a major flight of June beetles, and if you have not had grub problems in recent years, this treatment probably will not be needed.

Allowing fallen leaves to accumulate over lawn risks spread of disease.

White grub worm (larval form of June beetle)

- **Take-all root rot (TARR)**

  Grasses affected: St. Augustine primarily, bermuda occasionally, other grasses less often

  Timing: late March, April, May

  Symptoms: grass is yellowed and lethargic, even to the point of dying in irregular areas. Runners and blades pull loose together, similar to damage of grub worms, but grubs are not found in soil. Low-powered magnification will reveal fungal strands around runners.

  Control: fungicides have shown to be of little or no benefit. Application of any brand of sphagnum peat moss (sold by the cubic foot and in compressed bales) in a 1-inch layer across the top of the soil will help quickly and dramatically. The TARR fungus does not thrive in acidic conditions. Greening will happen within just a few weeks. Repeat a year or two later as needed. Remember that TARR is not a hot-weather disease. Many confuse it with other maladies of the summer.

- **St. Augustine decline (SAD)**

  This virus moved into Texas lawns in the 1960s and '70s, killing almost all of the St. Augustine. Up to that point, there were few varieties, and the "common" St. Augustine that we had all disappeared. Symptoms were mottled yellow blades, lethargic growth and large areas of dying grass. The virus was spread on lawn mower blades and other turf maintenance equipment. All of the varieties introduced since that time (Floratam, Raleigh, Delmar, Palmetto and others) are resistant to SAD, so we rarely see it any longer.

- **Smut**

  Grasses affected: bermuda (seed heads)

  Timing: early summer

  Symptoms: seed heads develop black, oily coating that transfers to shoes, cuffs and other clothing; no damage done to turf, but quite unattractive.

  Control: remove seed heads physically by mowing frequently; apply nitrogen fertilizer to promote vigorous new leaf and runner growth; soon runs its course as the grass stops blooming.

St. Augustine battles TARR

TARR "before"   TARR "after"

St. Augustine decline (SAD) virus less common due to resistant varieties

Chinch bug damage in St. Augustine

Chinch bugs in sunniest part of yard

Gray leaf spot on St. Augustine blades

Harmless slime mold coating leaf blades

- **Chinch bugs**

  Grasses affected: St. Augustine primarily; others rarely

  Timing: mid-summer into early fall

  Symptoms: first signs will be dried-looking grass that does not respond to irrigation. Chinch bugs will always be in the hottest, sunniest part of the yard, and they will come back to the same places year after year.

  Control: as you see grass that fails to respond to irrigation, and if it's in full, hot sun, part the grass with your fingers and look for small black insects with irregular white diamonds on their backs. They will be most active in the interface between dead and dying grass. Treat with properly labeled turf insecticide immediately. Left untreated, chinch bugs can kill large areas within a week or two.

- **Gray leaf spot**

  Grasses affected: St. Augustine

  Timing: June through early September

  Symptoms: diamond-shaped, gray-brown lesions on the midribs of the blades and occasionally on the runners themselves; most prevalent following applications of nitrogen; yellowed leaves that look like they need more nitrogen

  Control: turf fungicides may help somewhat, but also avoid nitrogen fertilizers (in spite of the lawn's yellowed appearance) from summer until first cool spells of early fall.

- **Slime mold**

  Grasses affected: St. Augustine and other grasses

  Timing: summer

  Symptoms: hand-sized patches of gray material appear on blades; resembles dusting of cigarette ashes; only damage would be from temporary shading of the coated blades.

  Control: wash spores off with water; mow lawn to remove them; brush them off with your shoe.

- **Pythium/cottony blight**

  Grasses affected: most common on bermuda, but occasionally other turf types

  Timing: late summer

  Symptoms: withered, oily looking patches of grass that die and turn brown over a matter of only a few days; affected areas may grow together to disfigure large portions of lawn.

  Control: improve drainage; reduce thatch; do not overfeed; do not water at night; apply properly labeled turf fungicide.

- **Brown patch**

  Grasses affected: primarily St. Augustine, also fescue, occasionally others

  Timing: St. Augustine in fall; fescue in spring

  Symptoms: grass blades first turn yellow, then browned and shriveled in round patches 12 to 24 inches across; blades pull loose easily from runners; dead leaf tissue can be seen at bases of leaf sheaths, where leaves attach to runners; runners and root systems are unaffected.

  Control: water only in mornings; apply labeled turf fungicide.

  Note: Brown patch may show up in spring in South Texas, where St. Augustine blades have not been browned by winter cold. Brown patch is also threatening to fescue turf, particularly in late spring. Because fescue has no runners, the entire plant dies when its leaves are killed, leaving bare areas in the lawn.

- **Frost damage in bermuda**

  This is a strange-looking situation, but the good news is that it's not a disease or insect problem, and it's not especially damaging. This is the mosaic that the first frost of fall or a late frost in spring can bring to bermudagrass. This happens when low temperatures are near, but not below 32 F. (At freezing, all of the grass would turn brown.) It doesn't show up every year, but when it does, it can be quite disconcerting.

Pythium blight in bermuda (late summer)

Brown patch in St. Augustine (fall)

Brown patch decay at bases of blades

Frost patterns in bermuda turf

Mushrooms and toadstools sprout up wherever organic matter accumulates in the soil.

Almost complete "fairy ring" of mushrooms has developed over the years.

Weed Control in Home Lawns

A highly respected turf professor once told our college class, "Weeds are invited guests into home lawns. We encourage their growth by neglecting some element of proper lawn management. Weeds are not the real problem. They're a symptom of some other problem. Once that problem is solved, most of the weeds will go away."

Commit that thought to your memory, and the next time you're facing weeds in your lawn (dallisgrass and nutsedge excluded), try to figure what you could do better in terms of watering, fertilizing, mowing (frequently and at proper height) and pest management to discourage weed growth and development.

Categorize your weeds

Most weeds fit into fairly specific groupings. You don't always have to know the precise name of the weed to be able to control it. You just need to be able to assign it to its proper category with reasonable accuracy. These three pairs of questions will get you there in almost all cases.

First clue

- Is the weed *annual* (germinates, grows, blooms, goes to seed and then dies in one growing season)?

  or…

- Is the weed *perennial* (persists from year to year by means of fleshy storage roots, bulbs, etc.)?

Second clue

- Does the weed grow most actively in late spring, summer and early fall (warm-season weed)?

  or…

- Does the weed grow most actively from October through March or April (cool-season weed)?

Third clue

- Is the weed some type of grass (parallel veins in its leaf blades) with dry and chaffy seed heads?

  or…

- Is the weed a "broadleafed" weed, that is, a weed that is not a grass – in most cases, a weed that has "regular" broad, flat leaves?

A few important terms explained

Gardeners often get confused by turf management terms, most notably by the products intended to kill weeds (herbicides). Here are explanations of three phrases that you'll want to understand.

Pre-emergent weedkillers. These are products that form a barrier across the soil surface to prevent the actual germination of annual grassy or broadleafed weed seeds. If they do their job, you will never see the weeds at all.

Most consumer pre-emergent herbicides are granular. Commercial lawn management companies frequently use liquid forms as sprays.

Your local Texas Master Certified Nursery Professional will show you several types and brands of pre-emergent herbicides for prevention of crabgrass and grassburs in spring, also of annual bluegrass (*Poa annua*), rescuegrass and ryegrass in the fall. He or she will also be able to show you another type of pre-emergent herbicide for prevention of clover, dandelions, chickweed and henbit in the fall.

Timing is obviously critical for these to be effective. They must be applied before germination. If you can see the weeds, a pre-emergent won't control that round of weeds.

CRITICAL TIMING

If you're applying pre-emergents, here are the three critical times:

- For warm-season weeds, make your first application a week or two before the average date of the last killing freeze in your area.

- Because Texas has a long growing season, you will need a second application ("booster shot") 90 days after the first treatment. That should prevent the warm-season annual weeds for the entire spring and summer. Critical fact – if you did not make the first application, the second treatment will be of no value.

- For cool-season weeds, apply your pre-emergent in the first week of September. It's often still hot then, and property owners forget how quickly winter weeds germinate with the first rain and cool spell of fall. It's better to be a week or two early with this treatment than just one day too late.

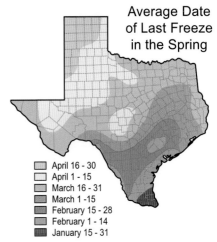

Average Date of Last Freeze in the Spring

☐ April 16 - 30
☐ April 1 - 15
☐ March 16 - 31
☐ March 1 -15
☐ February 15 - 28
☐ February 1 - 14
☐ January 15 - 31

FAQ

Q If I'm applying fertilizer and also one or two types of pre-emergent weedkillers in September, what is the sequence I should use? When do I water, and how heavily?

A Mow your lawn in early September (first week) and apply your fertilizer. Water deeply. Wait a day or two, then apply the pre-emergent weedkiller granules and water lightly to spread them across the soil's surface. From that point on, treat the lawn normally.

A wide assortment of broadleafed weeds shows that not all in this group have truly "broad" leaves. Some can actually be very small, even wiry. But they are not grasses (as confirmed by their flowers and seeds), so broadleafed weedkiller products will control them.

Q I have a bermudagrass lawn. The neighbor's St. Augustine is beginning to grow into my grass. How can I eliminate it without hurting my bermuda?

A Unfortunately, we no longer have a weedkiller that will do that for us. Your best option is to establish some type of boundary between your two lawns. It could be a shrub or perennial bed, or it could be some type of straight-line neutral area an inch or so wide, where you use a line trimmer to feather down to bare soil. Otherwise, you're either going to have to pull it up by hand, spot-treat each runner with a glyphosate herbicide or accept St. Augustine as your new lawngrass. It will crowd out the bermuda.

Post-emergent weedkillers. Use these products to kill existing weeds that can be seen growing actively in the turf.

Broadleafed weeds These can easily be eliminated by one of the several sprays available from nurseries and hardware stores. Read and follow the directions on the product label to avoid damaging nearby trees and shrubs. Pump sprayers are more efficient than hose-end sprayers at coating the entire leaf surface. They use less total herbicide. However, once you use a sprayer for a weedkiller, you should never use it for anything else. You can never be sure you have gotten all of the residue out of the spray tank.

Grassy weeds We no longer have a selective post-emergent herbicide that will safely eliminate a weed grass without harming our turfgrass, so we have to refine our treatments.

For *annual grassy weeds* such as crabgrass and grassburs, we must depend entirely on pre-emergent prevention.

For *perennial grassy weeds* such as dallisgrass, our only choices are to spot-treat with a total-kill material such as a glyphosate spray, or to remove the invading grass by hand.

Total-kill weedkillers. Sometimes you want to eliminate all existing vegetation prior to putting in a new vegetable, flower or landscape bed. Your nurseryman will have several options. These products should be applied during the growing season. Choose a type that does not contaminate the soil with a long-lasting herbicide. Let your nurseryman know that you want "contact" weed control and not "residual."

Other times you may want to eliminate all existing weeds and prevent their coming back for several months. That's where you want the more residual types of total-kill herbicides. Use care that the spray residues cannot be carried off-site by heavy rains.

Four Weeds that Require Special Attention

- **Nutsedge: a weed like no other.** It's not a broadleafed weed, and it's not a grass (in spite of the fact that people call it "nutgrass"). But it's perhaps the most tenacious weed in Texas lawns and landscapes. You can tell nutsedge from a true grass by rolling its stem between your index finger and thumb. Sedges have triangular stems. All grasses have round stems.

  It's almost impossible to eliminate nutsedge by pulling or digging. Talk to your nurseryman about products specifically designed to eliminate it. There are several on the market. All are used during the warm months (mid-May through mid-September). Follow label directions carefully.

- **Smilax briar control.** This glossy-leafed and thorny vine grows natively over much of the eastern half of Texas. It defies conventional weedkiller control because it has few leaves and very extensive root systems. Mowing or hoeing will eliminate probably 98 percent of the plants. Those few that do come back should simply be dug out with a sharpshooter. Sometimes a very woody root system will be involved, and other times a large, woody tuber. Removing the roots manually is quick and permanent. Spraying is quite ineffective.

- **Poison ivy requires special precautions.** Learn to recognize poison ivy, either by its three-leaflet leaves or, in the winter, by its stems. All parts of the plant can cause allergic reaction to its oils. Broadleafed weedkillers will eliminate it during the growing season, or you may have to dig it out very cautiously, being careful not to touch any plant tissues. See Vines, page 131 for more information.

- **Dealing with dallisgrass.** It's a tough-rooted, runner-less perennial grass that forms dense clumps of dark green leaves. Dallisgrass sends up flower stalks and seed heads only days after you have mowed, and its seeds are all viable (do not require pollination to be fertile). It's a bad news combination, and it's important that you eliminate dallisgrass as soon as you see it. Your choices are to hand-dig it with a sharpshooter spade or carefully to spot-spray it with a glyphosate herbicide. Mow frequently to keep its seed heads from maturing.

Nutsedge in bermuda

Smilax briar leaves and thorns

Poison ivy

Dallisgrass

Johnsongrass (W/G/P)

Gallery of Other Common Weeds

C: cool-season (winter)

W: warm-season (summer)

B: broadleafed

G: grass

A: annual

P: perennial

Henbit (C/B/A)

Dandelion (C/B/A)

Chickweed (C/B/A)

Bur clover (C/B/A)

White clover (C/B/P)

Dichondra (W/B/P)

Roadside aster (W/B/A)

Oxalis (W/B/A)

Spurge (W/B/A)

Grassburs (sandburs) (W/G/A)

Crabgrass (W/G/A)

Annual bluegrass (Poa annua) (C/G/A)

Annuals

Once you have the more-or-less permanent parts of your plantings (trees, shrubs and turf) in place, it's time to turn to the fun part of landscaping – garden color. Annuals, whether flowers, foliage or even with fruit, are the best color tools in your toolbox.

Pinks, petunias, pincushion flowers and sweet alyssum combine to fill a cheery patio pot.

Moss rose (portulaca)

Zinnia linnearis, ornamental sweet potato and purple fountaingrass

*A*nnual flowers and foliage bring zing to their surroundings. Nurseries race to sell the newest and best, and transplants are available virtually every week of the year. With urban landscapes getting smaller and smaller, we all have been striving to find ways to make ours stand out. Annuals provide a means to that end. But success with annuals does require planning and patience. I can't do much to grant you the patience, but I can surely help with the planning. This is my favorite topic in all of horticulture. This is my chance to share it with you!

What is an "annual?"

If you're looking for a purely botanical explanation of the term "annual," it's a plant whose entire life cycle is completed within one 12-month period. It goes from seed, through germination, into a mature plant that blooms, sets seeds and then dies. Only the dormant seed persists from one growing season to the next.

Gardeners embellish that meager concept greatly. For us, annuals are those fabulous plants that we set out already in bloom or with colorful foliage, and that we enjoy for many months thereafter. They fill our beds, pots and baskets. We surround ourselves with annuals, because we know that a garden without annuals is like a pizza without toppings.

Celosias, zinnias and angelonias

Sundance tropical hibiscus

Wax begonias, coleus and dusty miller

Brugmansias are perennials in South Texas, tropical annuals in North Texas.

Comparing annuals to perennials

Asking a plant person to choose between annuals and perennials is like asking a parent to choose between children. Here are a few of the primary differences.

- Annuals must be planted, then replaced, at least a couple of times every year. Some high-visibility commercial landscapes do these "change-outs" every few months, some even more often.

- But here's the kicker! Annuals are at their colorful best for several months in succession. Name five perennials that bloom more than four weeks out of each year. There are precious few of them. So if you need maximum color for maximum time, annuals should be your choices.

- Annuals have another decided advantage, and that is that you can rework the soil every time you prepare to replant. You'll probably take them all out at the same time, so the bed will be entirely empty at least a couple of times every year. As we will discuss with perennials in their own chapter, once you have perennials established and growing, you may never again have access to the entire bed of plants at the same time. That makes for a lot of handwork with perennials – work that will be easier with annuals.

Ageratum and Marguerite ornamental sweet potato

Nicotiana Lime Green

Calendula in spring

Fan flower (scaevola) in summer

Gold Star esperanza blooming in summer

Types of Annuals

As much as anything, these explanations are intended to create a few mindsets and to explain a few terms that may or may not be obvious to you.

Cool-season. Annuals that are tolerant of frosts, light freezes or perhaps even full-blown mid-winter cold fall into this list. As you'll see in our charts, some types are planted in October and November for color all winter and well into spring. Other, more cold-sensitive types that can handle only light freezes (28 or 30 F) are planted a few weeks ahead of the average date of the last killing freeze.

Warm-season. This group isn't as hard to explain. These plants like heat. You plant them in mid-spring (or later), and they're colorful through the summer and into the fall. Of course, some plants hold up to July and August hot weather better than others, and those become mainstays of Texas landscapes. They're probably already your buddies, but check our charts for some new ones to try.

Tropical. These could be lumped in with the "warm-season" crowd, but they're just a bit different. These are plants that are, in many cases, woody shrubs and vines in their tropical native homes. But because they won't stand freezing weather, we use them as annuals, letting them die with the first freeze in the fall. We also tend to use them just a little differently. Since most are grown from cuttings, they tend to cost more than standard annuals, so we're more likely to showcase them in smaller numbers in pots. We may even try to overwinter them indoors.

Flowering. This is the most obvious category of them all. Pure and simple, we grow these annuals for flowers. Some may also have decorative foliage, but flowers rule with this group.

Foliar. Sometimes our landscapes benefit more from a plant's leaves than from its flowers. In fact, some of our most dependable long-term annual color actually comes from highly variegated plants that never produce flowers of any consequence.

You'll find recommendations for the best plants in all these categories later in this chapter.

Copper plants' intense colors in fall's cooler weather

Using Annuals in the Landscape

Don't just buy annuals at the garden center, cart them home and then try to find a place for them. Plan things ahead of time. There are several considerations along the way.

Where will you get the most impact?

Don't feel like you have to plant thousands of annuals to be successful in showcasing them. Indeed, if you're careful in choosing where you use them, just a few dozen strategically placed plants can create quite a show.

Use annuals to accent prime focal points in your gardens. In the front yard, that would be near the entry. In the backyard, it might be near the pool, around a statue or fountain, or surrounding the patio.

Consider colors and the impacts they make

Colors work subtly. Some color differences are far more obvious than others, and you can put those differences to work in your plantings.

"Warm colors advance." That means they seem to come forward visually. Colors such as yellows, oranges, reds and hot pinks show up better, and they appear to be closer. Use them for color beds set back into the garden – beds that might otherwise go unnoticed as people pass by. Or use them as attention-getters in otherwise uninteresting settings.

"Cool colors recede." If you want small spaces to appear larger, put purples, lavenders, soft pastels and even greens to work in your gardens. They're delightful in zero-lot-line landscaping, and they also can be charming around intimate patio gardens. Many of us use them more broadly, however, simply because we like the soothing effects they bring to mid-summer landscapes, when nature alone provides us all the "warm color" that we want.

"White" is the enigma. White gardens are pristine and clean, second to none – and beloved for settings enjoyed at twilight and in the evening. But when you start to mix pure white in with other colors, it can leave visual "holes" in the plantings. If you're planting a mixture of colors in a particular garden, give thought to whether white will truly contribute or not.

Firebush (behind the perennial chrysanthemum plantings) becomes quite showy in cool fall weather.

Warm yellow of Gold Star esperanza advances visually, while cool purple of Mexican bush salvia recedes.

Wax begonias with Marguerite ornamental sweet potato

White sweet alyssum provides continuity in bed of mixed colors.

Begonias, coleus and potted annuals

White and blue fan flowers, wax begonia

Castor beans (poisonous), fountaingrass and other annuals

Massed color bed of angelonia

Color beds of red wax begonias and yellow variegated tapioca

"Massing" vs. "mixing" colors

For many years, gardeners would dedicate large beds to only one variety and color of annual plants, but in more recent years, there has been a swing to planting beds filled with mixtures of compatible colors. In many cases, breeders have blended their seeds into glorious combinations, so that when you buy the transplants, you already have a guarantee of a beautiful look. Before you make your final selection, take a look at what others have done, and borrow ideas from them.

Have a color scheme for your landscape

Think of your landscape as consisting of "rooms." In that respect, it will be similar to the inside of your house. And, just as you have a color scheme for your interior decorating, you should have one for your landscape as well. Each "room" that you enter as you walk through your landscape can have its own separate colors, but it's important that all of the shades in one line of sight be compatible.

That color scheme can change through the seasons. Perhaps you'll want cheery Easter-egg colors in spring. By summer, you'll be ready to swing over to cooling lavenders and soft pinks. Then for fall, rich shades of orange, yellow and red might come to the forefront.

Those seasonal changes should happen fairly quickly, so that your color scheme doesn't become muddled in the interims. That's where the quick change-outs you can get with annual color will be your best ally.

Minimize the "down" time

Nurseries offer annual plants in 4-inch, 6-inch, quart and gallon pots, so it's possible to have an entirely new look to a garden bed within just a few hours. However, it's usually best to put some thought into your choices before you go shopping.

Professional landscaping color designers draw grids of their beds to scale. In extreme cases, they'll replicate those grids week by week, showing what color plantings will come and go in each square foot over the course of a year. They often know 12 months ahead what annuals they'll need to have ready to fill spaces as they become open.

You're probably not going to go to that extreme in your home landscape, but you'll still want to have some type of plan for the change outs. It's hard to have a color scheme without it. If you care to draw each bed to scale on graph paper, you'll be able to use that as a record of when you planted each crop, how many transplants you bought, and when you had to replace them.

Zinnias allow quick color changes.

Displays of annuals at North Haven Gardens, Dallas

Impatiens in shade bed in spring, fall

Purple fountaingrass and pentas

Trailing periwinkles in raised bed

Cultural Requirements for Annuals

Give your annual flowers and foliage a great chance in your gardens. Know their needs, and do your best to meet them.

Bed preparation prior to planting

Because of their much more limited root systems, annual plants demand more careful bed preparation than trees and large shrubs.

- Plant in raised beds. These allow perfect drainage during periods of prolonged wet weather. While you certainly don't want to cover weep holes in brick or make contact with siding, elevating beds by as little as 3 or 4 inches can make a huge difference.

- Remove existing vegetation, including turfgrass before you do anything else. If you're preparing the bed during the growing season, there will be weedkillers that you can use for the purpose. During the winter, you will have to remove the grass and weeds manually.

- Rototill the new bed 12 to 14 inches deep. If there are shrubs, groundcovers and other flowers nearby, you can use a mini-tiller to make the job easier.

- Add 5 or 6 inches of organic matter to the top of the bed, including a couple of inches of sphagnum peat moss and 1 inch each of finely ground pine bark mulch, compost and rotted manure, then rototill again to blend the amendments into the freshly tilled soil. If you are amending a clay soil, include 1 inch of expanded shale with the rest of the ingredients.

- If you are reworking an existing bed in preparation for a new crop of color plants, repeat the process above, but cut the amount of organic amendments by half. Organic matter decays during the growing season, and you must replenish it to maintain a good soil mix for the next generation of plants. The expanded shale will need to be supplemented no more often than every two or three years.

- Rake the bed to a smooth grade, with the slope draining away from the side of the house. You can actually taper the planting mix down to the grade of the adjacent grass if necessary. That will be visually preferable to having some type of unattractive edging sticking up in the landscape.

Reseeding petunias and larkspur in spring at Antique Rose Emporium in Independence (Brenham)

Red Feather kale in late winter garden

Deep orange marigold in spring or fall

Getting the best start

There are several things you can do to help your plants zoom out of the starting blocks.

Choose annuals that are appropriate for the time of year in which you'll be planting. It's amazing how often people make the mistake of planting cool-season annuals late in the spring. Learn not to be tempted by the bargains or the remaining display of blooms as one season winds down and another begins.

Buy transplants that are "acclimated," that is, that have been grown and held at the nursery in generally the same kind of conditions that they'll be encountering when you take them home and plant them into your garden.

Look for healthy, vigorous transplants. Bargain annuals that have gotten too dry or that are generally root-bound will probably never do well.

If you're choosing flowering annuals, it's sometimes best to buy them in bud, rather than in full bloom. That's especially important for marigolds, zinnias and other large-flowering annuals. It isn't a concern with begonias, lantanas, pansies, pinks and many others.

Have the beds ready before you go shopping. Plant the annuals as soon as you get home from the nursery. Nothing good happens while annuals are sitting in pots waiting to be planted.

Bee harvests pollen from zinnia.

Pink wax begonia

Alternanthera's colorful summer foliage

Hyacinth bean with Marguerite sweet potato

Sun-tolerant coleus

Care after planting

Keep your annual plants growing vigorously. In most cases, that will involve watering them regularly and fertilizing them every three or four weeks. High-nitrogen granular fertilizers similar to those you apply to your lawn will usually be good. Use a hand-held spreader to distribute them, then either blow or wash the granules off the plants' leaves.

Most of our best types of annual flowers and foliage plants will have few, if any, pest problems. However, it's always a good idea to examine your plants several times weekly, and if a problem crops up, to identify it immediately. If some control measure is warranted, it should be applied right away.

A few annuals will tend to grow tall and may benefit from occasional pinching to remove their growing tips. That's true with coleus and copper plants, and it can even apply to flowering annuals such as lantanas and begonias as the season wears on.

Trailing lavender and white lantanas

Annuals for Container Color

Growing flowering annuals and colorful foliage plants in patio pots and hanging baskets makes great sense for any landscape, large or small. It's fun, and it's easy to get started.

Advantages of container color

- Every plant becomes a star when it's elevated by a decorative plant stand or pot.

- Container plants are portable, so they're easily moved into position for a quick spot of color. They are just as easily moved out of sight in the "down" times.

- Potted flowering plants can be placed where you wouldn't otherwise be able to build a flowerbed (on top of pavement or tree roots, or within established groundcover beds, etc.). They are perfect for patio homes and apartment balconies.

- Having plants in pots allows you to provide precise types of potting soil for the various plants that you're growing.

- Container gardening, when tall pots are used, is easier for the physically challenged gardener, since the plants are elevated by 15 to 25 inches or more.

Elephant ears, coleus and ornamental sweet potatoes

Garden Tip

If you're placing a grouping of three or five large patio pots within a groundcover bed, place concrete stepping stones where the pots will rest. During the growing season, they'll provide good bases for the pots. During the winter, you can remove and empty the pots and store them "out back," out of sight. The concrete stones will become neutral flat elements in the garden design.

Coleus and variegated Moses-in-the-rushes

Croton Picasso's Paintbrush

Terra cotta and concrete pots

Terra cotta bowls, tubs and pots

Glazed ceramic pots and urns

Nice variety of container options

Choosing the best pots

Every container must have one or more drain holes. That's the only way excess water can drain away, and it's also the only way you can leach accumulations of mineral salts out of the soil before root damage is done. If a pot you're considering doesn't have a drain hole, ask the nursery if they are able to drill one for you. (It's better that they take the risk of breaking the pot.)

If they cannot drill the hole for you, and if you are certain that you still want the pot, you can give it a try yourself. Use a variable speed drill and a medium-sized masonry bit. Set the pot upright on a solid piece of scrap lumber, and drill very patiently from inside the pot (assuming the pot is large enough). Keep the bit constantly lubed with oil. Continue to drill slowly, applying very little pressure. When you feel the masonry bit penetrating the bottom of the pot, turn the pot over and drill very slowly from the outside to clean up the opening. (You may want to practice on an inexpensive pot first.)

Pots come in all shapes and sizes. Plants don't really care if they're growing in large black nursery pots or in highly ornate ceramic containers, but you do need to consider the impacts the pots themselves will make on the look of the landscape.

Many designers prefer to use only simple, elegant pots, so that the containers won't detract from the good looks of the plants that are growing in them. You'll find beautiful glazed and terra cotta pots, also concrete, glass, plastic and fiberglass, metal and wood containers. Whatever you choose, buy for quality and durability.

Picking a great potting soil

The best growing mix for a container garden is always going to be described as "lightweight." When you pick up a bag, you should be surprised that it doesn't weigh more than it does. Heavy potting soils drain slowly and produce poor results.

In case you're considering mixing your own potting soil, here are some of the common ingredients and some general guidelines for quantities you might want to consider.

Sphagnum peat moss. Top-quality greenhouse mixes often contain 50 percent peat moss.

Finely ground pine bark. Add it in with the peat moss, but to no more than 20 or 25 percent of the total volume.

Expanded shale. This heat-treated clay product adds ballast against wind, and also good aeration. Use up to 10 percent by volume.

Horticultural perlite. Use to provide aeration and drainage, up to 10 percent by volume.

Washed brick sand. In the absence of expanded shale, use up to 10 percent sand.

Note: you may have noticed that "topsoil" is not listed as an ingredient of the best potting soils. That's because there is no precise definition of what "topsoil" really is. It could be everything from clay to sandy loam, and you don't want that great unknown when you're working in the specialized world of container gardening.

When a crop is finished and has been sent to the compost pile, remove and remix the potting soil before replanting. Add more peat and bark as you reblend it. After you have used potting soil two or three times, work it into flowerbeds or vegetable gardens and start with new potting soil in your containers.

If you are reusing pots, you'll probably be fine simply emptying them out, perhaps using a dry scrub brush to loosen any remnants of the old soil mix, and starting with new potting soil. If, however, there have been issues with algae or diseases, you may want to soak and scrub the pots. A light swabbing or spray of chlorine bleach will stop algal growth, but be careful not to let the bleach drift out onto vegetation or patio or walk surfaces. Rinse thoroughly, and allow the bleach a couple of weeks to volatilize before replanting.

Petunias well suited to pots

Faux terra cotta bowl filled with caladiums

Salvia Victoria intermingled with pink pentas

Normally wildflowers, winecups are being grown in a hanging basket.

Garden Tip

Have a special event coming up soon? Looking for a quick and great look in a large patio pot? Buy a full and lovely hanging basket. Carefully remove the hanger. Turn the basket upside-down and remove the plant carefully. Set it into the patio pot, add more potting soil as needed, and presto: instant color and beauty.

Designing the container garden

Landscape color specialists who use potted plants in their plans call for "thrillers," "fillers" and "spillers." The larger the pot, the more important that formula becomes.

Thrillers are tall, vertical plants that go to the centers of decorative plantings. They may be spike-form flowers, or they can be plants whose leaves have a distinctly upright habit.

Fillers are the flowers and foliage that make up the bulk of most patio pot and bowl plantings. They're usually somewhat rounded in their plant forms, but their textures and colors can be anything from bold and brilliant to soft and muted. They're the intermediate plants of the container design.

Spillers are trailing and cascading plants that go around the edges of the pots, tumbling down as the season progresses. They tie the plantings to the pots visually.

The number of plants required will depend on the size of the container. For a very large (e.g., 24-inch) pot you will need one to three of the thrillers in the center or at the back of the pot. Surround the thriller element with several of the fillers and several of the spillers. Water immediately after you plant them.

Caladiums "fill" garden urn as English ivy "spills."

Tapestry of coleus, begonias and other annuals planted alongside mums for fall color

Combinations of annual color in large urns

Special needs of container plantings

- Keep the soil moist. Plants being grown in pots will dry out more quickly than their in-ground counterparts. Drip irrigation systems are efficient ways of keeping the plants properly watered. You can also water by hand with a hose and a water wand. Attach either a water breaker or bubbler to the end of the wand to prevent the potting soil from being washed out of the pots.

- Fertilize every second or third time that you water. Use a water-soluble or liquid plant food applied according to label directions. You can also put timed-release fertilizer beads on top of the soil for sustained feeding over a several-month period.

- Should some of your plants begin to falter prematurely, you may be able to dig them out individually and replace them with new and fresh plants.

- If you're growing cold-hardy plants in pots over the winter, remember that you lose 10 to 20 degrees' worth of cold hardiness when plants' roots are above ground in soil that could freeze. If temperatures are expected to fall into the low and mid-20s, you may want to use a dolly to shuttle the pots into protection until the weather warms.

Caladiums are colorful all summer.

Coleus in large terra cotta pots

Amaranthus

Snapdragons in early spring

Dwarf banana, elephant ears in summer

Bright Lights mixed Swiss chard

Cardoon and Redbor kale

Best Plants for Container Color

The options are almost limitless, even extending well beyond annual color plants. However, to get you started, here are some of the best.

Thrillers

- Redbor kale
- Larkspur
- Snapdragons (tall)
- Ornamental Swiss chard
- Cardoon
- Amaranthus
- Cockscomb (tall)
- Copper plant
- Fountaingrass
- Mealy cup salvia
- Dwarf banana
- Elephant ear
- Lemon lollipop (yellow shrimp plant)
- Crotons

Fillers

Angelonia
Dusty miller
English daisies
Pinks
Snapdragons (intermediate)
Alternanthera
Wax begonias
Caladiums
Coleus
Cosmos
Dahlberg daisies
Firebush
Gerbera daisies
Gomphrenas
Joseph's coat
Lantana (bush)
Marigolds
Ornamental peppers
Perilla
Periwinkles
Zinnias
Verbena bonariensis
Chenille plant
Pentas
Mexican heather
Plumbago

Spillers

Pansies and violas
Petunias
Sweet alyssum
Lantana (trailing)
Moss rose
Hybrid purslane
Periwinkles (trailing)
Fan flower (Scaevola)
Ornamental sweet potato

Angelonia Serena Purple

Dahlberg daisy

Blackie ornamental sweet potato

Maximillian sunflower in early fall.

Indian paintbrush among bluebonnets

Blue-eyed grass in spring

Wildflowers as Annuals

Most wildflowers complete their life cycles in one growing season, and it's natural that we might consider using wildflowers in our floral gardens. Here are the critical pointers.

- Plant at the correct season. You'll probably be starting these from seed, so time your plantings as nature would do. Wildflowers that bloom in March and April mature their seeds by May and June, but most of those seeds don't germinate until early fall, so that's the ideal time to sow the seeds that you've either gathered or bought. Too many people assume that spring-blooming wildflowers like bluebonnets and Indian blankets can be seeded in spring, but that does not allow them enough time to establish and grow. Their seeds must be sown in the fall.

- Plant into dedicated beds, but don't overdo things. It may be that all you will need to do is a light cultivating of the soil. If you give wildflowers too much bed preparation and fertilizer, your plants will "go all to leaves," failing to produce a really good floral display.

- Don't make the mistake of overseeding your lawn with your wildflowers. If you think about where wildflowers grow in nature, you'll almost never see them growing where grasses compete. They're down in the washes and on the gravelly hillsides.

- Learn what your wildflower seedlings look like when they're really young. That way you'll not accidentally damage or destroy them as you work around them.

- Water during periods of extreme drought, but otherwise, let the plants fend for themselves. Do not apply fertilizers to them, or you'll end up with nothing but foliage.

- Let the plants die and dry completely following flowering. Give them time to produce viable seeds for the next year's crop.

- If you're going to collect and save seeds, store them cool and dry until planting time rolls around. Put them into a sealed jar in the vegetable bin of the refrigerator. Most types of Texas wildflowers can be saved that way for one to several years.

Texas-Friendly Annuals

Gardeners in the Lone Star State can grow many of the same annuals that thrive in other parts of the country. However, not all plants will tolerate our weather extremes. You need to know which types will be best and easiest for you, and that's the purpose of the following lists.

QUICK LIST
Best Winter-Hardy Annuals

Cool-season annuals' ability to withstand cold weather varies from crop to crop. Here is a list in order of decreasing cold tolerance.

Very cold-resistant
(Single digits and teens)

> Violas
> Pansies

Cold-resistant
(Teens and low 20s)

> Redbor kale
> Pinks

Moderately cold-resistant
(Low to mid-20s)

> Iceland poppies
> Dusty miller
> Ornamental cabbage, kale
> Snapdragons
> Sweet alyssum

Somewhat cold-resistant
(Frosts and light freezes into high 20s)

> Cardoon
> Swiss chard
> Stocks
> English daisies
> Petunias
> Foxglove
> Larkspur
> Wallflowers
> Lobelias

Iceland poppies in early spring

Lobelia Techno Blue

Foxgloves in spring

Jewel-like hues of pansies

Ornamental peppers in various stages of ripening

QUICK LIST
Best Annuals for Summer's Heat

- Alternantheras
- Celosias
- Copper plants
- Crotons
- Dahlberg daisies
- Firebush
- Gaillardias (vegetatively propagated types)
- Gold Star esperanza
- Gomphrenas
- Lantanas
- Moss rose
- Pentas
- Peppers (ornamental)
- Periwinkles
- Purslane
- Zinnias (Profusion and *Zinnia linearis*)

Dwarf Buddy gomphrena

Reseeding heirloom celosia

Alternanthera Brazilian Redhots

Nicotiana (flowering tobacco) Perfume

Red Dragon Wing begonia

QUICK LIST
Best of the Shade-Tolerant Annuals

Begonia, Dragon Wing

Begonia, wax

Bloodleaf (Iresine)

Caladiums

Coleus

Elephant ears

Impatiens (mildew-resistant types)

Lemon lollipop (yellow shrimp plant)

Nicotiana

Perillas

Persian shield

Persian shield

Magilla perilla

Cutting-grown coleus

Elephant ears' bold leaves

Hardy cyclamen

Mixed reseeding larkspurs

Apricot pansy

Cool-season annuals

In Overall Ratings (column at far right), the number 1 indicates the highest recommendation.

PLANT AND COMMENTS

Color key (COLORS): Red, Orange, Pink, Blue, Yellow, Purple, Lavender, Green, White, Gray

Sun/Shade key: Sun, Partial Sun, Shade

Plant and Comments	Peak Months	Colors	Form	Sun/Shade	Height (inches)	Spacing (inches)	Overall Rating
Bachelor button (*Centaurea cyanus*) — Strong-growing spring flower; reseeds	J F **MAM** J J A S O N D	Pink, Blue, Purple, White	Rounded	Sun, Partial Sun	16-24	10-15	3
Cabbage/kale, ornamental (*Brassica oleracea*) — Protect below 20 F; grown for foliage	**JF** M A M **JJA** S O **ND**	Red, Pink, Green, White	Heads	Sun	12-14	12-16	2
Calendula (*Calendula officinalis*) — Protect below 20-28 F	**JFMAM** J J A S O N D	Orange, Yellow	Rounded	Sun	12-20	12-16	2
Cardoon (*Cynara cardunculus*) — Very large, bold, silver foliage	**JFMAM** J J A S O N D	Gray	Rounded	Sun	30-42	24-36	2
Cyclamen (*Cyclamen hederifolium*) — Protect below 28 F	**JF** M A M J J A S O **ND**	Red, Pink, Purple, White	Clumping	Sun, Partial Sun	8-14	6-10	2
Dusty miller (*Senecio cineraria*) — Several types, all with gray foliage	**JFMAM** J J A S O N D	Gray	Rounded	Sun	10-16	10-14	2
English daisy (*Bellis perennis*) — Pots, floral borders; protect below 25 F	**JFMAM** J J A S O N D	Red, Pink, White	Rounded	Sun	8-10	8-10	2
Foxglove (*Digitalis purpurea*) — Background flower; containers; used as cool-season annual in Texas.	**JFMAM** J J A S O N D	Red, Pink, Lavender, White	Upright	Sun	24-36	12-15	2
Larkspur (*Consolida ajacis*) — Old types reseed, or transplant late winter	**JFMAM** J J A S O N D	Pink, Blue, Purple, White	Upright	Sun	24-36	8-12	2
Lobelia (*Lobelia erinus*) — Handsome flowers during cool months	**JFMAM** J J A S O N D	Blue	Rounded	Sun	8-12	6-8	3
Nasturtium (*Tropaeolum majus*) — Flowers used in salads	**JF** M A M J J A S O N D	Red, Orange, Yellow	Spreading	Sun	8-10	10-12	3
Pansy (*Viola x wittrockiana*) — Fragrant; most winter-hardy annual; rebounds after hard freezes	**JFMAM** J J A S O **ND**	Red, Orange, Pink, Blue, Yellow, Purple, Lavender, White	Rounded	Sun	8-10	10-12	1
Petunia (*Petunia x hybrida*) — Small-flowering types bloom heavily	**JFMAM** J J A S O N D	Red, Pink, Blue, Yellow, Purple, White	Spreading	Sun	8-10	10-12	2

Cool-season annuals CONTINUED

PLANT AND COMMENTS	PEAK MONTHS	COLORS	FORM	SUN/SHADE	HEIGHT (INCHES)	SPACING (INCHES)	OVERALL RATING
Phlox (*Phlox drummondii*) Many flowers with contrasting eyes	JFMAMJJASOND		Rounded	Sun	6-8	6-8	3
Pinks (*Dianthus chinensis* and *D. barbatus*) Fragrant; very cold-hardy; banded with eyes	JFMAMJJASOND		Rounded	Sun	8-15	8-12	1
Poppy, California (*Eschscholzia californica*) Direct-sow seeds in October	JFMAMJJASOND		Rounded	Sun	8-12	8-10	2
Poppy, Iceland (*Papaver nudicaule*) Open, graceful habit; bright colors	JFMAMJJASOND		Clumping	Sun	14-16	10-12	2
Primrose (*Primula* spp.) Good in pots; contrasting eyes	JFMAMJJASOND		Clumping	Partial Sun/Shade	8-12	8-10	3
Snapdragon (*Antirrhinum majus*) Many varieties and sizes	JFMAMJJASOND		Upright	Sun	8-36	8-14	2
Stock (*Matthiola incana*) Fragrant; thick stalks and floral spikes	JFMAMJJASOND		Upright	Sun	12-16	10-12	3
Sweet alyssum (*Lobularia maritima*) Fragrant; rich color mixes	JFMAMJJASOND		Spreading	Sun	3-4	10-12	1
Sweet pea (*Lathyrus odoratus*) Fragrant; plant very early spring	JFMAMJJASOND		Vine	Sun	60-96	12-16	3
Swiss chard, ornamental (*Beta vulgaris*) Beautiful large red, lavender, gold and green leaves	JFMAMJJASOND		Upright	Sun	14-16	10-14	1
Wallflower (*Erysimum* x *hybrida*) Cheerful flower with some resistance to frosts	JFMAMJJASOND		Rounded	Sun	12-18	10-12	3
Viola (*Viola* x *hybrida*) Multi-flowering pansy cousins; very winter-hardy	JFMAMJJASOND		Rounded	Sun	8-10	10-12	1

Golden California poppy

Bed of mixed annual pinks

New Look dusty miller

Warm-season annuals

In Overall Ratings (column at far right), the number 1 indicates the highest recommendation.

PLANT AND COMMENTS	PEAK MONTHS	COLORS	FORM	SUN/SHADE	HEIGHT (INCHES)	SPACING (INCHES)	OVERALL RATING
Ageratum, floss flower (*Ageratum houstonianum*) Spider mites problem in summer	JFMA**MJJAS**OND	Pink, Blue, White	Rounded	Partial sun, Shade	10-15	10-12	4
Alternanthera (*Alternanthera dentata*) Striking deep maroon foliage	JFMA**MJJAS**OND	Red, Green	Rounded	Sun	14-20	12-16	1
Amaranthus (*Amaranthus spp.*) Ambitious grower; stunning foliage and flowers	JFMA**MJJAS**OND	Red, Orange, Pink, Yellow	Upright	Sun	15-36	10-15	3
Angelonia, summer snapdragon (*Angelonia angustifolia*) Blooms all summer; resembles miniature snapdragon flowers	JFMA**MJJAS**OND	Red, Pink, Purple, Lavender, White	Upright	Sun	12-16	10-12	1
Begonia, Dragon Wing (*Begonia x hybrida*) Outstanding source of shade color; large glossy green leaves	JFMA**MJJAS**OND	Red, Pink, White	Rounded	Shade	16-24	12-15	1
Begonia, wax (*Begonia semperflorens*) Bronze-leafed varieties most tolerant of sun	JFMA**MJJAS**OND	Red, Pink, White	Rounded	Partial sun, Shade	8-15	10-15	1
Bloodleaf, Irisene (*Iresine herbstii*) Little-used but brilliant; yellow variegated type also sold	JFMA**MJJAS**OND	Red	Rounded	Partial sun, Shade	10-15	12-15	2
Blue daze (*Evolvulus glomeratus*) Gray foliage; good in containers; flowers close after noon	JFMA**MJJAS**OND	Blue, Gray	Spreading	Sun	6-8	10-12	2
Caladium (*Caladium bicolor*) Requires warm soils; remove flower buds; grown for brightly colored foliage	JFMA**MJJAS**OND	Red, Pink, White	Clumping	Partial sun, Shade	10-16	8-12	1
Candletree (*Cassia alata*) Fall-blooming; large background plant	JFMAMJJ**ASO**ND	Yellow	Shrubby	Sun	60-72	36-48	2
Castor bean (*Ricinus communis*) Very bold foliage; seeds extremely poisonous	JFMA**MJJAS**OND	Red	Shrubby	Sun	60-120	48-60	2
Cleome, spider flower (*Cleome hassleriana*) Bold plant with wispy blooms; reseeds	JFMA**MJJAS**OND	Red, Pink, White	Shrubby	Sun	36-48	24-36	2
Clock vine, black-eyed Susan vine (*Thunbergia alata*) Leaf miners may tunnel through foliage; twines vigorously	JFMA**MJJAS**OND	Orange, Yellow	Vine	Partial sun, Shade	96	36-48	3

Blue Daze evolvulus

Pink moss rose

Candletree

Cosmos at garden gate

Firebush in full bloom

Gerbera daisies

Warm-season annuals CONTINUED

PLANT AND COMMENTS	PEAK MONTHS	COLORS	FORM	SUN/SHADE	HEIGHT (INCHES)	SPACING (INCHES)	OVERALL RATING
Cockscomb (*Celosia argentea*) Crested and feathery types; also does well in fall	JFMAMJJASOND		Rounded		12-36	10-18	2
Coleus (*Solenostemon scutellarioides*) Cutting-grown types are superior; pinch out flower buds as they appear	JFMAMJJASOND		Rounded		16-30	16-20	1
Copper plant, copper leaf (*Acalypha wilkesiana*) Coppery in summer, more red in fall	JFMAMJJASOND		Shrubby		24-36	16-20	1
Cosmos (*Cosmos bipinnatus*) Open growth, showy blooms	JFMAMJJASOND		Rounded		12-36	12-18	2
Cupflower (*Nierembergia scoparia*) Use in front of floral borders or in pots	JFMAMJJASOND		Spreading		6-8	8-10	2
Cypress vine, Cardinal climber (*Ipomoea quamoclit*) Thick growth, fern-like foliage	JFMAMJJASOND		Vine		72-96	12-16	2
Dahlberg daisy (*Thymophylla tenuiloba*) Fine foliage, multitudes of blooms	JFMAMJJASOND		Rounded		10-12	8-10	2
Euphorbia hybrids (*Euphorbia hypericifolia*) Small, wispy flowers; used as fillers	JFMAMJJASOND		Rounded		12-24	8-12	1
Firebush (*Hamelia patens*) Reddish leaves, salmon-red blooms	JFMAMJJASOND		Rounded		16-24	15-20	1
Purple fountaingrass (*Pennisetum setaceum*) Maroon leaves and floral plumes; perennial in South Texas	JFMAMJJASOND		Upright		18-24	10-12	1
Geranium (*Pelargonium x hortorum*) Best in pots; struggles in summer	JFMAMJJASOND		Rounded		14-18	14-16	3
Gerbera daisy (*Gerbera jamesonii*) Blooms best in spring; Drakensburgs are most reliable in Texas conditions	JFMAMJJASOND		Clumping		12-14	10-12	3

COLORS: RED ORANGE PINK BLUE YELLOW PURPLE LAVENDER GREEN WHITE GRAY

SUN/SHADE: SUN PARTIAL SUN SHADE

PLANT AND COMMENTS	PEAK MONTHS	COLORS (Red, Orange, Pink, Blue, Yellow, Purple, Lavender, Green, White, Gray)	FORM	SUN/SHADE (Sun, Partial Sun, Shade)	HEIGHT (INCHES)	SPACING (INCHES)	OVERALL RATING
Globe amaranth, bachelor's buttons (*Gomphrena globosa*) Everlasting flowers; dwarf forms available; not to be confused with Centaurea cyanus	JFMA**MJJAS**OND	Red, Orange, Pink, Lavender, White	Rounded	Partial Sun	12-24	10-12	1
Hollyhocks (*Alcea rosea*) Some types annuals, others biennial; spider mites; coarse	J**FMAMJJ**ASOND	Red, Pink, Yellow, White	Upright	Partial Sun, Shade	18-48	15-20	4
Hyacinth bean (*Dolichos lablab*) Maroon foliage, flowers, fruit	JFMA**MJJAS**OND	Red	Vine	Sun	72-96	18-20	1
Hybrid Impatiens (*Impatiens x hybrida*) Several types bred for resistance to downy mildew, tolerance of morning sun	JFMA**MJJAS**OND	Red, Orange, Pink, Lavender, White	Rounded	Partial Sun, Shade	12-18	12-15	1
Impatiens (*Impatiens walleriana*) Subject to fatal downy mildew (improved varieties showing resistance); poor bloom in heat	JFMA**MJJAS**OND	Red, Orange, Pink, Lavender, White	Rounded	Partial Sun, Shade	12-18	12-15	3
Joseph's coat (*Alternanthera ficoidea*) Green foliage turns brilliant shades in fall	JFMA**MJJAS**OND	Red, Orange, Green, Gray	Spreading	Partial Sun, Shade	12-16	15-18	2
Lantana (*Lantana* spp.) Extremely heat-tolerant; attracts hummingbirds	JFMA**MJJAS**OND	Red, Orange, Pink, Yellow, Lavender, White	Rounded, trailing	Sun	8-36	10-24	1
Marigold (*Tagetes erecta* and *T. patula*) Spider mites in summer; exceptional color in fall with August planting	JF**MAMJJAS**OND	Orange, Yellow	Rounded	Sun	10-36	10-20	2
Melampodium (*Melampodium paludosum*) Heat-tolerant; daisy-like blooms	JFMA**MJJAS**OND	Yellow, White	Rounded	Sun	8-10	10-12	2
Mexican sunflower (*Tithonia rotundifolia*) Strong-growing plant; floral favorite of butterflies	JFMA**MJJAS**OND	Orange, Yellow	Rounded	Sun	24-36	20-24	3
Moonflower, angel's trumpet, devil's trumpet (*Datura metel*) Coarse-textured growth, fragrant white flowers at night; flowers poisonous	JFMA**MJJAS**OND	White	Shrubby	Sun	36-40	24-30	2
Moonvine (*Ipomoea alba*) Vigorous growth; fragrant nocturnal flowers	JFMA**MJJAS**OND	White	Vine	Sun	60-72	18-24	3
Morning glory (*Ipomoea tricolor*) Vigorous growth; blooms open in mornings	JFMAMJJ**AS**OND	Red, Blue, Lavender, White	Vine	Sun	60-72	18-24	3
Moss rose, portulaca, rose moss (*Portulaca grandiflora*) Heat-resistant; flowers close mid-afternoon	JFMA**MJJAS**OND	Red, Orange, Pink, Yellow, Lavender, White	Rounded	Sun	6-8	8-10	1

Colorful fall pods of hyacinth beans

Pink lantana and black swallowtail

Morning glory in fall

Ornamental peppers

Mixture of purslane colors

Small-flowering sunflower

Warm-season annuals CONTINUED

Plant and Comments	Peak Months	Form	Sun/Shade	Height (inches)	Spacing (inches)	Overall Rating
Pentas *(Pentas lanceolata)* — Multitudes of flowers all summer	JFMA**MJJAS**OND	Rounded	Partial Sun / Shade	12-16	10-12	1
Pepper, ornamental *(Capsicum annuum)* — Many varieties with varying fruit	JFMA**MJJAS**OND	Rounded	Sun	10-15	12-18	2
Perilla *(Perilla frutescens)* — Maroon or multicolored foliage resembles coleus	JFMA**MJJAS**OND	Rounded	Sun	16-24	12-16	2
Periwinkle, annual vinca, Madagascar periwinkle *(Catharanthus roseus)* — Heat-tolerant, free-blooming; serious disease problems, although resistant varieties are available	JFMA**MJJAS**OND	Rounded	Sun	8-12	10-12	2
Purslane *(Portulaca oleracea)* — Extreme heat tolerance; flowers close late afternoon	JFMA**MJJAS**OND	Spreading	Sun	8-10	10-12	1
Sage, mealy cup *(Salvia farinacea)* — Short-lived perennial that is best used as annual	JFMA**MJJAS**OND	Upright	Sun	12-16	10-12	1
Scaevola, fan flower *(Scaevola aemula)* — Trailing; baskets or borders, blue varieties are best	JFMA**MJJAS**OND	Spreading	Sun	8-10	12-14	1
Sunflower *(Helianthus annuus)* — Coarse textured; smaller types bloom longer	JFMA**MJJAS**OND	Upright	Sun	36-120	15-30	2
Swan River daisy *(Brachyscome iberidifolia)* — Bright daisy-like flowers, generally blue; not common	JFMA**MJJAS**OND	Rounded	Sun	8-10	8-10	2
Sweet potato, ornamental *(Ipomoea batatas)* — Several varieties with stunning foliage	JFMA**MJJAS**OND	Trailing	Sun	10-12	18-20	1
Tobacco, flowering *(Nicotiana alata)* — Fragrant, free-flowering	JFMA**MJJAS**OND	Upright	Partial Sun / Shade	15-48	15-20	3
Verbena *(Verbena spp.)* — Perennial types better than seeded annuals	JFMA**MJJAS**OND	Trailing	Sun	8-15	8-12	3
Wishbone flower *(Torenia fournieri)* — Floral border, containers	JFMA**MJJAS**OND	Rounded	Partial Sun	6-8	8-10	3
Zinnia *(Zinnia elegans)* — Rich colors, less mildew when planted in late summer	JFMA**MJJAS**OND	Rounded	Sun	8-42	8-24	2

Orange bougainvillea

Cherub brugmansia

Chenille plant

Tropical annuals

In Overall Ratings (column at far right), the number 1 indicates the highest recommendation.

PLANT AND COMMENTS	PEAK MONTHS	COLORS	FORM	SUN/SHADE	HEIGHT (INCHES)	SPACING (INCHES)	OVERALL RATING
African bush daisy *(Euryops chrysanthemoides)* — Bright yellow blooms all summer and early fall	JFM**AMJJASO**ND	yellow	Rounded	partial sun/shade	24-30	20-24	2
Allamanda *(Allamanda cathartica)* — Huge tubular blooms against bold green foliage	JFM**AMJJASO**ND	yellow	Leaning	partial sun/shade	48-60	15-20	1
Banana *(Musa spp.)* — Bold leaves; some types variegated red and green	JFM**AMJJASO**ND	red, yellow, green	Tree-like	partial sun	48-150	24-36	1
Bougainvillea *(Bougainvillea glabra)* — Stunning in bloom, but sporadic flowering	JFM**AMJJASO**ND	red, orange, pink, purple, white	Leaning	partial sun	36-48	36-48	3
Brugmansia *(Brugmansia spp.)* — Coarse; tubular downward-facing flowers open evenings	JFM**AMJJASO**ND	orange, yellow, white	Shrubby	partial sun	48-96	30-48	2
Chenille plant *(Acalypha hispida)* — Red catkin-like flowers persist for weeks; sister of copper plant	JFM**AMJJASO**ND	red	Rounded	partial sun	18-24	18-24	1
Croton *(Codiaeum variegatum)* — Brilliantly variegated leaves	JFM**AMJJASO**ND	red, orange, yellow, green	Rounded	partial sun/shade	48-72	36-54	1
Dipladenia *(Dipladenia sanderi rosea)* — Dark green foliage; compact growth; resembles mandevilla	JF**MAMJJAS**OND	red, pink, white	Vine	shade	72	30-36	2
Elephant ear *(Colocasia esculenta)* — Green- and purple-leafed varieties; usually perennial in South Texas	JF**MAMJJAS**OND	green	Clumping	shade	30-42	16-20	1
Esperanza *(Tecoma stans)* — Buttery yellow flower clusters all summer; will be perennial in South Texas	JF**MAMJJAS**OND	yellow, green	Leaning	partial sun	30-48	20-24	1

Bright variegation of crotons

Brugmansia double yellow

Orange esperanza

Bloodleaf (Iresine)

Lemon lollipop (yellow shrimp plant)

Cape plumbago

Tropical annuals CONTINUED

PLANT AND COMMENTS	PEAK MONTHS	COLORS	FORM	SUN/SHADE	HEIGHT (INCHES)	SPACING (INCHES)	OVERALL RATING
Hibiscus, tropical *(Hibiscus rosa-sinensis)* Large blooms last one day but continue all summer	JF**MAMJJAS**OND		Shrubby		36-48	20-24	1
Lemon lollipop, yellow shrimp plant *(Pachystachys lutea)* Light yellow floral spikes all season	JF**MAMJJAS**OND		Rounded		18-22	14-16	3
Mandevilla *(Mandevilla splendens)* Large blooms contrast with dark green leaves	JF**MAMJJAS**OND		Vine		48-60	15-18	1
Mexican heather *(Cuphea hyssopifolia)* Elegant, fine-textured border plant	JF**MAMJJAS**OND		Rounded		12-15	10-12	1
Papaya *(Carica papaya)* Bold-textured foliage; good in containers	JF**MAMJJAS**OND		Tree-like		72-96	36-48	1
Persian shield *(Strobilanthes dyerianus)* Iridescent purplish leaves	JF**MAMJJAS**OND		Rounded		12-18	10-12	2
Plumbago *(Plumbago auriculata)* Perennial in southern third of Texas	JF**MAMJJAS**OND		Rounded		24-36	10-12	2
Princess flower *(Tibouchina urvilleana)* Showy purple blooms; prune to avoid legginess	JF**MAMJJAS**OND		Shrubby		42-60	36-48	2
Shrimp plant *(Justicia brandegeana)* Robust plant; shrimp-like flowers atop foliage	JF**MAMJJAS**OND		Rounded		14-16	12-14	2
Stephanotis *(Stephanotis floribunda)* Deep green foliage sets off fragrant white blooms	JF**MAMJJAS**OND		Vine		48-60	12-16	2
Variegated tapioca *(Manihot esculenta 'Variegata')* Brilliantly variegated yellow foliage; focal point of its garden; pest-free	JF**MAMJJAS**OND		Shrubby		36-42	42-48	1

Wildflowers

Texas is renowned for its native wildflowers. While some types are perennials, most are annuals, so we have chosen to include them here. In Overall Ratings (column at far right), the number 1 indicates the highest recommendation.

PLANT AND COMMENTS	PEAK MONTHS	COLORS	FORM	SUN/SHADE	HEIGHT (INCHES)	SPACING (INCHES)	OVERALL RATING
Black-eyed Susan *(Rudbeckia hirta)* Free-blooming; reseeds freely	JFMAMJJASOND	yellow	Rounded	Sun	14-16	8-10	1
Bluebonnet *(Lupinus texensis)* Do not plant in turf areas; do not fertilize; all species of bluebonnets native to Texas are declared the official state flower.	JFMAMJJASOND	blue, purple, white	Rounded	Sun	8-12	6-8	1
Blue-eyed grass *(Sisyrinchium montanum)* Grows from small bulbs; dormant rest of year; is a perennial wildflower	JFMAMJJASOND	blue	Clumping	Sun	6-8	5-6	1
Coreopsis, goldenwave *(Coreopsis basalis)* Graceful annual is prettier than cultivated perennial types	JFMAMJJASOND	yellow	Rounded	Sun	12-14	8-10	1
Evening primrose *(Oenothera speciosa)* Invasive in beds, so plant separately; is a perennial wildflower	JFMAMJJASOND	pink, yellow, white	Spreading	Sun/Shade	8-10	12-14	1
Indian blanket *(Gaillardia pulchella)* Establishes well, reseeds freely	JFMAMJJASOND	red, orange, yellow	Rounded	Sun	8-12	6-8	1
Indian paintbrush *(Castilleja indivisa)* Beautiful, but difficult to establish	JFMAMJJASOND	red	Upright	Sun	8-10	6-8	3
Maximillian sunflower *(Helianthus maximiliani)* Forms large clumps; is a perennial wildflower	JFMAMJJASOND	yellow	Upright	Sun	18-60	36-48	1
Mexican hat *(Ratibida columnaris)* Attractive flowers; easily grown	JFMAMJJASOND	red, yellow	Rounded	Sun	14-20	10-12	1
Winecup *(Callirhoe involucrata)* Lovely short bloomer; is a perennial wildflower	JFMAMJJASOND	purple	Spreading	Sun	4-6	6-8	1

Bluebonnets and paintbrushes on Texas roadside

Goldenwave coreopsis

Pink evening primrose

Perennials

Gardeners who plan perennials into their landscapes bring magic to their surroundings. There's something enchanting about a seemingly delicate flower that can return year after year, even against the odds of Texas soils and climate.

Morden Pink loosestrife (rear) and Goldsturm gloriosa daisy are two of Texas' most dependable perennial flowers.

Naturalized jonquils blanket acres of "downtown" Edom each February.

Blue bearded iris

Daylilies in summer sun

Disbudded mum: lower flower buds on stem pinched off, resulting in one large head.

*P*erennials *were the first flowers I ever planted. In fact, my first recollection of gardening at all was alongside my dad as we planted a rose garden for Mom. I was 4.*

By the time I was 13, I'd fallen in love with jonquils and daylilies. To finance my obsession, I rode my bike, pulling our mower behind me, to mow yards all across east College Station for two bucks apiece. However, a couple of the ladies paid me in daylilies – $5 worth! I suspect they just enjoyed seeing my glee as I pedaled back home, mower in tow and daylilies in hand. That was a grand time in my life. Perennials *and* Neil *have a long history together.*

What is a "perennial"?

As a horticulturist, I have a rather simplistic definition of the term. I use it to refer to plants (mostly flowering) that persist for more than two years without having to be replanted. That distinguishes perennials from annuals (which complete their full life cycle within 12 or fewer months) and biennials (which grow normal stems and leaves for their first year, then flower and set seed the second year).

Most of the plants that I'm calling perennials are herbaceous plants (non-woody), although technically, trees and shrubs are perennials, too. As a gardener, I generally think of perennials as being plants that grow vigorously part of the year, flower, and then die back to a persistent root system, bulb or other fleshy plant part – a storage organ to get the plant through the tough times of cold, heat or drought.

And, in a state as large and diverse as Texas, there is one other pertinent distinction. What actually might be a shrub in warm South Texas can behave more like a perennial (dying to the ground in winter) in Central Texas, and it might even be used as an annual in northern parts of the state. Lantanas are a great example. So, depending on where you garden in the Lone Star State, your lists of what are annuals and what are perennials may differ from the comparable lists of someone living only a few counties away.

Planning the Perfect Perennial Garden

It's easy to design a showy garden of annuals. Perennials require more forethought and planning. They're at peak bloom for much shorter times (seldom more than three or four weeks), so you have to include several types to ensure a full season of color.

Here are your most important considerations:

- Pick the best location. Full, or nearly full sun is best for most types. Good drainage is essential.

- Be aware that perennial gardens are usually better when seen from across the landscape. Because there will be extended periods when the plants are either dormant or not in bloom, it's usually better not to have them alongside the patio or at the front door.

- Consider planting in dedicated perennial beds. They usually work best because they allow you to focus on the needs of the specific types of plants that you're growing.

- Prepare the soil carefully. Eliminate all existing weeds and grasses, either by spraying with a glyphosate-only herbicide during the growing season or by digging during the winter. Rototill the native soil to 12 to 14 inches, then incorporate 5 or 6 inches of a variety of organic matter (sphagnum peat moss, compost, rotted manure, shredded pine bark mulch, etc.), and if you're amending a native clay soil, 1 inch of expanded shale. Rototill again to blend all the components together.

- Install bed edging almost flush with the top of your lawngrass, then rake the tilled soil in the perennial bed to establish a 5- or 6-inch crown in the middle, tapering down to the level of the edging. That slight slope will ensure good drainage later.

Goldsturm gloriosa daisy

Cannas, golden yarrow, purple heart and (lower right) skullcap

Morden Pink loosestrife

Golden gaillardia

Salvia greggii (Autumn sage)

Perennials at the nursery

Fall perennials with late-season annuals

- Have a few anchoring evergreen shrubs within the bed of perennials. That's especially important in winter, when most of your perennial plants will have died back to the ground. Without those constants, the perennial bed can quickly become a blank, lifeless space.

- Make a list of your favorite perennials and the amount of room they will require. List the prime bloom times for those you're going to be buying. Plan for a sequence of blooms from spring until frost. Remember that not all perennials will be available at the same time. Some are more readily available in spring, others in fall.

- Plan for pockets of color within your overall landscape. Distribute these pockets around the landscape based on bloom times, so that your perennial color will always be evenly balanced from one end of the yard to the other.

- Have a color scheme for your plantings. As with annual flowers, your perennial garden may lean toward one family of colors in spring, another in summer, and yet another come fall.

- Know your desired plants' recommended planting spacings. Do the math to determine how many plants you'll need to buy. Notice that, in contrast to annuals, many perennials are sold at the nursery as larger starter plants – in quarts and one-gallon pots. Others will be dug and moved bare-rooted. You may find them in protective plastic bags or packed in moist sawdust.

- Shop in unexpected places. Sometimes you'll find better selections of particular perennials if you go to local shows, plant societies' sales, and collectors' personal home gardens. That will be especially true with plants such as iris and daylilies. Other times you'll have the best luck if you find someone who is already growing a particular plant and who will give you "a start." That's a great way, for example, to get St. Joseph's lily (hardy amaryllis), oxblood lilies and fall crocus. You will almost never find them in nurseries.

- Use annuals to add spots of color to your perennial beds. Annuals can help pull your lovely garden through its lean times when few of the perennials are blooming.

Enchantment lily (in Texas!)

Louisiana phlox

Hardy red mallow hibiscus

Gloriosa daisies

Maintaining Your Perennials

By the time you've gone to the trouble of planning the garden, then finding and planting your perennial favorites, you'll immediately need to start caring for them. It's not difficult in most cases, but it certainly is essential. As much as some people might have you believe, you can't plant perennials and then forget them.

John Fanick summer phlox

- Watering is critical. Without it, most perennials will start to fail. They may hang on for a while, but they'll perform at a fraction of their potential. Water deeply when you do irrigate, to encourage deeper, more vigorous roots. Use low-angled sprinklers and sprinkler heads or drip irrigation. Overhead irrigation leads to diseases, and it can also weight down and ruin the flowers.

- Fertilize regularly. Again, your goal is to keep your plants healthy and vigorous, and nutrients are keys to success. Unless a soil test directs you to do otherwise, apply a high-nitrogen or all-nitrogen plant food. Keep the granules off the flowers and foliage, and water immediately to soak nutrients down to the roots. Feed your perennials in anticipation of upcoming growth. That would mean in late winter, again in late spring or early summer, and a third time in early September. Those dates might need to be adjusted slightly, depending on the types of perennial plants that you're growing.

Flame anisacanthus

Hardy ageratum and visitor

- Mulch your beds of perennials. Weed control can be especially difficult in perennial gardens, because you never get a second chance to rototill the beds. Mulches choke out many of the weeds that are already there, and they discourage or prevent germination of new ones. They conserve valuable water, and they protect against rapid changes in soil temperature. That can be critical when you're growing perennials that are a little bit tender to either winter's cold or summer's heat.

- Weeds can be a real issue in perennial gardens. Everyday invaders like spurge and annual bluegrass or crabgrass aren't of much concern, but nutsedge, Johnsongrass and bermudagrass can be simply awful. Learn what the various types of young weeds look like, and take immediate action to eliminate them. In most cases, merely scraping the surface of the soil with a sharpened hoe will eliminate the majority of the weeds. Other times, you may have to apply a weedkiller by spot-spraying or by "painting" the herbicide on with a foam rubber paintbrush. If you opt to try spraying, use cardboard baffles to protect desirable foliage while you're addressing the weeds.

- "Deadheading" to a gardener means removing spent foliage and flowers, plus seed heads as they develop. You may need pruning shears to accomplish this task, or you may be able to pinch off the old plant parts with your fingers. Removing faded flowers and leaves makes a huge difference in the look of the garden and in repeat blooming.

Herbstsonne rudbeckia is tall, easy and dependable.

Pink oxalis in shaded bed

Blue Dutch iris

Confederate rose hardy hibiscus

When Things Become Crowded

Dig and divide your perennials as needed. Some (Shasta daisies as examples) may need to be dug every year, perhaps every two. Others can go on for many years before they become crowded enough to require thinning and dividing.

Work on your beds in the plants' "off season." If they bloom in the fall, divide them in the spring, and if they bloom in spring, fall is your time to dig and reset them. Use a sharpshooter or nursery spade to dig up the clumps. Either cut them into smaller clumps with the spade, pruning shears or a machete, or carefully break them apart between your two hands.

Prepare the planting soil anew before you reset the plants. Space them at the recommended distances. In other words, avoid the temptation to crowd them. If friends can use the overflow, share your plants with them. If not, either create new beds for them, or send them to the compost.

Homestead purple perennial verbena

Preparing to dig hardy amaryllis

Daylily

Hardy amaryllis

Sign at the Antique Rose Emporium in Independence (Brenham)

The Easy Elegance rose Sunrise Sunset

Mermaid rose's blooms are captivating, but the strong vines are extremely thorny.

Roses for Texas

Queen of all flowers, the rose was among the first plants brought into cultivation during the days of the Republic of Texas. Today, roses are still riding that same wave of popularity, and recent research and new introductions have merely strengthened the swell.

Choosing the site

With a little luck, your rose plantings should be in place for many years, so it makes perfect sense to put your best efforts forward in selecting the location and preparing the soil.

- **Full sun.** Roses need sun to grow to their full potential. They need sun to bloom heavily. They can tolerate two or three hours of light shade in the afternoon, but be careful planting near trees. Trees have a habit of growing larger and casting more shade.

- **Perfect drainage.** Most roses struggle in waterlogged soils, particularly if the overly wet conditions persist more than a day following heavy rains. You can always add water when conditions are dry, but it's difficult to remove water from saturated soil. For that reason, you might want to choose a slightly uphill site for your bed.

- **Dedicated bed.** Some types of roses blend well into the landscape, but many of the popular cut-flower types really show better and are more easily maintained if you'll grow them in beds created solely for them. Beds that are out in the landscape (not against the side of the house) usually look best, especially if you have a dark evergreen shrub background behind them.

- **Good air circulation.** Fungal diseases, especially black spot and powdery mildew, are serious threats to many types of roses. Keep the leaves dry as you water, and even more importantly, plant in areas where there is good movement of winds.

- **Highly organic soil mix.** Rototill to a depth of 12 to 15 inches. Remove all roots and rocks you turn up in the process. Spread 2 or 3 inches of sphagnum moss, and 1 inch each of pine bark mulch, well-rotted manure, and compost. If you're amending a clay soil, also include 1 to 2 inches of expanded shale. Rototill again, to blend the amendments into the 12 to 15 inches of tilled topsoil.

- **Raised bed surface.** As you rake the well-amended rose planting bed soil, leave it 6 to 10 inches above the surrounding grade. You may want to use river rock, bricks or pressure-treated wood as an edge to the bed, or you can taper it gently back down to ground level, in which case you would want to have baked enamel metal edging installed almost flush with the ground. Leave enough edging visible that you'll be able to run the trimmer up against it.

- **Drip irrigation** works especially well in rose beds. The plants will be staying in place for many years, so you won't have the problem of having to retrofit the drip lines to fit new types of plants every year. (That can be a problem with vegetables and flowers.) Drip irrigation also keeps the foliage completely dry, and drip systems are given extra allowances during periods of water restrictions.

Choosing your roses

There are two key times to purchase the highest-quality, best-graded rose plants. You'll find them either bare-rooted in January and early February or container-grown in late March, April and early May.

If you're buying bare-rooted stock, be sure it has been held in cool, bright surroundings outdoors, and buy the plants soon after they arrive in the nursery. You don't want them to have dried out or been exposed to hard freezes, and you certainly don't want to buy plants that have sprouted and started to grow while still in their bare-root packaging. Be particularly careful not to buy "bargain" bare-rooted roses at end-of-season closeouts. The plants themselves, after all, represent a small fraction of the cost of getting the bed growing.

Container roses that you buy in April or May were probably bare-rooted plants that the nurseryman potted up in January and grew on site, so that they could be sold in full bud and bloom later that spring. That is perfectly acceptable, because it allows you to compare the colors and flower forms, and it also allows you to see the vigor of the plants. Most home gardeners now prefer to buy their roses this way.

Tyler Municipal Rose Garden's raised planting bed

Public gardens are great places to choose roses you like best. (Tyler Municipal Rose Garden in October)

Goldmarie rose

Climbing red roses belong on white picket fences.

Garden Tip

Granular products are the best means of applying nutrients to rose beds. Liquid foliar feedings work only for short periods of time. They also put the leaves and buds at risk of sunscald if the mineral salt/water mix is still beaded up on the leaves when the sun strikes them. Adding moisture to rose leaves also increases likelihood of black spot and powdery mildew. All of these issues can be avoided by applying granular fertilizers directly to the soil.

Setting the plants

Have the planting beds ready before you go shopping, and set the plants into their new spots as soon as you arrive home with them. Check the labels and other resource information to determine their full sizes at maturity, and allow them 6 inches more space for extra measure. Remember that different classes of roses grow to very different sizes as they mature, so adjust plant spacings accordingly.

Set the plants at the same depth at which they were previously grown. If you're planting bare-rooted roses, remove all of the packaging material and trim away any damaged roots. In fact, it's good for the plants if you'll take time to soak their roots in a bucket of water for an hour prior to planting.

If you're planting roses from pots, remove them from the containers. If the pots are said to be a "biodegradable" type that will decay over time, it's still a good idea to slice through the pot walls with a knife or even to peel away as much of each container as possible once you have the plants set down into the planting holes.

Water your new roses immediately after they have been planted. Water slowly and deeply to eliminate all pockets of air in the planting soil. The second time that you water them, apply a liquid root-stimulator fertilizer and repeat that one month later.

Feeding established rose plantings

The only way to know for sure what your roses will need in the way of nutrition will be to have a reputable lab run a test on the planting soil.

There are many fine products listed as "rose foods" in the nursery marketplace, and most will be just fine for the first couple of years. However, most of them are comparatively high in phosphorus (middle number of the fertilizer analysis), and phosphorus can accumulate in Texas soils to harmful levels. Don't be surprised, as a result, if the soil test suggests that you switch over to a product that is all nitrogen, half or more of it in slow-release form.

Roses hit peak bloom in mid-spring and mid-fall in Texas.

Brilliant Pink Iceberg rose

Petals of the butterfly rose (Mutabilis) change colors as they age.

Pruning roses

We use pruning to keep rose plants at manageable sizes. We also use pruning to eliminate weak and damaged branches and to direct growth of the plants.

- Bush roses, whatever their types (Hybrid Teas, Floribundas, Grandifloras, even miniatures) are pruned by half early each February. Each cut should be made directly above a bud that faces out from the center of the plant. That will encourage more open, spreading growth. This pruning stimulates new growth and best spring flower production. You will want to do a similar thinning and reshaping in early August as you prune the plants back by one-third, to encourage a round of blooms in September and October.

- Climbing roses produce their flower buds on canes that grew the prior year, so don't prune them until after their big spring bloom has finished. At that point, remove weak canes that won't contribute to the plants' long-term beauty. Remove canes that extend out from their supports. It would be difficult to pull them back into shape. As the growing season progresses, remove unwanted canes as they appear.

Honey Bouquet rose

You'll also have ongoing pruning tasks as the plants finish rounds of blooms. Remove spent flowers on Hybrid Teas and other cut-flower roses by trimming their canes back to the second set of five-parted leaves. Prune floribundas during the growing season by snipping just a few inches below the inflorescences after all flowers in the spray have bloomed – particularly if the variety can be expected to rebloom. Cease deadheading toward the end of the season if you want to enjoy the hips in the winter garden.

Old-fashioned Blaze climbing red rose

Pest control for your roses

Several insects and diseases bother our roses. Learn to identify them, and take quick steps to control them.

- **Black spot** is a fungal leaf disease. It is common on most varieties of roses, but it's far worse on some. Dark brown, almost black spots will be surrounded by haloes of yellowed tissues. Leaves will soon drop and the plants will be bare. Keep foliage dry, and apply a labeled fungicide weekly to slow the disease's progress.

- **Powdery mildew** is often seen along with black spot. It looks like a dusting of flour from the kitchen, and you'll see it during periods of high humidity. The same fungicide that you use for black spot will probably control the mildew.

- **Aphids** congregate on new growth in the spring. You'll see clusters of their pear-shaped bodies on buds and new leaves. Most organic and inorganic insecticides will eliminate them.

- **Thrips** disfigure rose flowers. They are almost-microscopic sliver-shaped insects that proliferate inside the buds just before they try to open. Petals will be singed around their edges, and the buds will fail to open properly. Those that do manage to open will develop small light spots on dark roses and dark spots on the light-colored petals. Systemic insecticides will control thrips if applied about the time buds begin to be visible.

Winter Sunset rose from Iowa hybridizer Griffith Buck

Unusual color and form for roses

Rio Samba rose

A WORD ABOUT ROSE ROSETTE VIRUS

RRV has become quite common in several parts of Texas, most especially on Knockout roses. Gardeners' first observations are that their plants aren't blooming properly, and that the new shoots are misshapen, dark, mottled and clubby looking – a pattern of growth often described as "witch's broom."

This disease is extremely damaging to rose populations, and we do not yet have a reliable control for the virus. Recommendations of rosarians and pathologists alike are that we dig and destroy all parts of affected plants. That will remove them as sources of inoculation of other roses in our gardens and in the neighborhood. Pruning to make the plants look better will simply prolong the problem until it has had time to spread to other roses nearby.

Rank, clubby growth of RRV infection

Fewer and poorly formed flowers due to RRV

Tyler Municipal Rose Garden is a good place to study different types and colors of roses.

Climbing Pinkie rose clambers over arbor. It has been designated as an Earth-Kind® rose selection.

Types of roses

There are dozens of classes of roses. Real rose lovers probably dip into several of the categories to find types that they like.

- **Hybrid Teas** are the long-popular cut-flower roses. They have perfectly formed buds filled with many petals. They generally produce one bud per stem, so they're ideal for floral design. The plants grow to be 4 to 6 feet tall and 4 to 5 feet wide.

- **Floribundas** are popular landscape roses that bear multiple blossoms in large clusters. Ranging from compact and low-growing to large and open, they make striking massed plantings or blooming hedges.

- **Grandifloras** are less common, but they are types of roses that grow strongly to 5 or 6 feet tall and wide. They produce large, handsome flowers that are well suited to cutting.

- **Miniature roses** are novelties in the group. They have all the same assets and liabilities as their larger counterparts, so the care that you give them should be exactly the same. You just have to scale it all back proportionate to their plant size.

- **Climbing roses** come from several different groups. The thing they all have in common is that they lack the means of supporting their stems. You have to provide them a substantial trellis, arbor or fence along which they can be trained.

- **Antique roses** fall into dozens of categories, so much so that entire books have been written on them alone. Many of these old varieties are "found" roses that have been collected by rose "rustlers" from abandoned homesites and cemeteries, where they often have grown unattended for decades. Many are highly fragrant, and many can be grown as landscaping shrubs.

A SPECIAL NOTE ABOUT EARTH-KIND® ROSES

This is a mixed group of antique and modern roses that have been rigorously tested against one another and against other popular rose varieties, first in Texas and then across America. Those that proved after several years of testing to be superior performers with minimal maintenance were selected as being Earth-Kind®.

This program was begun by Dr. Steve George of the Texas AgriLife Extension Service of Texas A&M, and it has been carried forward by rose researchers from the academic world, nursery industry, and rose societies across America. These roses carry special identification tags. The most current information on them can be found online at the Earth-Kind® website.

Garden pool at Dickson Brothers, Mesquite

Tropical water lily

Water Gardening

The legions of Texas water gardeners are growing faster than almost any other population of plant people. If you are among them, you will be dealing with a different group of plants in different types of plantings. Here are the basics.

- Start with a bright location. Aquatic plants need full or nearly full sunlight.

- Plan a lovely geometric or formal water feature to complement your home, or nestle the pond into a natural-looking watercourse, to make it look like a little spring-fed pool in the Texas Hill Country. Either way, be sure it's not accessible to free-roaming young children.

- Plan to elevate the pond at least slightly from its immediate surroundings, so that debris won't wash into it during rainstorms.

- To make things easier, use a pre-formed pool from a garden center or pond gardening source. There are many sizes and shapes available.

- If you prefer something more unusual, dig your own free-form pond, then assure water retention by installing a heavy vinyl pond liner. Your pond will need to be 15 to 24 inches deep. In cutting and fitting the liner, allow 10 or 12 extra inches of vinyl around the outer edges of the pool. Fill with water, allowing the weight of the water to pull the vinyl farther down into the hole. Make your final trim, leaving 5 or 6 inches of vinyl encircling the pond. Conceal and weight the liner edges with river rock, ledgestone pavers or other heavy material. You may want to build a ledge specifically to allow space for container plants at water's edge.

Horsetail equisetum is popular alongside garden pools.

- Provide for good aeration of the pond water to lessen the likelihood of algae. Small bubbling fountains work well, and moving water adds soft, natural sounds to the garden. If the water travels through a filtration system as it flows, so much the better. Talk to your water garden supplier about the size of pump you'll need for your pond.

- Choose the best mix of plants for your water garden. There are scores of bog plants of all sizes, forms, colors and textures. You may want something as simple as one water lily, or you might prefer an exciting variety.

- Consider adding fish. Colorful koi are as much a part of backyard ponds as shells are to the seashore. Some of the most prized specimens of koi can cost a great deal, but you can have lovely fish for a modest amount.

- Enjoy your water garden into the evening by adding night lighting, either from tree limbs overhead or through submersible lights within the pond itself (or both). Since you may be combining water and electricity, you'd be wise to call in a pro.

- If you like the sounds of moving water, but you're not up to the effort of digging a pond, at least buy yourself a nice fountain. Position it against a dark background of brick, stone or evergreen shrubs that will allow you to see the bubbling water. You can either install a receiving pool and recirculating pump, or you can buy a totally self-contained fountain (a "plug-and-play" model).

However you decide to bring water to the landscape that surrounds you, you're sure to be pleased with the outcome.

Hardy water lily

Arrowhead

Aquatic plants

Colony of hardy water lilies

Author's fountain and pool

Colocasias ready to head pond-side

Cleopatra canna

Pink hardy hibiscus (mallow)

Coronation Gold yarrow

Most Durable Perennials for Sun

Summer foliage of Autumn Joy sedum

Amaryllis, hardy
Artemisia, Powis Castle
Canna
Chrysanthemum
Daylily
Fall aster
Gloriosa daisy
Grasses, ornamental
Hibiscus (mallows)
Iris
Pinks
Purple coneflower
Purple heart
Red yucca
Rock rose
Salvias
Sedums
Shasta daisy
Thrift
Yarrow

Hameln dwarf fountain grass

Daylily garden

Anemone-form chrysanthemums

Goldsturm gloriosa daisy

Best Perennials for Shade

- Columbine
- Fern, autumn
- Fern, Japanese holly
- Fern, southern wood
- Four o'clocks
- Gingers
- Hellebores
- Hostas
- Leopard plant
- Oxalis
- Oxblood lily
- Resurrection lily
- Spider lily
- Summer phlox
- Summer snowflake
- Spiderwort
- Sweet violet
- Umbrella plant (paper plant)

Leopard plant

Texas Gold columbine

Best Perennials for Foliar Interest

- Artemisia, Powis Castle
- Elephant ears
- Fern, autumn
- Fern, Japanese holly
- Fern, southern wood
- Grass, dwarf fountain
- Grass, maiden
- Grass, Mexican feather
- Grass, Gulf muhly
- Hostas
- Lamb's ear
- Leopard plant
- Purple heart
- Umbrella plant (paper plant)

Collection of hostas

Variegated silver grass

ZONE 6 — USDA Hardiness Zones
ZONE 7
ZONE 8
ZONE 9

Find Texas Hardiness Zones information page 5.

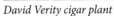

David Verity cigar plant

Balloon flower

Flowering Perennials

In Overall Ratings (column at far right), the number 1 indicates the highest recommendation.

Best Zones In Texas
6 7 8 9

PLANT AND COMMENTS	PEAK MONTHS	COLORS	FORM	SUN/SHADE	HEIGHT (INCHES)	SPACING (INCHES)	OVERALL RATING
Anisacanthus, flame (*Anisacanthus quadrifidus* var. *wrightii*) Tubular flowers are hummingbird favorites	JFMAMJJASOND		Shrubby		36-48	30-45	2
Balloonflower (*Platycodon grandiflorus*) Graceful, pretty; better in northern areas	JFMAMJJASOND		Clumping		18-24	12-16	3
Bee balm (*Monarda didyma*) Strong growers; better in North Texas	JFMAMJJASOND		Shrubby		24-30	18-24	3
Blackfoot daisy (*Melampodium leucanthum*) Intermittent bloomer; daisy-like flowers	JFMAMJJASOND		Clumping		6-12	6-10	2
Blue plumbago (*Ceratostigma plumbaginoides*) Hardy cousin to tropical annual	JFMAMJJASOND		Trailing		4	15-18	2
Bouncing Bet (*Saponaria officinalis*) Phlox-like pink blooms; heirloom plant known also as soapwort	JFMAMJJASOND		Spreading		15-18	15-18	3
Butterfly weed (*Asclepias tuberosa*) Tuberous wildflower perennial; favorite of butterflies	JFMAMJJASOND		Rounded		18	15	2
Candytuft (*Iberis sempervirens*) Lovely border or rock garden plant; shear lightly after bloom to keep plant compact	JFMAMJJASOND		Spreading		18-60	12-15	1
Canna (*Canna x generalis*) Bold texture; many with variegated foliage	JFMAMJJASOND		Upright		18-60	12-16	1
Catmint (*Nepeta x faassenii*) Foliage attracts cats; attractive floral sprays	JFMAMJJASOND		Spreading		16-24	15-18	2
Chrysanthemum (*Dendranthema x grandiflorum*) Many sizes and forms of "garden" mums	JFMAMJJASOND		Rounded		15-42	15-24	1
Cigar plant, firecracker plant (*Cuphea ignea*) Also blooms in spring in South Texas	JFMAMJJASOND		Upright		36-42	15-18	2

Butterfly weed

Coreopsis

Purple coneflower

Flowering Perennials CONTINUED

Best Zones In Texas* — 6 7 8 9 *See Zones Map page 222.

Plant and Comments	Peak Months	Form	Sun/Shade	Height (inches)	Spacing (inches)	Overall Rating
Columbine (*Aquilegia chrysantha* var. *hinckleyana* 'Texas Gold') — 'Texas Gold' is a superior selection	JF**MAM**JJASOND	Rounded	Shade	15-20	12-15	2
Coneflower, giant (*Rudbeckia maxima*) — 6-inch flowers; great for back of garden	JFMAMJJASOND	Clumping	Partial Sun	60-72	24	2
Coneflower, Herbstsonne (*Rudbeckia nitida* 'Herbstsonne') — 5-inch flowers; flowers with green centers	JFMAMJ**JA**SOND	Upright	Partial Sun	48-60	24	2
Coreopsis (*Coreopsis verticillata* and other species) — Golden daisy-like flowers	JFM**AM**JJASOND	Rounded	Partial Sun/Sun	15-24	12-18	2
Daylily (*Hemerocallis* spp.) — Unlimited choices; many reblooming types	JFM**AM**JJASOND	Clumping	Sun	12-48	12-24	1
Fall aster (*Symphyotrichum oblongifolium*, formerly *Aster oblongifolius*) — Tip-prune in May to keep plants compact	JFMAMJJ**ASO**ND	Rounded	Partial Sun/Sun	18-24	15	2
Four o'clocks (*Mirabilis jalapa*) — Flowers open late afternoon	JFM**AMJJAS**OND	Shrubby	Partial Sun/Shade	24-30	18-24	2
Gaillardia (*Gaillardia* x *grandiflora*) — Perennial form of wildflower Indian blanket	JFM**AMJJAS**OND	Rounded	Partial Sun/Sun	10-20	12-14	3
Gaura (*Gaura lindheimeri*) — Airy plants carry small flowers	JFM**AMJJAS**OND	Clumping	Partial Sun/Sun	20-28	14-18	3

Sizes and colors of daylilies

Fall aster

Double gaillardia

Flowering Perennials CONTINUED

Best Zones In Texas* — 6 7 8 9   *See Zones Map page 222.

Best Zones In Texas (6 7 8 9)	Plant and Comments	Peak Months	Colors	Form	Sun/Shade	Height (inches)	Spacing (inches)	Overall Rating
6 7 8 9	Gayfeather (*Liatris spicata*) — Dramatic purplish-pink bloom spikes	JFMAM**JJA**SOND	Pink, Purple/Lavender	Spikes	Sun	18-24	16-24	2
8 9	Gingers (*Zingiber, Alpinia, Hedychium* and other genera) — Bold leaves; many variegated types; showy blooms	JFMAM**JJAS**OND	Red, Pink, Blue, Yellow, White	Clumping	Partial Sun, Shade	24-72	18-36	2
6 7 8 9	Gloriosa daisy (*Rudbeckia hirta* and other species) — *R. fulgida* var. *sullivantii* 'Goldsturm' one of the most dependable types; resembles annual wildflower black-eyed Susan	JFMAM**JJAS**OND	Yellow	Clumping	Sun	15-18	10-12	1
6 7 8 9	Gregg's mist flower (*Eupatorium greggii*) — Resembles annual ageratum; spider mites; butterfly favorite	JFM**AMJJAS**OND	Blue	Upright	Partial Sun, Shade	12-18	18-24	2
6 7 8 9	Hellebores, Lenten rose (*Helleborus* x *hybrida*) — Unusual flowers during late winter; evergreen	**JFM**AMJJASOND	Red, Pink, Purple, White, Gray	Clumping	Partial Sun, Shade	15-30	18-24	2
6 7 8 9	Hibiscus (*Hibiscus* spp.) — Coarse texture; tropical look; several types	JFMAM**JJAS**OND	Red, Pink, White	Clumping	Sun	24-60	30-48	1
6 7 8 9	Hypericum, St. John's wort (*Hypericum perforatum*) — Shows iron chlorosis in alkaline soils	JF**MAM**JJASOND	Yellow	Shrubby	Partial Sun, Shade	24-36	24	3
6 7 8 9	Iris, bearded (*Iris hybrida*) — Hundreds of varieties	JF**MA**MJJASOND	Red, Orange, Pink, Blue, Yellow, Purple, Lavender, White	Clumping	Partial Sun, Shade	12-36	10-18	1
7 8 9	Iris, Louisiana (*Iris* spp.) — More upright than bearded; tolerate wet soils; dramatic foliage; five species in group	JF**MA**MJJASOND	Red, Orange, Pink, Blue, Yellow, Purple, White	Clumping	Partial Sun, Shade	20-42	12-18	1
6 7 8 9	Jerusalem sage (*Phlomis fruticosa*) — Resembles sage; flowers in whorls along stems	JFMA**MJJAS**OND	Orange, Yellow	Shrubby	Partial Sun, Shade	36-48	36-42	2
8 9	Mexican mint marigold (*Tagetes lucida*) — Fall bloomer; fragrant leaves	JFMAMJJ**ASO**ND	Yellow	Clumping	Partial Sun, Shade	18-30	15-18	2

Variegated ginger

Hellebores

St. John's wort (Hypericum)

Ozark primrose

Pavonia (rock rose)

Penstemon

Flowering Perennials CONTINUED

Best Zones In Texas*
6 7 8 9

PLANT AND COMMENTS *See Zones Map page 222.	PEAK MONTHS	COLORS	FORM	SUN/SHADE	HEIGHT (INCHES)	SPACING (INCHES)	OVERALL RATING
Mexican oregano (*Poliomintha maderensis*) Tubular flowers become lighter in color as they age	JFMA**MJJAS**OND		Shrubby		24-30	24-30	2
Mexican petunia (*Ruellia simplex*) Species good, but invasive; dwarf types popular	JFMA**MJJAS**OND		Clumping		10-30	12-18	2
Obedient plant (*Physostegia virginiana*) Snapdragon-like spikes; usually lavender-pink	JFMAMJJA**S**OND		Clumping		24-30	12-16	2
Oxeye daisy (*Leucanthemum vulgare*) Traditional white daisy blooms	JFMA**MJJAS**OND		Rounded		18-24	12-14	1
Ozark primrose (*Oenothera macrocarpa*) Large yellow blooms; native to Central Texas	JFMA**MJJAS**OND		Spreading		8-12	12-15	2
Pavonia, rock rose (*Pavonia lasiopetala*) Hibiscus relative; 1-inch blooms	JFMA**MJJAS**OND		Shrubby		24-36	36	2
Penstemon (*Penstemon* spp.) Related to snapdragons, foxgloves	JFMA**MJJAS**OND		Clumping		15-36	12	2
Peony (*Paeonia* spp.) Suited only to colder areas of Texas	JFMA**MJJAS**OND		Clumping		18-24	24-30	3
Phlox, Louisiana (*Phlox divaricata*) Lovely border plant; greener foliage than thrift	J**FMA**MJJASOND		Spreading		4-6	15-18	2
Phlox, summer (*Phlox paniculata*) Rose-red heirloom form, magenta 'Victoria' and pink 'John Fanick' are two of best	JFMA**MJJAS**OND		Clumping		30-36	12-15	2
Pincushion flowers (*Scabiosa* x *hybrida*) Tufted flowers; this one is non-invasive	JFMA**MJJAS**OND		Clumping		12-24	12-24	2
Pinks (*Dianthus* spp.) Fragrant carnation relatives; several good perennial selections	JF**MAM**JJASOND		Sprawling		6-15	8-12	2

Pride of Barbados (Mexican bird of paradise)

Mexican bush sage

Red hot poker

Flowering Perennials CONTINUED

Best Zones In Texas* (6 7 8 9) — *See Zones Map page 222.

PLANT AND COMMENTS	Best Zones (6 7 8 9)	PEAK MONTHS	FORM	HEIGHT (INCHES)	SPACING (INCHES)	OVERALL RATING
Pride-of-Barbados, red bird of paradise (*Caesalpinia pulcherrima*) — Used as shrub or perennial in South Texas, annual in North Texas; drought-tolerant; brilliantly colored flowers; attracts butterflies	8 9	JFMAMJJASOND	Shrubby	96-120	96-120	1
Purple coneflower (*Echinacea purpurea*) — Native Texas daisy-like wildflower; many highly improved selections in many different colors.	6 7 8 9	JFMAMJJASOND	Clumping	16-30	8-12	1
Purple loosestrife (*Lythrum salicaria*) — Spike form with purplish-pink flowers	6 7 8 9	JFMAMJJASOND	Clumping	18-24	18	2
Red hot poker (*Kniphofia uvaria*) — Red-and-yellow spikes atop grass-like clumps	6 7 8 9	JFMAMJJASOND	Clumping	16-30	12-18	2
Red yucca (*Hesperaloe parviflora*) — Drought-tolerant; attractive in massed plantings	6 7 8 9	JFMAMJJASOND	Clumping	36-48	16-24	1
Russian sage (*Perovskia atriplicifolia*) — Fine-textured leaves; lavender-pink sprays	6 7 8 9	JFMAMJJASOND	Clumping	30-40	24-30	2
Salvia, anise (*Salvia guaranitica*) — Deep-blue flower spikes	7 8 9	JFMAMJJASOND	Clumping	36-42	18-24	1
Salvia, autumn sage (*Salvia greggii*) — Longest-flowering perennial; prune back by half late winter	6 7 8 9	JFMAMJJASOND	Shrubby	18-24	18	1
Salvia, Henry and Augusta Duelberg (*Salvia farinacea* 'Henry Duelberg' and 'Augusta Duelberg') — Very dependable perennials; 'Henry Duelberg' is blue; 'Augusta Duelberg', silvery white	7 8 9	JFMAMJJASOND	Shrubby	24-30	30-36	1
Salvia, Indigo Spires (*Salvia* x 'Indigo Spires') — Deepest purple-blue spikes	7 8 9	JFMAMJJASOND	Shrubby	36-42	24	1
Salvia, Mexican bush (*Salvia leucantha*) — Pinch growing tips late spring to keep plants compact; variety 'Santa Barbara' is dwarf	8 9	JFMAMJJASOND	Clumping	24-36	18-24	1

Flowering Perennials CONTINUED

Best Zones In Texas* (6 7 8 9)	PLANT AND COMMENTS *See Zones Map page 222.	PEAK MONTHS	COLORS	FORM	SUN/SHADE	HEIGHT (INCHES)	SPACING (INCHES)	OVERALL RATING
■■■■	Showy stonecrop (*Hylotelephium spectabile*) Fall-blooming upright succulent	JFMAMJJA**S**O**ND**	■	Clumping	●	16-24	16-24	2
■■■■	Shasta daisy (*Leucanthemum x superbum*) Many forms and sizes; some double-flowering	JF**MAM**JJASOND	□	Clumping	●●	12-36	10-18	1
■	Shrimp plant (*Justicia brandegeana*) Heavy-flowering; pink shrimp-like blooms; used as annual in other zones	JFMA**MJJAS**OND	■■■	Rounded	●●	18-24	15	2
■■■	Skullcap (*Scutellaria suffrutescens*) Compact mounds of tiny foliage covered in small flowers	JFMA**MJJAS**OND	■ □	Rounded	●	12-18	12-24	2
■■■■	Speedwell (*Veronica* spp.) Deadhead spent flowers for longer bloom	JF**MAMJJAS**OND	■■ ■ □	Spreading	●●	10-20	12-24	2
■■■■	Spiderwort (*Tradescantia* spp.) Sprawling wandering Jew relative	JF**MAMJJAS**OND	■■ ■ □	Spreading	●●	15-24	15-24	2
■■	Sundrop (*Calylophus* spp.) Evening primrose-like; 1-inch flowers	JFMA**MJJAS**OND	▪	Spreading	●●	8-10	10-24	2
■■■■	Thrift (*Phlox subulata*) Showy spring blooms; good in rock gardens and borders	**JFM**AMJJASOND	■ □	Spreading	●●	6-8	18-20	1
■■	Turk's cap (*Malvaviscus arboreus* var. *drummondii*) Rolled red blooms are hummingbird magnets	JFMA**MJJAS**OND	■ ■ □	Shrubby	●	48-84	48-60	1
■■■■	Verbena, perennial (*Verbena* spp.) 'Blue Princess,' 'Homestead Purple' are best types	JFMA**MJJAS**OND	■ ■ ■■ □	Spreading	●	6-12	12-18	2
■■■■	Violet, sweet (*Viola odorata*) Very fragrant; spider mites and nematodes	**JFM**AMJJASOND	■■ ■ □	Clumping	●	6-10	8-12	3
■■■■	Yarrow (*Achillea millifolium*) Fern-like foliage; flowers can be dried	JFM**AMJJ**ASOND	■ ■ ▪ ■ □	Spreading	●●	12-36	12-18	1
■■	Zexmenia (*Zexmenia hispida*, formerly *Wedelia hispida*) Tough native with yellow daisy-like flowers	JFM**AMJJASO**ND	▪	Shrubby	●●	24-36	12-18	2

Color key: RED ORANGE PINK BLUE YELLOW PURPLE LAVENDER GREEN WHITE GRAY
Sun/Shade key: SUN PARTIAL SUN SHADE

Spiderwort

Shasta daisies

Turk's cap

Flowering Perennial Bulbs

In Overall Ratings (column at far right), the number 1 indicates the highest recommendation.

Best Zones In Texas* — 6 7 8 9

PLANT AND COMMENTS   *See Zones Map page 222.

Color legend: RED, ORANGE, PINK, BLUE, YELLOW, PURPLE, LAVENDER, GREEN, WHITE, GRAY

Sun/Shade legend: SUN, PARTIAL SUN, SHADE

Best Zones (6 7 8 9)	Plant and Comments	Peak Months	Colors	Form	Sun/Shade	Height (inches)	Spacing (inches)	Overall Rating
8 9	Amaryllis, hardy; St. Joseph lily (*Hippeastrum x johnsonii*) — Heirloom Texas garden flowers; seldom sold in nurseries	JF**MA**MJJASOND	Red	Bulb	partial sun, shade	20-24	12-16	1
6 7 8 9	Byzantine gladiolus (*Gladiolus communis* spp. *byzantinus*) — Magenta flowers; compact clumping form of glads	JF**MA**MJJASOND	Pink	Corm	partial sun, shade	24-30	4-6	1
6 7 8 9	Chinese ground orchid (*Bletilla striata*) — Terrestrial orchid; striking foliage	JFM**AM**JJASOND	Lavender, White	Bulb	shade	18-24	8-10	2
6 7 8 9	Crinum (*Crinum* spp.) — Glossy leaves; lily-form flowers	JFM**AMJJA**SOND	Red, Pink, White	Bulb	partial sun, shade	30-40	30-48	2
6 7 8 9	Fall crocus, lily-of-the-field (*Sternbergia lutea*) — Brilliant fall flowers; naturalizes	JFMAMJJ**AS**OND	Yellow	Bulb	partial sun, shade	4-6	4-6	1
7 8 9	Gladiolas (*Gladiolus spp.*) — Usually treated as annuals; require staking (at time of planting)	JFM**AMJJA**SOND	Red, Orange, Pink, Purple, Lavender, Green, White	Corm	sun	30-48	4-6	2
6 7 8 9	Grape hyacinth (*Muscari armeniacum*) — Blankets of miniature bluebonnet-like flowers	JF**M**AMJJASOND	Blue	Bulb	partial sun, shade	4-6	2-3	1
6 7 8 9	Lily (*Lilium* spp.) — Most true lilies are not suited to Texas summer heat; some local nurseries and specialty online sources of bulbs may offer them.	JFM**AMJJA**SOND	Orange, Yellow, White	Bulb	partial sun, shade	15-42	12-15	3
9	Lily-of-the-Nile (*Agapanthus orientalis*) — Tropical bulb for South Texas only	JFMA**MJJAS**OND	Blue, White	Bulb	partial sun, shade	15-36	15-20	2
8 9	Montbretia (*Crocosmia x hybrida*) — Showy flowers atop gladiolus-like leaves	JFM**AMJJA**SOND	Red, Orange	Bulb	partial sun, shade	36-42	6-8	2
6 7 8 9	Narcissus, jonquils, daffodils (*Narcissus* spp.) — Early- and small-flowering types best naturalizers	JF**M**AMJJASOND	Orange, Yellow, White	Bulb	partial sun, shade	6-18	3-6	1
6 7 8 9	Ornamental onion (*Allium x hybrida*) — Large northern types not dependable in Texas	JFM**A**MJJASOND	Lavender, White	Bulb	partial sun, shade	12-24	8-12	3

Crinum

Gladiolus byzantinus

Fall crocus, lilies-of-the-field

Oxblood lilies

White oxalis

Perennialized Tulipa praecox

Flowering Perennial Bulbs
CONTINUED

Best Zones In Texas* 6 7 8 9 / PLANT AND COMMENTS *See Zones Map page 222.	PEAK MONTHS	COLORS	FORM	SUN/SHADE	HEIGHT (INCHES)	SPACING (INCHES)	OVERALL RATING
Oxalis (*Oxalis crassipes*) Long-popular, low border flower	JFMAMJJASOND	■ □	Bulb	●●	10-12	6-10	1
Oxalis, purple-leafed (*Oxalis triangularis*) Showy leaves; attractive flowers	JFMAMJJASOND	■	Bulb	●●	10-12	6-10	2
Oxblood lily, schoolhouse lily (*Rhodofiala bifida*) Heirloom perennial; dark-red, nodding flowers early each fall	JFMAMJJASOND	■	Bulb	●●●	10-12	3-4	1
Peruvian daffodil, Shoal's spider lily (*Hymenocallis coronaria*) Lovely graceful plant near water gardens	JFMAMJJASOND	□	Bulb	●	30-36	18-24	2
Rain lily (*Zephyranthes* spp., *Cooperia* spp.) Bloom 3 to 4 days after summer or fall rain	JFMAMJJASOND	■ ■ □	Bulb	●●	8-12	3-4	2
Resurrection lily, naked lady lily (*Lycoris squamigera*) Large leaves appear in late winter, soon disappear; flowers appear without foliage	JFMAMJJASOND	■	Bulb	●	16-20	6-8	2
Spider lily (*Lycoris radiata*) Red form is showiest	JFMAMJJASOND	■ ■ □	Bulb	●●	15-20	8-12	1
Spring starflower (*Iphieon uniflorum*) Light- to dark-blue, star-shaped blooms	JFMAMJJASOND	■ ■	Bulb	●●	5-6	4	2
Star of Bethlehem (*Ornithogalum umbellatum*) Six-petaled, star-shaped blooms; grass-like leaves	JFMAMJJASOND	□	Bulb	●●	8-10	3-4	2
Summer snowflake (*Leucojum aestivum*) Delicate bell-shaped, drooping blooms; jonquil-like leaves	JFMAMJJASOND	□	Bulb	●●	12-18	8-10	1
Tulip (*Tulipa* spp.) Several species types perennialize in Texas; large hybrids should be treated as annuals	JFMAMJJASOND	■■ ■■ □	Bulb	●●	10-15	3-4	3

Powis Castle artemisia | *Purple heart* | *Lamb's ear*

Foliage Perennials

In Overall Ratings (column at far right), the number 1 indicates the highest recommendation.

Best Zones In Texas* — 6 7 8 9

PLANT AND COMMENTS — *See Zones Map page 222.

Best Zones In Texas (6 7 8 9)	Plant and Comments	Peak Months	Colors	Form	Sun/Shade	Height (inches)	Spacing (inches)	Overall Rating
6 7 8 9	Artemisia, wormwood (*Artemisia ludoviciana* and hybrids) — Ferny gray/green leaves; 'Powis Castle' is best	JFMAMJJASOND	gray	Clumping	sun	8-30	10-24	1
7 8	Elephant ear (*Colocasia esculenta*) — Showy caladium relatives, also grown from tubers; used as annuals in colder regions; dark purple-leafed types especially showy	JFMAMJJASOND	purple, green	Clumping	shade	36-54	18-24	1
6 7	Hosta, plantain lily (*Hosta* spp.) — Small-leafed types better suited to Texas heat	JFMAMJJASOND	lavender, white	Clumping	shade	12-24	12-16	2
6 7 8 9	Lamb's ear (*Stachys byzantina*) — Soft leaves; may melt in summer; remove flower buds as soon as they are visible	JFMAMJJASOND	gray	Spreading	sun, partial	10-12	12-15	2
6 7 8 9	Leopard plant (*Farfugium japonicum*) — Dramatic leathery green leaves blotched yellow; solid-green form 'Gigantea' is showy	JFMAMJJASOND	green	Clumping	partial, shade	18-24	15-18	2
6 7 8 9	Moneywort (*Lysimachia nummularia*) — Sprawling plant; small leaves and yellow blooms	JFMAMJJASOND	yellow	Trailing	partial, shade	4	18-24	2
7 8	Paper plant, umbrella plant (*Cyperus alternifolius*) — Unusual palm-like leaves; good near water gardens	JFMAMJJASOND	green	Clumping	partial, shade	30-42	12-15	1
7 8 9	Purple heart (*Setcreasea pallida*) — Purple-leafed cousin of wandering Jew; dies to ground in winter but returns	JFMAMJJASOND	lavender	Spreading	sun, partial	12	15-18	1
7 8	Santolina, lavender cotton (*Santolina chamaecyparissus, S. virens*) — Border plant; remove flowers to keep plants compact; gray- and green-leafed types	JFMAMJJASOND	green, white, gray	Shrubby	sun	16-20	16-20	2
6 7 8 9	Sedum, trailing (*Sedum* spp.) — Low border or rock garden plant; many types	JFMAMJJASOND	red, green, gray	Trailing	sun	3-8	8-12	2
6 7 8 9	Yellow archangel (*Lamiastrum galeobdolon*) — Long runners spread quickly; seldom flowers	JFMAMJJASOND	yellow, green	Trailing	partial, shade	10-12	12-18	2

Perennial Grasses

In Overall Ratings (column at far right), the number 1 indicates the highest recommendation.

Best Zones In Texas* (6 7 8 9)	PLANT AND COMMENTS *See Zones Map page 222.	PEAK MONTHS	COLORS	FORM	SUN/SHADE	HEIGHT (INCHES)	SPACING (INCHES)	OVERALL RATING
▪ ▪ ▪	**Bloodgrass, Japanese** (*Imperata cylindrica*) Reddish leaves on trailing runners	JF**MAMJJAS**OND	Red	Spreading	◐◐	8-10	15-18	2
▪ ▪ ▪ ▪	**Dwarf fountaingrass** (*Pennisetum alopecuroides*) 'Hameln' has white plumes; 'Moudry' has black	JF**MAMJJAS**OND	White	Clumping	◯	18-30	15-18	1
▪ ▪ ▪	**Feather reed grass, Karl Foerster** (*Calamagrostis* x *acutiflora* 'Karl Foerster') Popular and proven ornamental grass for drama in background of perennial garden	JF**MAMJJAS**OND	Green/White	Upright	◯	30-36	18-24	1
▪ ▪ ▪ ▪	**Maiden grass** (*Miscanthus sinensis* 'Gracillimus') Graceful leaves; showy plumes; several types	JF**MAMJJAS**OND	Green/White	Clumping	◐◐	48-72	48-60	1
▪ ▪ ▪	**Mexican feather grass** (*Nassella tenuissima*) Extremely fine-textured; gracefully flowing foliage; silvery-tan flowers and seeds in summer	JF**MAMJJAS**OND	White/Green	Arching	◯	18	10	1
▪ ▪ ▪ ▪	**Muhly, Gulf** (*Muhlenbergia capillaris*) Pink, airy fall plumes	JF**MAMJJAS**OND	Pink/White	Clumping	◐◐	24-30	30-36	2
▪ ▪ ▪ ▪	**Muhly, Lindheimer** (*Muhlenbergia lindheimeri*) Wiry clumps; stout upright plumes	JF**MAMJJAS**OND	White	Clumping	◯	36-48	42-48	2
▪ ▪	**Pampas grass** (*Cortaderia selloana*) Extremely strong grower; showy silvery plumes	JF**MAMJJAS**OND	Green/White	Clumping	◯	60-96	72-120	1
▪ ▪ ▪ ▪	**Variegated Japanese silver grass** (*Miscanthus sinensis* 'Variegatus') Showy white-striped variegation	JF**MAMJJAS**OND	Green/White	Clumping	◐◐	48-60	36-48	1
▪ ▪ ▪	**Zebra grass** (*Miscanthus sinensis* 'Zebrinus') Yellow crossbanding on leaves	JF**MAMJJAS**OND	Green/White	Clumping	◐◐	60-84	48-60	2

Pampas grass

Zebra grass

Maiden grass

Autumn fern

Southern wood fern

Holly fern

Perennial Ferns

In Overall Ratings (column at far right), the number 1 indicates the highest recommendation.

Best Zones In Texas* — *See Zones Map page 222.

Best Zones In Texas* 6 7 8 9	PLANT AND COMMENTS	PEAK MONTHS	COLORS	FORM	SUN/SHADE	HEIGHT (INCHES)	SPACING (INCHES)	OVERALL RATING
	Autumn (*Dryopteris erythrosora*) Evergreen clumps with bronze new growth	JFMAMJJASOND	▮	Clumping	●●	18-24	12	1
	Cinnamon (*Osmunda cinnamomea*) Prefers moist, acidic soils	JFMAMJJASOND	▮	Clumping	●●	18-30	12-18	2
	Dixie wood (*Dryopteris x australis*) Fast-growing; evergreen in warmer areas	JFMAMJJASOND	▮	Clumping	●●	48-60	18-24	1
	Japanese holly (*Cyrtomium falcatum*) Bold clumps of holly-like evergreen leaves	JFMAMJJASOND	▮	Clumping	●●	18-30	12-18	1
	Japanese painted (*Athyrium niponicum* var. *'pictum'*) New foliage is silver and burgundy	JFMAMJJASOND	▮	Clumping	●●	8-20	10-12	3
	Ostrich (*Matteuccia struthiopteris*) Upright grower; best in eastern sandy areas	JFMAMJJASOND	▮	Clumping	●●	24-72	18-24	3
	Royal (*Osmunda regalis*) Prefers moist, acidic conditions	JFMAMJJASOND	▮	Clumping	●●	18-30	24-60	3
	Southern wood (*Dryopteris ludoviciana*) Fast-growing, graceful fern	JFMAMJJASOND	▮	Clumping	●●	18-30	12-16	1
	Tassel (*Polystichum polyblepharum*) Deep-green leathery foliage	JFMAMJJASOND	▮	Clumping	●●	12-24	10-12	2
	Asparagus fern (*Asparagus densiflorus* 'Sprengeri') Not a true fern, but an ornamental asparagus; mixes well as perennial border greenery	JFMAMJJASOND	▮	Arching	●●	15-24	24-30	1

Fruit

There is something very special about harvesting fresh fruit from your own garden. It's a goal that is certainly achievable, and best of all, many of the crops that you grow can be worked into attractive home landscapes, giving you double use from the plants.

Many of our most popular fruit crops are well suited to Texas conditions.

Choose crops that will do well in your part of Texas.

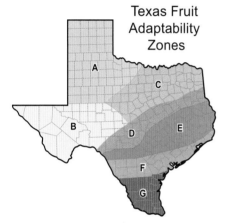

Texas Fruit Adaptability Zones

Use this map to find the best fruit types and varieties both from our chart on page 237 and from the information on each crop that you'll find in the remainder of this chapter.

One of the joys in raising fruit is to find a tree that is handsome in the landscape as well as being productive as a fruit source. Hachiya persimmon fills that bill.

Growing fruit and nut crops in Texas gardens can be rewarding, or it can just as easily be frustrating. Before you start planting, you need to do your homework. Choose types that are adapted to your part of Texas. Buy healthy plants, and tend them carefully – not just until they're established and growing, but pretty much as long as you have them. You'll find the details in the pages that follow.

Zones of Fruit Adaptability

Texas A&M has broken the state of Texas into seven distinct zones of fruit crop adaptability. This map is distinct from any other landscaping or plant hardiness map to which we refer. Locate your county and make note of your zone. If you are near a boundary of two zones, odds are that you can choose crops from either zone.

Establishing the Home Orchard

Some things are non-negotiable when you're determining where best to grow your fruit trees, bushes and vines. Here are the essentials.

- **Sunlight.** Full sun is best. Be careful in planting fruit crops near shade trees that might grow to overtake your fruit plants.

- **Good soil.** You'll want a depth of 3 to 4 feet for most types, more for large trees. Choose sites that drain well during extended periods of rainfall. For most types of fruit and nut plantings, sandy loam soils are best.

- **Good air circulation.** Leaf and fruit diseases are typically spread in still, moist settings. Equally important, frost damage can occur in early spring if plants are situated in low spots, where air movement is poor.

- **Accessible water.** You'll need it to get the plants established, and you'll need it to keep the plants vigorous thereafter. Fruit size and quality are dependent on constantly moist soils.

Buying your plants

Fruit plants are available in best selection from late December into early spring. You would be wise to know the types you want as you enter that period, and to buy when you find good plants available. If you are ordering fruit plants to be shipped to you, you may be able to book your order ahead of the digging and shipping date, to be sure you get the varieties you want.

- **Bare-rooted**. These are dug while the plants are dormant in winter. Their roots are trimmed, then packed in moist sawdust or shavings. You'll find bare-rooted stock in retail nurseries in January and early February, or the plants can be ordered online for shipment from the nursery to your door. These are the least expensive, so they're the most affordable way to establish a larger orchard. But they also suffer the greatest setback due to transplant shock. Choose fruit trees that are 3 to 5 feet tall and pecan trees that are 4 to 6 feet tall. Larger sizes will be available, but they will be slower to recover. All bare-rooted trees should be pruned by 50 percent immediately after they are planted. Like fruit trees, grapes and brambleberries are commonly sold bare-rooted. However, they are smaller plants, and the only pruning that is usually needed is to remove broken roots and stems.

- **Balled-and-burlapped**. Fruit trees can be dug and sold with soil balls intact around their root systems. Pecans are not usually sold this way. Balled-and-burlapped plants have somewhat better survival rates than bare-rooted stock. Still, they are not common in nurseries, and the benefits don't measure up to the increased costs.

- **Container-grown**. More and more often you'll find desirable varieties grown and sold in nursery pots. Selection will still be best in late winter and spring, but you can plant at other seasons if you find the recommended varieties. One caution: check the soil balls to be sure the plants have actually been grown in the pots, not just dug and planted into them a month or two earlier. Resist the temptation to buy very large fruit trees in pots, because you will still need to prune them back to train them to establish the proper branching structure.

Fruit trees may be sold growing in pots.

Garden Tip

Before heading out to buy your fruit trees:

1. Determine types of crops your family likes.
2. Identify those varieties that grow best in your area. (See information in following pages and check with local Extension offices.)
3. Buy from local independent retailers whenever possible. Beware of varieties being sold by large national chain stores. They are often bought nationally and may not be adapted to your area.
4. Buy from reputable online or mail order sources when necessary.

Young pecan trees, still showing the bud unions, will be ready for digging (bare-rooted) after one to two years.

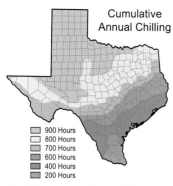

Cumulative Annual Chilling

900 Hours
800 Hours
700 Hours
600 Hours
400 Hours
200 Hours

Adapted from map prepared by Texas A&M University

CHILLING FACTS

To be successful in growing fruit, you need to be familiar with the term "chilling requirement" as you choose your varieties. It will be expressed as the number of hours that the temperature must be below 45 F before that variety will set buds and come into flower. This map shows you the average number of chilling hours for the various regions of Texas. Find your county, and determine the number of chilling hours your plants will receive. Check the variety listings later in the chapter and choose types that are a good match for your county. You have leeway of up to 100 hours above and below what is shown for your county. However, if you choose a variety that requires a much higher number of hours than your county gets, odds are that it will never come into flower. If you choose a variety that has a much lower chilling requirement, its needs for cold weather will be met too soon, and it will come into bud and flower before the winter is actually over for your county. Its fruit will almost always be cut down by late freezes.

Keys to Selecting Fruit Crops

To help you choose the best fruit crops for your plantings, this chart will compare the following categories.

- **Best suited.** Fruit zones on the map for which each type of fruit is best adapted.

- **Spacing.** Distance between plants. If you are planting different varieties, use the distances for the larger types. Crowded fruit crops do not bear well.

- **Pollinator needed?** Many types of fruit and nut crops require that two distinctly different varieties be planted close enough to one another that pollen can be shared. They may not be receptive to pollen from the same variety, as is the case with many apples, peaches, plums and other fruit crops. Or, in the case of pecans, pollen on a given tree may be produced before or after the time the female flower parts are receptive to it. If there are other varieties in neighboring gardens, you may not have to plant the second variety of a given type of fruit or nut crop yourself. But, if you have room, it never hurts.

- **Years to first harvest.** Assuming good vigor of the stock at planting, and appropriate care thereafter, this is an indication of the time required for the first meaningful harvest (not a scattering of fruit).

- **Insects.** Are there significant pests that threaten either the plant or its fruit?

- **Diseases.** Are there significant diseases that threaten either the plant or its fruit?

- **Dependability.** Factors include how reliably the plant bears once it starts producing, also the average size of its harvest, the expected quality of the fruit, and the productive life expectancy of the crop. These are indicated by our star ratings in this column. They are based on observations and opinions of professional horticulturists and veteran gardeners, but they are still subjective and are offered only as a beginning point for your consideration. They are intended to give you a rough idea of your chances of succeeding with any given crop, although you are always encouraged to find reliable local advice. Contact your local independent retail garden center or your county office of the Texas A&M AgriLife Extension Service.

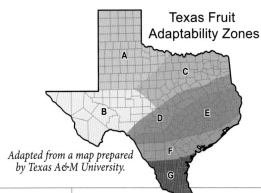

Texas Fruit Adaptability Zones

Adapted from a map prepared by Texas A&M University.

Compare your favorites with fruit types that are best suited to your region.

Fruit

CROP	BEST SUITED* Compare your county to these entries to find the best fruit types for your area.	SPACING (FEET) Plants should be set at least these distances from one another.	NEEDS POLLINATOR? See explanation of pollinators on facing page.	YEARS TO FIRST HARVEST	INSECTS OF MAJOR CONCERN	DISEASES OF MAJOR CONCERN	DEPENDABILITY SCORE*
Apples	A-D, limited E	25-30 (standard), 10-15 (dwarf)	Yes	3-4	Limited	Yes	★★★
Apricots	A-D	15-18	Recommended*	5	Yes	Yes	★★
Blackberries	A-G	3-4 (rows), 8-10 (between rows)	No	2	Limited	Limited	★★★★★
Blueberries	Eastern third of C-F	8-10	Yes	4	No	No	★★★
Cherries	A	15-18	No	5	Limited	Yes	Zero
Citrus	F-G	15-25	No	5	Yes	Limited	★★★★
Figs	Southern half of B, C; all of D-G	15-20	No	2-3	Limited	Limited	★★★★
Grapes	A-F	10-20	No	3	Limited	Yes	★★★
Grapes, Muscadine	Eastern portions of D–F		Recommended	3	Limited	No	★★★
Jujube	A, B and G; western portions of C-F	20-25	Recommended	5-8	No	No	★★★★
Olives	F-G	25-30	Recommended*	3-4	No	Yes	★★
Peaches and nectarines	A-G	18-25	No	3	Yes	Yes	★★★
Pears	A-F	25-30	Recommended*	4-5	Yes	Yes	★★★★
Pecans	A-G	40-50	Recommended*	6-10	Yes	Yes	★★★★
Persimmons	B-F	15-25	Recommended*	4	Yes (foliage)	No	★★★
Plums	A-E	15-18	Recommended*	2-3	Yes	Yes	★★★★
Pomegranates	B-G	10-15	No	4	No	No	★★★★
Strawberries	A-G	12-18 inches	No	1	Yes	Yes	★★
Walnuts	Eastern half of C-E	35-40	Recommended*	8-10	Yes	Yes	★
	* Varieties vary with region		* Depends on variety				* Varies with regions

Apples are suited to much of Texas, as long as you choose varieties that are suited to your region.

Garden Tip

Apples typically do not develop deep red color as they ripen in warm Texas weather. The red anthocyanin pigment comes to the forefront only when it gets cold. In Texas, apple harvest may occur two or three months before cold arrives in mid-fall. Regardless of color, flavor will not be impacted in any way.

Apples are attractive in the landscape and on the table.

Apples ★★★

Best varieties

For medium- and high-chill areas of Central and North Texas (listed in general sequence of ripening)

Gala is a high-quality gold/red variety. Crisp, flavorful. Needs constant supply of moisture as fruit is developing to produce maximum size. Has produced as far south as College Station.

Jonagold is, as you might guess, a cross between Golden Delicious and Jonathan. Its flesh is crisp. The apples are best used soon after harvest. Good for sauce and pies.

Mollie's Delicious requires less chilling than many apples, so it is good for Central and South Central Texas. It has a yellow skin that is heavily blushed with red. Its fruit is of high quality, and it stores well in refrigeration. It is an outstanding pollinator.

Fuji produces medium-sized fruit with yellow-green skin and significant red striping. Fruit has good texture and crisp, white flesh. Refrigerates well. Has produced as far south as College Station.

Honeycrisp produces red fruit with a yellow mottled background. The flesh is very crisp, sweet and aromatic. Good for fresh eating and stores well.

For low-chill areas of South Texas

Anna produces large, yellow-skinned fruit with a red blush. It is slightly tart, and it's good eaten fresh or made into pies or applesauce.

Dorsett Golden has a very low chilling requirement. Its fruit is medium-sized, yellow with an orange-red blush. It is a good pollinator for Anna.

Cultural requirements

Pollinator needed: Yes.

Special soil needs: Well-draining neutral or slightly acidic soil is best for good production.

Special climatic needs: Cold winters, relatively dry growing seasons for best yields.

Size to buy: 3 to 5 feet (bare-rooted); 4 to 6 feet (container).

Pruning at planting: If single trunk ("whip"), prune by half. Encourage development of side branches 26 to 30 inches from soil.

Subsequent pruning: Second year, select four or five main branches at or near 90-degree angles to trunk. Ultimate goal with pruning is to develop Christmas-tree shape with strong, open branching that allows good light penetration. After tree is well established, little regular pruning is needed except to remove damaged branches and strongly vertical shoots ("watersprouts"). Prune in winter.

Thinning required: Yes. Thin when fruit is marble-sized and leave them 6 inches apart.

Fertilizing: Apply high-nitrogen or all-nitrogen fertilizer (one-half pound per inch of trunk diameter) as the plants start to grow in late winter/early spring. Repeat every 6 to 8 weeks until early August.

Primary insect pests

Stinkbugs, tarnished plant bug, apple maggot, borers, scale are all occasional problems.

Primary diseases

Cotton root rot is a soil-borne fungal disease that kills a wide range of landscape and orchard plants. Apples are at the top of the list. Affected trees turn dark brown very suddenly. Because cotton root rot kills the root system, the entire tree is impacted at the same time. The disease will spread slowly from tree to tree. It occurs only in alkaline soils, so it's of concern primarily near and west of I-35.

Fire blight is a bacterial disease that shows up on apple branches. It causes sudden browning of individual 12- to 18-inch twigs in spring and summer. It can be somewhat disfiguring, but it is seldom fatal to apple trees. Prune out infected wood, cutting back into healthy stem tissue several inches down from the dieback. Disinfect your pruning tools by dipping them into a solution of 10 percent chlorine bleach and 90 percent water between each cut. To prevent rust, oil the tools before putting them away.

Other fungal diseases of apple foliage and fruit will appear on occasion, including apple scab, cedar-apple rust and powdery mildew.

Blush of red comes to apples as they ripen in summer in Texas.

This apple tree's branches must be supported due to failure to thin fruit adequately early in season.

Apricots bloom with first warm days of late winter and often lose flowers or fruit. As a result, count on good harvests only one or two years out of five. Apricots are attractive landscape trees.

It's curious to note that all of these fruit crops (as well as pyracanthas, photinias, loquats, cotoneasters and roses) are members of the horticulturally rich rose family.

FAQ

Q When a pollinator plant is recommended for a fruit crop, how close does that second variety have to be?

A If bees will be carrying the pollen (as with apples, pears, plums, peaches, strawberries, blackberries and most other fruit crops), the two plants should be within 100 yards, closer if possible. If the wind is carrying the pollen (as with pecans and other nut crops), pollen will be carried much greater distances (up to a mile and much farther).

Visit Neil's FAQ pages at www.neilsperry.com

Apricots ★★

Best varieties

Bryan is the most reliable producer in Texas, although its fruit is susceptible to brown rot.

Moorpark produces high-quality fruit on very vigorous trees.

Cultural requirements

Pollinator needed: Recommended.

Special soil needs: Well-draining, neutral or slightly acidic soil is best.

Special climatic needs: Frost-free weather late in winter and early spring, because late frosts and freezes catch apricots in bud, bloom or even with young fruit. Unfortunately, this happens a high percentage of years.

Size to buy: 3 to 5 feet (bare-rooted); 4 to 6 feet (container).

Pruning at planting: Trim tops back to 24 to 30 inches from soil.

Subsequent pruning: Encourage three scaffold branches 24 to 30 inches from soil. Maintain scaffold branching as trees mature by removing strongly vertical shoots.

Thinning required: Yes. If fruit set is strong, thin so that apricots will be 5 or 6 inches apart.

Fertilizing: Apply high-nitrogen or all-nitrogen fertilizer (1/2 pound per inch of trunk diameter) as the plants start to grow in late winter/early spring. Repeat every six to eight weeks until early August.

Primary insect pests and diseases

Plum curculio in fruit; peach tree borers in trunk. (See "Peaches" for controls.)

Brown rot fungal disease can affect fruit.

Blackberries ★★★★

Best varieties

Thornless (listed alphabetically)

Apache bears large, very sweet berries late in season. A small percentage of the drupelets will naturally be white, but they do not affect fruit quality or flavor.

Natchez produces the largest berries with high sugar content. Its fruit ripen early. The plants are semi-erect and do need to be grown in wire trellises.

Navaho produces comparatively small fruit abundantly. It has a high chilling requirement, so it is best suited to North Texas. Its fruit keep ripening for up to one month.

Ouachita (pronounced "wash-uh-taw") is a low-chill variety. It ripens in mid- to late season, producing large yields of very sweet berries.

Thorny (listed alphabetically)

Brazos is a long-time favorite variety with vigorous canes and large, early fruit. Brazos is the "father of all modern blackberries," having been used extensively in breeding programs since it was introduced. It is acidic and is recommended more for cooking than for fresh eating.

Chickasaw gives the highest yield of any blackberry, producing large, very sweet fruit and cylindrical black berries. It stores well compared to other varieties.

Kiowa is a heavy producer of the largest berries. As with other varieties with Native American tribal names, it is from the outstanding University of Arkansas breeding program. Very good along Gulf Coast.

Rosborough produces large berries sweeter than those of Brazos, often with better yields. It is ideal for East and South Central Texas.

Cultural requirements

Pollinator needed: No.

Special soil needs: Blackberries adapt to a variety of soils, but sandy, highly organic and constantly moist soils are best.

Blackberries are perhaps the easiest of all Texas fruit crops.

FAQ

Q How well will dewberries do in my garden? They grow wild over so much of Texas.

A Also known as "trailing blackberries," dewberries are really popular native fruits. They ripen several weeks ahead of upright blackberries, but they're not nearly as productive and they're much more work to maintain, primarily because they turn into unmanageable briar patches over time. The variety Austin is the one most commonly sold. Try it if you wish, but do include one or more of the upright blackberry varieties as well.

Blackberries ripen late spring into very early summer.

Texans enjoy blackberries fresh and preserved.

Special climatic needs: None.

Size to buy: Bare-rooted transplants or root cuttings in winter.

Pruning at planting: None

Subsequent pruning: Plants bear on canes produced the prior year. Once a cane bears, it will never bear fruit again, so prune it to the ground immediately after harvest. Pinch growing tips out of strong new canes in late spring to encourage side branching and to keep plants from growing too tall.

Train within trellises: For the tidiest blackberry patch, set posts in two rows, each row 12 inches away from the row of blackberry plants. On each row of posts, secure heavy wires at 24 inches from the ground and 48 inches from the ground. As new shoots develop on the plants, push them back within the wires. Trim off sprouts that come up from the ground if they are outside the wires.

Thinning required: No. Allow all fruit to develop.

Fertilizing: Apply high-nitrogen or all-nitrogen fertilizer as the plants start to grow in late winter/early spring. Repeat immediately after harvest.

Primary insect pests and diseases

Spider mites, thrips, stinkbugs and leaf-footed bugs, double blossom, crown gall.

Blueberries ★★★ (East Texas)

Best varieties

Austin ripens in June, producing medium-large fruit. It can be pollinated by Climax or Premier. 500 chilling hours.

Brightwell produces medium-large berries through June. Although it is a good pollinator for the popular Tifblue, Brightwell's fruit tends to split. It is sensitive to wet conditions. Austin and Premier are good pollinators for Brightwell. 400 chilling hours.

Premier produces medium-large berries in late May into early June. Its young limbs are quite limber and they do not fruit heavily. Austin is a good pollinator for it. 550 chilling hours.

Tifblue is outstanding and has been a favorite for home gardens in Texas for a long time. It produces somewhat smaller fruit than Woodard from late June into July. Brightwell is a good pollinator for it. 650 chilling hours.

Woodard is grown for its excellent quality and production. Fruit ripens quite early (late May into early June). Texas A&M lists the varieties Climax and Premier as good pollinators for it. 350 chilling hours, so well suited to Southeast Texas.

Cultural requirements

Pollinator needed: Yes.

Special soil needs: Highly acidic soil required (pH 4.5 to 5). Irrigation water must also be acidic – blueberries are very intolerant of salts in irrigation water. For those reasons, suited only to the East Texas (Piney Woods) soils. If soils are alkaline, blueberries must be grown in large containers filled with organic matter.

Special climatic needs: Blueberries are better suited to East Texas, not only for the acidic soils and water, but also for the higher humidity during the growing season.

Size to buy: Small transplants, often in 1- or 2-gallon pots.

Pruning at planting: No.

Subsequent pruning: Remove lower branches that would touch ground when laden with fruit. Remove strongly vertical shoots that develop. Thin older plants to encourage strong regrowth.

Thinning required: No thinning of fruit.

Fertilizing: Apply ammonium sulfate (21-0-0) in small amounts several times from spring through the summer.

Primary insect pests and diseases

Blueberry maggot, botrytis, anthracnose.

FAQ

Q Is it practical to grow a blueberry plant in a container, so that I can modify the planting soil as needed?

A You would need a 4- by 4-foot container that is 36 to 42 inches deep. Fill it with a mix of half sphagnum peat moss and half finely ground pine bark mulch. You will need a second variety in a similar container nearby to insure good pollination. It's much cheaper just to buy the berries.

Blueberries are well suited to Piney Woods soils.

Garden Tip

Blueberries are a fairly easy and productive crop in East Texas, but they are extremely difficult and challenging elsewhere due to alkaline soils and water. As readily available as high-quality, fresh blueberries are in the grocery throughout the year, growing them in the home garden doesn't make economic sense unless you're in East Texas.

Cherries are not recommended at all for most areas of Texas.

Garden Tip

Cherries are extremely poorly adapted to Texas climates. They have low winter heat requirements, meaning they will come into flower very promptly following a few warm days in mid- or late winter. Cherry cultivation of any degree is limited only to the Davis Mountains and northern Panhandle.

Hardy satsuma variety Bumper is large, delicious and seedless.

Cherries (Not recommended for Texas)

Best variety

Montmorency produces fruit that is large, red and tart. However, it is not productive in most of Texas.

Cultural requirements

Pollinator needed: No.

Special soil needs: No.

Special climatic needs: Cold winters (very high chilling requirement).

Size to buy: 3 to 5 feet (bare-rooted); 4 to 6 feet (container).

Pruning at planting: Single-trunk; otherwise, little pruning is needed.

Subsequent pruning: Only as needed to remove damaged branches.

Thinning required: No.

Fertilizing: Apply high-nitrogen or all-nitrogen fertilizer (1/2 pound per inch of trunk diameter) as the plants start to grow in late winter/early spring. Repeat every six to eight weeks until early August.

Primary insect pests and diseases

Borers. No disease problems.

Citrus ★★★★ (South Texas)

Best varieties

Best choice depends on your location. Types that are the most winter-hardy are kumquats, satsumas and Meyer lemons, but even these are best suited to Zones F and G. Check with your local county Texas A&M AgriLife Extension office for specific recommendations. Research by Texas A&M has earned Orange Frost hardy satsuma high recommendations.

Cultural requirements

Pollinator needed: No.

Special soil needs: Well-draining; otherwise, plant slightly above surrounding grade.

Special climatic needs: Winter hardiness varies greatly with type, but all are vulnerable to freeze damage.

Size to buy: 3 to 4 feet tall.

Pruning at planting: None.

Subsequent pruning: As needed to shape trees. Otherwise, no routine trimming.

Thinning required: Occasionally.

Fertilizing: Apply high-nitrogen or all-nitrogen fertilizer in early spring and again in early summer.

Primary insect pests and diseases

Scale, whiteflies. Sooty mold grows on leaves and fruit that have been coated with honeydew from whiteflies or scales.

Figs ★★★★

Best varieties

Celeste is small, brown fig of high quality for fresh eating and for use in preserves.

Texas Everbearing (also known as Brown Turkey) produces medium-sized to large fruit over an extended period of the summer.

Alma produces high-quality fruit, but it is the most susceptible to freeze damage, and therefore is adapted only to the southern half of Texas.

Cultural requirements

Pollinator needed: No.

Special soil needs: Deep, well-draining.

Special climatic needs: Damaged by winter temperatures, so adapted to southern half of Zones B and C, plus Zones D – G.

Hardy satsumas Arctic Frost (larger) and Orange Frost (smaller) extend the citrus region northward away from the Texas Gulf Coast.

Figs are large landscape shrubs. Choose varieties with closed "eyes" at ends of fruit.

Grapes are widely grown in Texas for fresh eating, preserves and production of wine.

Size to buy: 12 to 18 inches (bare-rooted); 5-gallon nursery container.

Pruning at planting: None. Allow young plants to grow into their natural shrubby, multi-trunked forms.

Subsequent pruning: Train as large shrubs, not as single-trunk trees. Do as little pruning as possible, primarily to eliminate errant branches and remove freeze-damaged portions. Heavy pruning lessens production of fruit. The vigorous regrowth is also more likely to suffer freeze damage. Light tip-pruning each winter results in side shoot growth and more fruiting.

Thinning required: No.

Primary insect pests and diseases

Dried fruit beetles enter through open "eyes" at the distal ends of the fruit. The varieties recommended have closed eyes that prevent entry.

Nematodes (soil-borne microscopic pests that feed off roots) result in knotty root galls and stunted growth. Mulching soil heavily (3 to 4 inches) will reduce impact of nematodes.

No disease problems.

Grapes ★★★

Best varieties

Choice of varieties is completely influenced by where you are located relative to Pierce's disease (PD). Most European, American and French-American hybrid varieties of grapes are susceptible to PD and should not be grown in the area of high likelihood of the disease (South and Southeast Texas). Black Spanish and Blanc du Bois grapes can be infected with the bacterium and still produce heavy crops, so they are the best choices for East, Southeast and South Texas.

Blanc du Bois was released in 1988 by the University of Florida, and it is one of the highest-quality white wine grapes. It is eaten fresh, and is also used in jellies. This variety shows tolerance of PD. Its fruit are round and light green. They typically ripen in early July along the Texas Gulf Coast and two or three weeks later farther north.

Black Spanish is a much older variety of unknown lineage, but South Texas plantings date back to 1889. Also known as Lenoir, this is a very high-quality red wine grape, also used for juice. It is tolerant of PD. Its vines are moderately vigorous, and the fruit clusters are large and dense with small grapes. They ripen in late July into early August. Black Spanish shows iron deficiency in alkaline soils.

Champanel is a large black grape that bears its fruit in loose clusters. It is most commonly used in making jelly. Developed by T.V. Munson in Dennison in the early 1900s, it is adapted to the northern two-thirds of Texas. Champanel is resistant to PD.

Other varieties cited by Texas A&M as showing PD resistance or tolerance include Victoria Red, Herbemont and Orlando Seedless.

Of special note…

In spite of their susceptibility to Pierce's disease, two varieties of grapes are very commonly planted in North and Northwest Texas, where PD is less of a threat.

Cabernet Sauvignon is a strong-growing variety that produces small purplish-black grapes. It is the most popular grape for red wine.

Chenin Blanc is an easily grown white grape that produces high yields of excellent-quality grapes. It ferments well, making it a popular white wine grape.

Choose grape varieties carefully to be sure you have a type that's adapted.

Cultural requirements

Pollinator needed: No.

Special soil needs: Well-draining soil is a must, preferably sandy loam. Good soils result in the most vigorous vine growth and highest fruit production. Grape vines are likely to show iron deficiency in chalky, highly alkaline soils.

Special climatic needs: Different types of grapes are adapted to almost all parts of Texas. In fact, of all species of grapes in the world, more than half grow natively in Texas. See "Best varieties" for more details on climatic needs.

Size to buy: 12 to 15 inches (bare-rooted); 15 to 18 inches (1-gallon pots).

Methods of training: You're going to have to decide how intensive you want your management program to be. Here are the options.

- **Home gardens:** Many homeowners choose to grow grapes on fences, overhead arbors or other existing supports. As long as those

Grapes are assertive growers. They twine vigorously around their supports, whether wires, wooden structures or even branches of nearby plants. Their tendrils give them superior climbing powers as the new growth reaches out to attach to a support.

Grapes are large plants that require substantial supports.

Garden Tip

If you're confused by the information on support structures and pruning of grapes, you're not alone. Volumes of information are available online, along with hundreds of illustrative photos. Include "university" as a key word in your searches, and you will end up with the most up-to-date details.

While they do require ongoing attention, grapes can yield meaningful rewards.

supports allow you to prune to remove old cane growth, they can be a satisfactory option.

- **Vineyard systems:** If you are establishing an actual home vineyard, however, you probably should use one or both of the two training techniques that the commercial growers use.

"Curtain canopy" training: Support wires for strong-growing varieties that produce trailing or dropping shoots should be at 5-1/2 feet from the ground. Those varieties include Cabernet Sauvignon, Champanel and Blanc du Bois. Following annual pruning each winter, these vines are allowed to cascade downward as they grow and bear fruit.

"Vertical shoot spacing" training: Support wires for upright varieties such as Chenin Blanc and Black Spanish are installed 2 feet from the ground. Two "catch" wires should be installed 14 and 28 inches above the support wire. As these varieties' upward-facing shoots develop from the two cordons, they should be tied to the catch wires with plastic plant ties.

Plant your grapevines 8 feet apart within their rows. Rows should be spaced 12 to 15 feet apart to allow room to work. At the time of planting, you will need to set posts and install the wires that will eventually support your vines. Use 12-1/2 gauge, high-tensile galvanized wire and heavy T-posts spaced 24 feet apart within the rows. Because of the weight of grapevines and their fruit, you will need to secure the trellis at each end with some type of earth anchor or tie-back post. You will set thinner grape stakes alongside each plant at the time of planting.

Pruning

- **At time of planting:** Trim each plant to leave three or four buds above the soil line. Allow all growth to develop the first year. Do not attempt to prune or tie the vines for the first growing season.

- **Second year:** Allow the two strongest stems to remain. Tie them to the support post or stake, and secure them in place as they grow to reach their support wires (see details above). As the two vines reach the support wire, train one branch (cordon) to grow horizontally along each side of the wire. Secure them with plastic plant ties until they twine around the wire and can support themselves. Train so that branch spurs are 5 to 6 inches apart on the cordons. Rub off any unwanted shoots that try to develop.

- **Third year:** Before the grape vines start to grow for their third year, cut each cane back to two or three buds. Allow no more than one cluster of grapes per cane for the third year.

- **Subsequent years:** Prune your grapes every winter. Dormant buds on 1-year-old canes (produced the prior growing season) will be the source of new (current season) canes on which grape clusters will be produced. That means that you must essentially replace all of the fruiting wood with new growth each year, and that will require removing 80 to 85 percent of the 2-year-old canes each winter, so that they can be replaced by 1-year canes.

As you are pruning, remove shoots that are growing in directions that are inconsistent with your training program. Each cordon should be allowed to grow no longer than 3 feet (6-foot total plant width). Prune each spur to leave two buds.

Note: The topic of pruning of grapes can be fairly confusing to novices. You will find well-illustrated university web pages with extensive additional information should you feel the need to search online.

Thinning required: Yes. In addition to the extensive pruning you'll do to your vines, you'll also want to remove some or many of the young clusters of grapes as they begin to develop in the spring. Your goal will be to have fewer clusters, but of greater size and quality, and thinning will be your prime way of accomplishing that. You will need to experiment with the extent of the thinning for your vines in your growing conditions, but again, decisions will relate to the vigor of the vines.

Fertilizing: Apply high-nitrogen or all-nitrogen fertilizer (1/2 cup per plant) as growth begins in early March. Repeat in early June.

Harvesting: Grapes are ready to be harvested when the desired flavor has been reached. Immature grapes will have an astringent puckering effect. Wine grapes should be harvested somewhat earlier, before their sugar content reaches its maximum.

Primary insect pests: Mites, lace bugs, phylloxera galls and several other insects may attack grapes, but these are usually kept in check by routine spraying done in the home orchard.

Of special note: The insect known as the glassy-winged sharpshooter is responsible for the spread of Pierce's disease. Learn to recognize it, and spray to eliminate it at once.

Garden Tip

Grapes can be a fun addition to a home garden in Texas, but variety selection and careful management of the vines are two critical aspects. Do your homework before you go shopping. Plant grapes where they can grow for many years, either in your home vineyard or within the landscape, then give them ongoing attention.

All the grape-growing care and attention pay off.

FAQ

Q Is it possible to grow grape vines on a chain link fence?

A Possible, but not advisable. The vines themselves will thrive, because they'll be able to weave in and out of the fencing. But pruning to remove 85 percent of the cane growth each winter, as is recommended if you are serious about growing high-quality grapes, will be almost impossible. The weight of the vines may also be sufficient to pull the fence down.

Pierce's Disease Probability

High
Little or no

Primary diseases

Black rot attacks grape clusters, also causing severe leaf spotting and stem damage. It causes the fruit to become black and mummified. Often only a few of the grapes in a cluster will be affected at one time. Apply a labeled fungicide in early spring according to homeowner spray recommendations from Texas A&M.

Pierce's disease (PD) is the most serious threat to grapes – one for which there is no control. It is most prevalent in hot, humid areas of the state. In general terms, it is a major factor in grape growing east of I-35 and, additionally, south of a line from Austin to Del Rio. It is spread by the glassy-winged sharpshooter insect, but selection of resistant varieties is your only current means of avoiding it in infested areas. Control of the insects alone will provide only limited help. When infected, grapes' leaves develop tip dieback and eventually dry completely. The dying canes will show lesions of the infection.

Jujubes ★★★★

Best varieties

Li is largest jujube grown in Texas, also best-flavored. Skin turns mahogany colored. Harvest before fruit wrinkles.

Lang is the most widely grown variety. It bears heavy crops of large pear-shaped, red-skinned fruit. It is a more spreading tree than Li.

Cultural requirements

Pollinator needed: Recommended.

Special soil needs: Quite adaptable. Even does well in very alkaline soils. Requires good drainage.

Special climatic needs: Better suited to western, drier parts of Texas.

Size to buy: 3 to 5 feet (bare-rooted or container).

Pruning at planting: Only as needed to compensate for roots lost in digging.

Subsequent pruning: Only as needed to remove damaged, dead or errant branches.

Thinning required: No.

Jujube trees are attractive in the home landscape.

Fertilizing: Nitrogen is all that needs to be added to jujubes, and then no more than 4 ounces per inch of trunk diameter for mid-sized trees and 1 pound per inch of trunk diameter for mature trees per year in the spring. They will get additional nutrition from turf and shrub feedings if the trees are a part of the landscape.

Primary insect pests and diseases

Primary insect pests: None

Primary diseases: None

Olives ★★

Best varieties

Alberquina is the most widely planted variety in Texas. It is self-fertile, and it grows to 12 to 15 feet tall at maturity. It has good cold hardiness, and while the fruit are small, they produce a high-quality oil.

Arbosana is a Spanish variety that grows well, but it has only moderate cold hardiness. Its fruit can be pressed for oil or processed. Alberquina is a good pollinator for it.

Manzanilla olives originated in Spain, but are widely grown in warmer parts of the United States. Pendolino is a good pollinator for it. The trees have average cold hardiness among olives.

Pendolino is an Italian olive that serves as a universal pollinator for all other varieties. It grows to 20 feet in height, and it is used primarily for oils.

Cultural requirements

Pollinator needed: With some varieties.

Special soil needs: Tolerant of soils ranging in pH from 5.5 to 8.5. Shallow roots, so deep soils are not required, but perfect drainage is.

Special climatic needs: Damaged by cold winter temperatures, so adapted only to Zones F and G. Young trees will be killed by 25 F temperatures. Smaller branches of established trees will die at 22 F, and entire trees will be lost at 15 F. As protection against cold, mound soil around the trees' roots to 12 to 15 inches during the trees' first several winters. Remove the mounds each spring.

Garden Tip

Jujubes are often called Chinese dates, but their flavor and texture more closely resemble those of apples. They were imported to the United States from the Middle East by the United States Department of Agriculture in 1875, as agronomists sought drought-tolerant fruit crops. Indeed, jujubes are very tolerant of a variety of conditions, and they make interesting landscape trees. They do send up root sprouts and can form thickets of plants if steps are not taken to control them.

Garden Tip

Olives are one of the newer fruit crops to Texas gardening, and still not proven on a long-term basis. Due to issues with winter cold, limit plantings to areas south of I-10.

Peaches are almost ready to harvest.

Size to buy: 1- to 5-gallon nursery containers. Space plants 20 feet apart.

Pruning: Remove dead or weak branches late in the winter. Earlier pruning risks cold-weather injury.

Thinning required: No.

Primary insect pests and diseases

Scale, nematodes, borers, thrips and occasionally, stinkbugs.

Cotton root rot in alkaline soils.

Peaches and Nectarines ★★★

Best varieties

High-chilling varieties, listed in approximate order of ripening

Springgold is very early, producing high yields of comparatively small fruit. The seeds are unusually large for the fruit size. Zones C and D, northern half of E. (750 hours)

Surecrop is a semi-freestone yellow peach that is excellent either fresh or in cooking. Ripens early to mid-June. Zones A – C. (1,000 hours, so best north of I-20)

Sentinel produces good crops of high-quality fruit. It is semi-freestone. Ripens mid-June. Zones C – E. (850 hours)

Harvester is a popular large freestone peach that ripens late June. Zones C – D, northern half of E. (750 hours)

Ranger is an excellent large, yellow-fleshed freestone peach. Vigorous trees. Fruit ripens late June. Zones A – C. (1,000 hours, so best north of I-20)

Redglobe gives good yield of high-quality fruit. Freestone with yellow flesh. Ripens early to mid-July. Zones A – D. (850 hours, so best north of I-20)

Dixieland produces high-quality freestone peaches that ripen in mid- to late July. Zones C and D, northern half of E. (750 hours)

Redskin peaches are large yellow freestones that ripen mid- to late July. Zones C and D, northern half of E. (750 hours)

FAQ

Q Are Elberta peaches good for Texas?

A No. In fact, Elberta peaches were developed more than 125 years ago, and many far better varieties have been introduced since. Because the name is almost a franchise of its own, some unscrupulous growers will slap an Elberta peach label on other varieties, so that you really won't know what you're getting anyway. Buy only from reputable nurseries, and stick with the varieties that are recommended for your region.

Medium-chilling varieties, listed in approximate order of ripening

Junegold is a yellow-fleshed cling peach that ripens in early June. Zone E, northern half of Zone F. (650 hours)

Flordaking is a medium-sized yellow cling that ripens in late May. Trees are strong and yields are good. Zones F and G. (450 hours)

TexKing is a large, firm yellow cling. Fruit ripens late May, early June. Zones F and G. (450 hours)

Texstar is a yellow semi-cling that produces heavily. Fruit ripens early June. Fruit tends to plug (part of flesh remains on tree when picked, exposing open wound). Zones F and G. (450 hours)

TexPrince ripens mid-June. It produces yellow freestone peaches reliably. Zones F and G. (550 hours)

TexRoyal produces yellow freestone peaches that ripen mid-June. Zones F and G. (600 hours)

La Feliciana is a yellow freestone variety that ripens mid-June. One of best mid-chill varieties. Fruit has considerable "fuzz." Zones F and G. (600 hours)

Dwarf peaches are interesting novelties, but standard peaches are far more productive – and the trees don't get especially large if they're properly pruned

Low-chilling varieties, listed in approximate order of ripening

Flordaprince is a cling peach that ripens in late May. Zone G. (150 hours)

Tropic Prince is a cling variety that ripens in early June. Zone G. (150 hours)

Tropic Beauty is a semi-freestone peach that ripens in mid-June. Zone G. (150 hours)

Cultural requirements

Pollinator needed: No, although planting two or more varieties ensures maximum pollination and can provide fresh fruit over a longer season.

Special soil needs: Sandy, slightly acidic soils are best, but trees will produce in clays. Good drainage is essential.

Special climatic needs: It is critical that you choose a variety that matches the number of chilling hours in your locale. (See map page 236). Plant where air circulation is good, to lessen chance of frost

This peach tree's branches must be braced for support. The fruit should have been thinned when they were marble-sized to be 6 or 7 inches apart.

Fresh peaches are among the most compelling of fruit.

Your goal in pruning peach trees each winter is to establish a cereal-bowl shape by removing strongly vertical branching.

Plum curculio worms invade both peaches and plums in spring.

damage when plants are in bud or bloom (or even when they have young fruit). Late frosts are the major threat to good peach production.

Size to buy: 3 to 5 feet (either bare-rooted or container).

Pruning at planting: Cut trunk at 24 to 26 inches from ground, regardless of tree height at time of purchase. Your goal will be to encourage three "scaffold" branches to develop at 22 to 26 inches and equally spaced (120 degrees apart) around trunk.

Subsequent pruning: Peaches bear only on 1-year-old shoots, so careful annual pruning to remove 35 to 40 percent of the wood will maintain good tree vigor and therefore maximize production. Maintain an open center to allow sunlight to reach ripening fruit. Prune to leave branches extending outward at 45- to 50-degree angles. Weight of ripening fruit will pull them downward, so that you will be able to harvest fruit without using a ladder. Remove all basal sprouts that arise from the rootstock.

Thinning required: Yes, to 6 or 7 inches between fruit. Late frosts will sometimes thin fruit by natural processes. Do manual thinning before fruit are marble-sized.

Fertilizing: Apply high-nitrogen or all-nitrogen fertilizer (1/2 pound per inch of trunk diameter) as the plants start to grow in late winter/early spring. Repeat every six to eight weeks until early August.

Watering: Keep trees moist at all times, particularly as fruit is developing.

Primary insect pests

Plum curculio are larval worms that invade both peach and plum fruit as they develop. Control with labeled insecticide sprays beginning at bud stage (before buds have begun to open), when three-fourths of the petals have fallen, and at 10-day intervals until harvest.

Stinkbugs sting ripening fruit, causing soft, rotted spots to develop. Routine spraying for other insects will offer some measure of control. No other spray is advised.

Peach tree borers result in the death of a majority of peaches and plums. They attack at ground level and tunnel through the trunk tissues, cutting off nutrients and water to the top. Follow Texas A&M AgriLife Extension horticulture prevention measures listed online.

Primary diseases

Scab and brown rot. For timing and product suggestions, see spray schedules from Texas A&M AgriLife Extension websites. A regular spray program that begins while the trees are in bud is critical.

About nectarines and almonds

Nectarines are merely "fuzzless" peaches, so their care is exactly the same. Without the protection of the fuzz, however, nectarines will show blemishes from abrasion of twigs and leaves, also insects. The variety Armking is a low-chill selection that is occasionally grown in South Texas.

Almonds do not produce well in Texas. They have low chilling requirements, and the plants come into flower too early. Late winter and early spring freezes almost always injure the flowers. Almonds closely resemble their close relatives, peaches. The pit is harvested and eaten as a "nut." However, the fruit are susceptible to brown rot and bacterial leaf spot.

FAQ

Q Can I plant a seed from a peach that was really good and grow my own peach trees?

A Yes. But definitely no. You will certainly get a peach tree, but it will not be genetically the same as the fruit that you ate. Peaches do not reproduce "true" from seeds. For all the time, space and effort you will be dedicating to your peach tree, you should buy a recommended variety from the lists you see here.

Pears ★★★★

Best varieties

Ayers produces high-quality fruit of small size. Fire blight resistant. May take trees 10 to 12 years to begin producing. Best in Zones A – C. Pollinator recommended.

Kieffer is an old and well-proven variety. Good fire blight resistance. Flesh contains many grit cells, resulting in hard fruit of fair quality for fresh eating. Fruit requires "after-ripening." Harvest them, then wrap them in paper and allow them to finish ripening in garage.

LeConte produces bell-shaped fruit of high quality. The tree grows vigorously and produces fruit reliably. Fire blight resistance.

Moonglow produces high-quality fruit with good texture and flavor. Excellent pollinator that is also self-fertile. Good fire blight resistance.

Orient is very resistant to fire blight. Reliable producer of large fruit of excellent quality over all of Texas. While not of the extreme quality of West Coast European-type pears, Orient is the most dependable pear for Texas. It also makes a handsome landscape tree. Pollinator required.

Moonglow pear is one of the best varieties for Texas.

Pears are among the few types of fruit that actually continue ripening after they are harvested. That process can add to their fresh-eating quality.

Pear trees and their fruit are longtime favorites in Texas landscapes and gardens.

Garden Tip

Pear trees are slow to flower (and therefore bear fruit) while their growth is vertical. Veteran gardeners often encourage more horizontal branching by hanging weights from the ends of the branches to pull them down.

Note regarding Asian pears: These produce fruit of very high quality, but all varieties are very susceptible, even highly susceptible, to fire blight. If you do decide to try one, the varieties Shinseiki and 20th Century are two of the better ones for much of Texas.

Cultural requirements

Pollinator needed: Varies (see descriptions of best varieties).

Special soil needs: Best in sandy, well-draining soils that are slightly acidic. May show iron deficiency in highly alkaline soils. Cotton root rot occurs in alkaline soils (primarily along and west of I-35).

Special climatic needs: Fire blight is more common in humid regions of South and East Texas.

Size to buy: 4 to 6 feet tall (bare-rooted or containers).

Pruning at planting: If you have bought a bare-rooted tree, remove 50 percent of top growth at planting. Trim container-grown trees to remove unneeded branches.

Subsequent pruning: Remove damaged or rubbing branches. (See precaution in fire blight discussion on next page.) Unlike many other types of fruit trees, no annual pruning is required. In fact, pruning stimulates new growth, which can be unnecessarily vulnerable to fire blight.

Thinning required: Yes, to allow 5 to 7 inches between fruit.

Fertilizing: Be careful not to stimulate vigorous leaf and stem growth that would be unnecessarily vulnerable to fire blight. Apply high-nitrogen or all-nitrogen fertilizer (1/2 pound per inch of trunk diameter) as the plants start to grow in late winter/early spring.

Primary insect pests

Stinkbugs puncture skin of ripening fruit, resulting in soft, deteriorated flesh.

Primary diseases

Fire blight is a bacterial infection that causes dieback of 12- to 18-inch twigs at ends of random branches in spring and summer. Leaves of affected twigs turn dark brown, almost black, within days. It is most common in years that bring frequent rainy days during bloom time. Some trees are reasonably resistant to fire blight and require little more than occasional pruning, but other varieties will likely be seriously impacted and even killed by it. Prune to remove dead branches, cutting back into healthy tissue. Disinfect pruning tools by dipping in 10-percent solution of chlorine bleach mixed with water. Dip between each cut to prevent spreading disease with pruning tools. Oil tools after you are finished to prevent rusting. Apply copper-based fungicide early in growing season to lessen severity of outbreaks.

Cotton root rot is a soil-borne disease to which pears being grown in alkaline soils are very susceptible. Affected trees may die suddenly (all leaves on the tree turning dark brown simultaneously), or it may take several months during which the tree will have drab green or even muted burgundy fall-like foliage. There is no prevention or control for this disease. Confirming its presence through the Plant Disease Lab at Texas A&M will help you know what types of plants can be used as replacements.

Fire blight is a serious threat to many varieties of pears in Texas gardens.

It's hard to resist a handful of freshly shelled Texas pecans.

Pecans ★★★★

Best varieties

East region

Caddo
Desirable
Pawnee
Kanza

Central region

Caddo
Desirable
Pawnee
Sioux
Wichita

West region

Pawnee
Western
Wichita

North region

Caddo
Kanza
Pawnee

Variety descriptions

Most pecan trees do not shed their pollen at the same time that the nutlets are receptive to that pollen.

Some shed pollen before the nutlets, and they are identified with "E" for early pollen production.

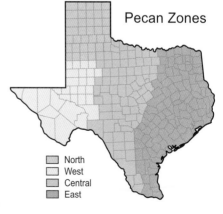

Pecan Zones

☐ North
☐ West
☐ Central
☐ East

Adapted from map prepared by Texas A&M University

Pecan adaptability varies with regions of Texas. Choose a type that is well suited to your area.

Others shed pollen after the nutlets have been produced, and they are identified with "L" for late pollen production.

If you do not have other pecans in your neighborhood, you may benefit from having at least one early (E) and one late (L) type.

Caddo (E) Well-adapted type that produces small- to medium-sized, football-shaped pecans of high quality. It is highly scab-resistant, making it perhaps the best choice for the eastern half of Texas.

Desirable (E) Old commercial variety that is still one of the most dependable. Reliable producer. Attractive tree that is good in landscape.

Kanza (L) Excellent variety, although kernels are somewhat small. Among the most winter-hardy of all pecans.

Pawnee (E) Increasing in popularity. Pecans ripen early. Well adapted to all regions of Texas.

Sioux (L) Small kernels of outstanding quality. Best adapted in western half of the state due to diseases, but grown in eastern Texas with regular applications of fungicides.

Western (E) For many years, the most popular commercial variety in western half of Texas. Bears at an early age.

Wichita (L) Important commercial variety in western half of Texas. Consistently productive, but requires regular applications of zinc.

Cultural requirements

Pollinator needed: Yes. However, pecans are wind-pollinated. Pollen blows from the male catkins onto the female flowers (nutlets). If you are in an urban area, there are probably many other pecans in the near vicinity. You may recall seeing a green dust over your car at the time that pecans are flowering. If so, that was pollen, and pollination may not be an issue.

Special soil needs: Deep (4 to 6 feet), well-draining soil. Pecan trees will not do well when planted atop alkaline caliche outcroppings. Due to the massive root systems pecan trees produce, it is not practical to attempt to amend the soil or to bring in additional soil. If you are growing pecans in alkaline soils, be prepared to apply zinc sprays to their leaves several times in late spring and summer.

Special climatic needs: Pecans grow well over almost all of Texas. Some types are not suited to the extreme winters of the Texas Panhandle, and other varieties that are highly prone to pecan scab are not well suited to the humid conditions of East Texas. Stay with varieties recommended for your region and you will have the best possible chance of success.

Size to buy: 4 to 6 feet tall (bare-rooted); 6 to 8 feet tall (containers).

Pruning at planting: For bare-rooted trees, to compensate for roots severed as the tree was dug, remove half of its top growth at the time of planting. That may involve removing unwanted side branches, but you may also end up cutting the central shoot back to 4 feet from the ground.

Subsequent pruning: Train the tree's new growth so that there will be one central trunk ("leader"). Side shoots will also develop, and you'll want to let them grow. Keep them tip-pruned to 8 or 10 inches out from the trunk. Known as "trashy trunk," this will aid the tree in developing a stronger trunk more quickly. As the tree grows, choose three or four scaffold branches 5 or 6 feet off the ground. After the third or fourth year you will be able to remove the trunk stubble. Once the tree has begun developing strong scaffold branches, you will have little regular pruning to do. Should limbs die or be damaged, you can remove them at any time. For quickest healing, always leave a short section (1/4 to 1 inch) of the branch collar where the limb joined the trunk. No pruning sealant is needed.

Thinning required: No.

Fertilizing: Apply 1 pound of high-nitrogen or all-nitrogen fertilizer per inch of trunk diameter around April 1. Repeat 30 and 60 days later.

Primary insect pests

Pecans do have a significant number of insect pests. If you're growing your pecan primarily as a shade tree, most of these won't be of much concern to you. However, if you're hoping to produce big crops of pecans each year, you'll want to invest in a power sprayer, and you'll want to be watching for these common invaders.

Pecan phylloxera galls. Small insects cause marble-sized galls on pecan leaflets in May and June. Affected leaves often fall to the ground, giving people great concern. By then, the galls have typically cracked open and the insects have flown away. These galls are of fairly minor long-term importance, but if you want to reduce their populations, you will need to apply dormant oil spray during January.

Pecans were named the official state tree of Texas in 1919, thanks to years of diligent work by Governor James Hogg.

FAQ

Q   If I just want my pecan as a nice big shade tree, do I have to spray for all the insects and diseases?

A   Not at all. As you read through the list of pests, you'll notice that almost all impact the pecan fruit. Pecan phylloxera galls attack the leaves, but they're fairly harmless. Webworms are a different story. You want to tip-prune to remove the new webs. If you don't address them, they'll disfigure your tree all through the growing season and well into the winter, when winds will eventually cause them to fall. Otherwise, most gardeners find it expedient simply to bypass almost all of the spraying regimen and to be grateful for the pecans that do survive the onslaught of pests.

Round Burkett pecans are among the most recognizable of all varieties. It has been a longtime favorite of Texas gardeners, although better varieties are available today.

Garden Tip

There are thousands of acres of native pecans in Texas.

If you are building a new home near native pecans, take care to protect them. Do not change the grade over their root systems. Just a couple of inches of fill soil can kill a mature pecan tree in a year or two. Instruct the contractor to stay outside the drip line of the tree as trenches are cut for utility lines, even if it means extra cost for additional pipe or wiring. Erect some type of temporary barrier around the drip line, and tell the contractor that no vehicles may come within the protected area.

Compaction can do serious harm to the trees. If you have to compromise on that, at least limit access to as small an area as possible. As the final grading is done, and if fill has been added elsewhere, be sure that water will not be trapped around the pecan tree. You must not change the soil water table (level of water in the subsurface soil) around a pecan.

Pecan nut casebearer. This small larval insect feeds on young pecans and tender new shoots. Insecticides labeled for casebearer control work well, but timing is critical. The five-day window during which sprays will be effective falls between mid-May and early June, depending on where you are in Texas. The farther south you are, the earlier the date will be. The date can vary by several days, depending on spring weather. Your local county Texas A&M AgriLife Extension office will have the precise information each year.

Twig girdlers. If you are finding small branches and twigs that look like they have been cut off with a pocketknife, littering the ground beneath your pecan (and some types of shade trees), that is damage of twig girdlers. The adult females deposit their eggs in the twig tissue. Then they move a foot or two farther out on the branch and score the bark with their very sharp mouthparts. The twig dies and falls to the ground, and the larvae complete the life cycle and emerge as flying adult beetles, all from the fallen twigs. Because the adult is there for such a short time, and because she doesn't actually feed on the plant tissue, there is no spray that will work on her as she's laying her eggs. The larvae are developing in dead twigs, so there isn't much reason to spray the little branches, either. Just pick them up and burn or discard them. You'll be reducing the population, although you'll never completely eliminate them. Their "damage" is quite minor in most cases.

Aphids. Several species of these very small pear-shaped pests visit pecans through the calendar year, and you'll always know when they're around by the sticky honeydew sap they excrete onto all surfaces below. Black sooty mold grows in that honeydew, and it will coat patio surfaces, outdoor furniture, plants' leaves and even cars that are left in place. Two aphids are common, although others may appear. Giant bark aphids (size is relative to other aphids – they're slightly larger than BB's) are present over the winter. Black pecan aphids visit the trees in late summer. In addition to the honeydew, they cause yellow spots to develop on the leaflets. You can control aphids with several common insecticides that are labeled for pecans, but finding a means to apply them will be your bigger challenge. You'll need a power sprayer.

Webworms. Eastern tent caterpillars and fall webworms devour pecan leaves in just a matter of days. If you're observant, you'll see basketball-sized webs encircling the ends of random branches. That's the time to try to control them, because you can easily clip off 12 or 18 inches of a branch without doing any significant damage to the tree. Use lopping shears for those close to the ground and a long-handled pole pruner for higher ones. Be aware of all power lines that are nearby. If you ignore the developing webworms for six or eight days, they'll engulf several feet of the branch, and pruning won't be an option. By that time, about all you can do is to reach into the web with some type of hook (wire coathanger on the end of PVC pipe works well) to pull the web open. That will expose the larvae to drying conditions and also to birds. It is difficult to reach high into trees with sprays, also to get the insecticide to penetrate the webs.

Hickory shuckworms. Larvae of this pest invade the outer shuck of the pecan during late summer, tunneling through and cutting off flow of water to the enlarging kernels. The nuts don't fill out properly, and they hang in the trees well beyond the normal time for pecans to drop in October and November. When they do fall, the dried shucks are often still attached to the pecans. This pest is controlled by spraying the first and last weeks of August with a labeled insecticide.

Pecan weevils. The larvae of this pest feed within the kernels in August and September. The spray you apply for hickory shuckworms will also prevent damage of the weevils.

Primary diseases

Pecan scab. This is a serious fungal disease that causes pecan husks to turn black. The pecans fall prematurely (August and early September), husks still in place, and the kernels quickly turn black and watery. Some varieties are far more susceptible to this disease than others, and that is the precise reason for the "east" and "west" zone recommendations you'll see in our variety list. You can include a labeled fungicide with every spray application you make from late spring until early fall to help reduce the incidence, but it's critical that you begin with one of the approved varieties for your area. If you don't address it directly, pecan scab can cause loss of more pecans than most of the insects mentioned earlier.

Pecan scab causes pecans to fall in late summer and very early autumn, long before they would normally be mature. The pecans are not usable.

FAQ

Q Can I start a new pecan tree from a pecan of very high quality?

A Remember that pecans are wind-pollinated. You know who the mother tree is, but you have absolutely no idea where the pollen originated, so your seedling tree will be nothing more than a native pecan. There will be no way to predict the quality of its fruit, the tree's disease resistance or any of the other critical features.

Hachiya persimmon is productive and handsome.

Pecan rosette Even though it is used in comparatively small quantities, zinc is one of the elements labeled as "essential" for good plant growth. As with some of the other minor elements, zinc becomes insoluble in alkaline soils. Pecans have critical need for it, and without it, tips of branches will die back and resprout repeatedly, resulting in what is called "witch's broom." The old recommendation for pecan trees being grown west of I-35 was that zinc be applied as a foliar spray every three or four weeks from mid-April into early July. Current recommendations have been broadened, suggesting that pecans in producing orchards all over Texas be sprayed according to that schedule. Your local farm supply store will have the materials you need.

Persimmons ★★★

Best varieties

Eureka is the most popular of all Oriental persimmon varieties. It produces medium-sized, tomato-shaped fruit of outstanding quality. It is self-fruitful, and it usually has seeds. It is best not to plant it with other varieties that are expected to be seedless. Eureka trees are the shortest of the Oriental persimmons. Zones B – F.

Fuyu bears flattened, orange, high-quality fruit, which is non-astringent (won't cause you to "pucker") and can be eaten before it has softened following freezes. Best suited to southern half of the state. Zones D – F.

Hachiya produces large, heart-shaped seedless fruit. The tree grows upright and with vigor, making it a fine landscaping tree. Zones B – F.

Tamopan fruit is easily recognized by its "waistline" constriction around its middle. The tree produces large orange fruit, and the trees are extremely vigorous and upright growing. Zones B – F.

Tane-nashi produces cone-shaped orange fruit. The trees are upright and vigorous, well suited to both orchards and home landscapes. It is seedless. Zones B – F.

Cultural requirements

Pollinator needed: This will depend on the variety. Eureka and Fuyu are both excellent pollinators, but they can also cause seedless varieties to produce fruit with seeds. Complicating things further, seedless fruit are quite likely to abort when facing environmental issues such as drought or sudden hot weather.

Special soil needs: Persimmons can be grown in a variety of well-draining soils, from sands to clay loams. The native American persimmon rootstock is resistant to cotton root rot (whereas Oriental persimmons are not), so it should be the rootstock that is used for any trees planted in the alkaline soils near or west of I-35.

Special climatic needs: None.

Size to buy: 3 to 5 feet (bare-rooted) and 4 to 5 feet (containers).

Pruning at planting: Remove half of top growth at time of planting.

Subsequent pruning: Train to grow in upright, pyramidal habit. Goal is to have three to five branches 10 or 12 inches apart, with the lowest branch somewhere near 36 inches from the ground. Once a strong scaffold branching system has been established, little annual pruning will be needed.

Thinning required: Probably not, especially with seedless varieties. Nature will take care of it. The seedless types are notorious for aborting fruit whenever hot or dry weather arrives suddenly.

Fertilizing: Apply high-nitrogen or all-nitrogen fertilizer (1/2 pound per inch of trunk diameter) as the plants start to grow in late winter/early spring. Repeat every six to eight weeks until early August.

Primary insect pests and diseases

Webworms on occasion. Use lopping shears to prune out.

Cotton root rot on Oriental varieties. It is important that they be grafted onto American persimmon rootstocks to have the native type's resistance to the soil-borne disease.

Most persimmon fruit are astringent until they have been exposed to at least one hard freeze.

Garden Tip

Persimmons are outstanding fruit trees for the urban landscape. The tree will be attractive, and fall color of the foliage is very good. Fruit ripens in fall and can actually stay in place on the tree well into the winter.

Persimmon yield can be very good.

Bruce plum is a longtime Texas favorite. It is well suited to most of the state.

Garden Tip

Every home garden has room for one or two plums (one of them being the variety Methley for pollination). Plums bear at a young age, and they are easy to grow compared to other fruit crops.

Plums ★★★★

Best varieties

Bruce is a large red plum that is a Texas favorite for both fresh consumption and jams. It is early ripening, and it's suited to the northern three-fourths of Texas. It must have a pollinator variety nearby, Methley being an outstanding one. Zones A – F.

Methley produces medium-sized purple fruit with red flesh. It is self-pollinating, and it makes an outstanding pollinator for other varieties. It is early ripening. Zones A – F.

Morris is a flavorful large red plum with red flesh. It must have 800 or more chilling hours, so it is adapted only to the northern half of Texas. It requires that a pollinator variety be planted nearby. Zones A – D.

Ozark Premier produces large fruit with mottled skin shades of purple, yellow and red. Its yellow flesh is extremely flavorful. It is a productive, self-pollinating variety. Suited to northern half of Texas. Zones A –D.

Cultural requirements

Pollinator needed: With some varieties.

Special soil needs: Plums do best in sandy loam, slightly acidic soils. However, they can be grown in clay soils as well, provided there is not a caliche layer close to the soil's surface. They need moist soil, but they are intolerant of poorly draining soils.

Special climatic needs: Plums, like their close relatives peaches, have a chilling requirement. (See map page 236.) Match your locale with the varieties recommended by your county Extension office.

Size to buy: 3 to 4 feet tall (bare-rooted) or 4 to 5 feet (container).

Pruning at planting: Trim top growth by half (to 22 to 24 inches) at planting. That will encourage branching as the tree begins to establish and grow in its first season.

Subsequent pruning: As with peaches, select three scaffold branches 20 to 24 inches from the ground and evenly spaced around the trunk. Prune each winter to remove strongly vertical shoots, always training to an open bowl-shaped habit. Mature trees should be kept at no more than 8 or 9 feet in height. With proper pruning they will spread to reach 14 to 16 feet in width.

Thinning required: Yes, when fruit are no larger than marbles, so that plums will be 4 or 5 inches apart on the branches.

Fertilizing: Apply high-nitrogen or all-nitrogen fertilizer (1/2 pound per inch of trunk diameter) as the plants start to grow in late winter/early spring. Repeat every six to eight weeks until early August.

Primary insect pests

Plum curculio are larval worms that invade both plums and peaches. Control with labeled insecticide sprays beginning at bud stage (before buds have begun to open), again when three-fourths of the petals have fallen, and at 10-day intervals until harvest.

Stinkbugs sting ripening fruit, causing soft, rotted spots to develop. Routine spraying for other insects will offer some measure of control. No other spray is advised.

Peach tree borers result in the death of a majority of plums and peaches. They attack at ground level and tunnel through the trunk tissues, cutting off nutrients and water to the top. Follow Texas A&M AgriLife Extension horticulture prevention measures listed online.

Primary diseases

Bacterial leaf spot causes a "shot-hole" effect on plum foliage. The spots are small and brown initially, but the dead tissue falls out, leaving many small holes in each leaf. You frequently will see the browned tissues that have only partially separated, almost as if a dull paper hole punch had been used. Apply labeled fungicide.

Bacterial stem canker attacks twigs and small branches. It results in cracks in the thin bark and subsequent oozing. Applications of copper-based fungicides just after leaf drop in fall will offer some help. Maintain good tree vigor.

Native Mexican plum fruit isn't much for fresh eating, but it's wonderful preserved.

Mexican plum trees are outstanding additions to the Texas landscape. They're suited to a wide variety of soils, and their spring blooms are long-lasting and highly fragrant.

Wonderful pomegranates are longtime favorites in Texas gardens. Several new types have now come into the market.

Garden Tip

Pomegranates are very attractive fruiting shrubs that have a place in every landscape in the southern two-thirds of Texas. They grow quite well on their own roots (not grafted), so they are started from pencil-sized cuttings taken in late winter.

Pomegranates are popular as fruit crops and handsome as landscaping shrubs.

Pomegranate ★★★★

Best varieties

Al-Sirin-Nar is a Russian variety with large, glossy red fruit. Good producer of sweet, tart fruit that ripen in late October. Southern half of Zones B and C, D – G.

Salavatski produces large fruit that is sweet with a slight tartness. From Russia. Good cold-hardiness. Ripens mid-October. Zones B and C, D – G.

Surh Anor is another Russian variety grown for its consistent production and large, sweet fruit. Ripens mid-October. Zones B and C, D – G.

Wonderful has been the most popular consumer and commercial variety for many years. It is not quite as winter-hardy as some. It bears red, somewhat tart, fruit that tend to split as they near maturity. Zones B and C, D – G.

Cultural requirements

Pollinator needed: No.

Special soil needs: Pomegranates will do well in any type of well-draining soil. They are among some of the finest fruit crops for the alkaline soils and arid climates of Southwest Texas.

Special climatic needs: Winter cold is the biggest adversary to pomegranates in colder parts of Texas. Some varieties have shown good cold resistance down to 10 F, but others are damaged at 16 to 18 F. Plants that suffer freeze damage usually will re-grow from their root systems, but with a delay of three or four years before they begin to produce fruit again.

Size to buy: 16 to 18 inches (bare rooted); 1- or 5-gallon pots.

Pruning at planting: No special pruning is needed other than to remove or trim damaged or errant branches.

Subsequent pruning: Pomegranates are shrubs, not trees, in Texas plantings. While they may develop as single-trunk plants, they should be pruned to three or four scaffold side branches fairly close to the soil line. Remove weak or damaged branches as you see them during the winter.

Thinning required: Usually not.

Fertilizing: Apply high-nitrogen or all-nitrogen fertilizer (1/2 pound per inch of trunk diameter) as the plants start to grow in late winter/early spring. Repeat every six to eight weeks until early August.

Primary insect pests and diseases

No insect pests of common occurrence.

Heart rot. Fungal disease (*Rhizopus arrhizus*) that ruins the fruit as it begins to ripen. Appears during especially rainy spells in early fall.

Strawberries ★★

Best varieties

Cardinal produces medium-sized berries with excellent flavor.

Chandler is an outstanding choice for Texas gardens. It is readily available, and it produces high-quality fruit with excellent yields.

Sequoia is a large, bright-red type with outstanding flavor. It is one of most popular home garden varieties for South Texas.

Cultural requirements

Pollinator needed: No.

Special soil needs: Perfectly drained and highly organic soil. Plant in raised beds that are 42 inches wide and 8 or 10 inches above the surrounding grade.

Special climatic needs: None.

Size to buy: Transplants, either bare-rooted or potted. Plant in late September or October. You will harvest fruit the following spring, at which time it is usually best to remove the plants and start anew in the fall.

Constructing low tunnels for protection: Gardeners in the northern three-fourths of Texas traditionally have planted strawberries in February, pinched off all flowers the first spring, then harvested their crop 14 months later. However, that was often very frustrating, as high summer temperatures weakened the plants severely, usually resulting in poor yields the following spring.

Tunnel production of strawberries has brought new excitement to growing this popular crop.

Strawberry jar is suited to this trailing crop, but it will produce small and sporadic yields.

Growing strawberries in Texas has always been difficult and frustrating. Tunnel production removes weather extremes as a source of crop failure.

Research has shown that if beds are covered with low hoop "tunnels" made from pre-formed electrical conduit, and if the tunnels are covered with clear polyethylene plastic film, fall plantings will prosper and bear fruit the following spring, even on the High Plains. The hoops should span the entire planting bed, and they should be 48 to 60 inches tall. Cut the plastic film to cover the hoops, with 12 inches of plastic to spare on either side and several feet of excess on each end. Lay stones, heavy pipe or even garden soil on top of the edges to weight it down. Drive a single stake 3 or 4 feet away from each end of the tunnel, and pull and secure the excess length of plastic tightly to it, both to prevent the cover from blowing off in the wind and also to make the tunnel virtually air-tight.

These low tunnel strawberry beds are useful from I-10 northward. Obviously, the farther south you go in Texas, the warmer the temperatures inside the tunnels may be on sunny winter days, so make provision for opening up one end or the side of the tunnel for temporary ventilation. Have simple drip irrigation lines running the lengths of the rows to allow occasional watering if necessary. When the plants begin to bloom in early spring, remove the cover to allow bees to pollinate the flowers. If you need short-term protection against cold from that point on, you can cover the tunnel with frost cloth.

Pruning: Pinch off any flower buds that try to develop in the fall soon after planting. Otherwise, no other pruning is required. Reposition runners that form so that new plants will fill the bed.

Thinning required: No.

Fertilizing: Apply a high-nitrogen or all-nitrogen granular fertilizer in fall, two or three weeks after planting. Repeat in late winter, as plants begin to grow. Follow each feeding with a thorough watering.

Primary insect pests

Pillbugs (sowbugs) will eat into fruit that is in contact with the soil.
Mites cause leaves to turn brown and crisp. Apply products labeled for insect control on strawberries for either pest.

Primary diseases

Fungal leaf spots develop during cool, wet weather. Apply labeled fungicide.
Nematodes may attack root systems of plants. If nematodes are confirmed, replant with new certified transplants into fresh soil elsewhere in your garden.

Vegetables

Growing your own produce is one of the most enjoyable parts of gardening. It feels good to bring a harvest to the table. You know those vegetables are nutritious, and you certainly know that they're fresh. You've nurtured them from seed or small transplants, and now – there they are, in front of your family. It's a great feeling for kids of all ages.

Vegetables in Texas come in all flavors and forms.

One of my first tomato transplants

I remember my very first garden. My dad was there beside me. I was just 8, and he was my hero. He brought the tools, and he bought the seeds. We spaded the garden together, but I suspect that he was a lot more tired at the end of the day's digging than I was. As my garden grew, he taught me to water. He sprayed the bugs. We weeded together, but again, I'm pretty sure that I took more credit than deserved.

*I learned a lot from my dad in that garden. Some of it was even about plants. It was **my** garden. Those were **my** vegetables when it came time to take the beans, corn and tomatoes in to my mother. I'll never forget how excited I was. My dad stood quietly off to the side – with a kind smile. Yep. I learned a lot from my dad, Omer E. Sperry, in that garden.*

Vegetable Gardening in Texas

We Texans love our state. However, we're also willing to admit that our soils and climate don't always make vegetable gardening easy here. Before we go into any more detail, here are the overriding keys to a heartier harvest.

The short list of steps to success

- Choose a good site.
- Plan a garden of manageable size.
- Prepare the soil deeply and carefully.
- Grow only crops that are well adapted to your part of Texas.
- Plant only at the recommended times.
- Nurture your crops from the moment they're planted.
- Watch for likely pests to make their arrival.
- Harvest at the peak of perfection.

Boiling it all down to those eight little statements makes it all sound so simple. But there are more details. Let's build them, referring back to these eight steps as our guides.

Picking the Perfect Garden Spot

If you were making a shopping list of the things you'd want in your garden plot, that list would include:

- *Full sunlight.* No crop really prefers shade. Some are just more tolerant of it.

- *Deep soils.* At least 12 to 15 inches of soil, preferably more, or make provisions to bring in some more.

- *Perfect drainage.* You can always add water to a soil; it's much more difficult to get it out of waterlogged soils that lack good drainage.

- *Location convenient to the house and to water.* Stick your garden "out back," and it's likely to become lost and forgotten.

- *Good air circulation.* This reduces the chance of frosts in early spring as well as late in the fall.

"Grow big" if space, time and energy allow.

Raised-bed gardens fit small spaces and are ideal for gardeners with physical limitations.

Determining the Best Size for Your Garden

Most first-time gardeners start too large, and too often, weeds and hard work serve to discourage. It's better to begin smaller and to choose crops wisely (avoiding types that require large amounts of space).

A plot that's 10 by 10 feet is a great start-up size, especially if a young gardener is involved. If things go well, that size can be doubled the following year. And, truth is, you can effectively double or triple the "size" of any garden by growing two or three crops in the same space each calendar year. Early-season vegetables can be out of the way in time for heat-tolerant crops. And fall is pretty much still an untapped opportunity for most Texas vegetable gardeners. So the gardener's mantra might be: "Start small, nurture nature, and keep the garden space filled."

If you eventually consider moving up to a still-larger garden, remember that nothing much changes in those eight initial steps to success. You still have to prepare the soil carefully, whether you're planting 100 or 1,000 square feet. You still have to be the caretaker, so don't bite off too much until you're sure of your abilities.

A small garden is best for young horticulturists.

Preparing the Soil

This is the foundation of your entire vegetable gardening success. The better the soil, the better the results. Here is your sequence:

- Lay out the garden plot.

- Eliminate existing weeds and grass. During the growing season, apply a contact herbicide spray to kill grasses without leaving residue in the soil. During winter, dig and remove grasses, including roots and runners.

- Rototill to a depth of 10 or 12 inches. Rear-tine tillers do a better job of pulverizing the soil.

- If you intend to build a raised garden using treated timbers, concrete blocks or interlocking concrete wall stones, this is the time to do so.

- If the garden is to be raised, bring in 4 to 8 inches of additional sandy loam topsoil. Ask for assurance that it does not contain nutsedge ("nutgrass"). Rototill again to blend all of the soils.

- For better drainage, either taper the soil down to ground level, or install some manner of enclosure. Large decorative river rocks are easy to place, attractive and very functional.

- Add 5 or 6 inches of a mix of organic materials – for example, 2 inches of sphagnum peat moss, and 1 inch each of finely ground pine bark mulch, compost and rotted manure. If you're amending a clay soil, also add 1 inch of expanded shale. Rototill again, to blend all of the ingredients together uniformly.

- Rake out roots, rocks and other debris. Till again if needed – until the soil is a uniform blend, free of debris and clods.

Good gardens start with good soil.

Raised planting beds need not be difficult.

Rear-tine tillers do best job of preparing garden soil.

Get supports in place before planting.

Choosing the Crops

It's hard to make all the right choices, but here are some important considerations.

Grow only crops that:

- Your family likes (and will eat),
- Are adapted to your soils and your climate, and
- Are adequately productive for the space you have available for them.

How Long Until Crops Mature

To help you plan your gardening year, here are the numbers of days you can expect from planting to maturity of the various crops. This depends, of course, on your planting at the proper times and caring for the plants regularly. It also depends on varieties chosen.

30 to 60 days	60 to 80 days	80 days or longer
Beets	Broccoli	Brussels sprouts
Bush beans	Cabbage	Bulbing onions
Leaf lettuce	Carrots	Cantaloupes
Kohlrabi	Cauliflower	Eggplant
Mustard	Chinese cabbage	Garlic
Radishes	Collard greens	Onions
Spinach	Corn	Potatoes
Summer squash	Cucumbers	Parsnips
Turnips	Green onions	Pumpkins
	Kale	Southern peas
	Okra	Sweet potatoes
	Parsley	Tomatoes
	Peppers	Watermelons
	Pole snap beans	Winter squash
	Snap peas	
	Swiss chard	

Garden Tip

Hybrid vegetable varieties will almost always outperform their inbred counterparts several fold. Seed hybridizers seek greater yields, better flavor and quality, and insect and disease resistance. Heirloom vegetables are nice curiosities, but they're often disappointing in terms of yields.

Garden Tip

Recommended varieties change annually, partly because new and better types come along, but also because of seed companies' mergers and acquisitions. The best lists of recommended types will come from Texas A&M vegetable specialists. Contact your county office of the Texas A&M AgriLife Extension or look at current TAMU websites.

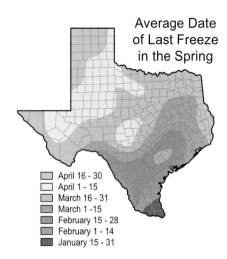

Average Date of Last Freeze in the Spring

- April 16 - 30
- April 1 - 15
- March 16 - 31
- March 1 -15
- February 15 - 28
- February 1 - 14
- January 15 - 31

Plant at the Right Time

Vegetable planting dates in Texas center around last freeze dates, arrival of summer heat, and dates of the average first killing frosts in the fall. Using the appropriate map and the information in these charts, you can determine the best timing for each crop in your locale.

For spring plantings

Six to eight weeks prior to average last freeze date

Onions
Snap peas

Four weeks prior to average last freeze date

Broccoli
Brussels sprouts
Cabbage
Cauliflower
Chinese cabbage
Kale
Kohlrabi
Potatoes, Irish

Two to four weeks prior to average last freeze date

Beets
Carrots
Horseradish
Lettuce, leaf
Mustard greens
Radishes
Spinach
Swiss chard
Turnips

On or up to two weeks after last freeze date

Beans, green (bush or pole)
Cantaloupes
Corn
Cucumbers
Pumpkins
Squash, summer
Squash, winter
Tomatoes
Watermelons

Two to four weeks after average last freeze date

Eggplant
Peppers

Four to eight weeks after average last freeze date

Okra
Southern peas
Sweet potatoes

A Comment from Neil

Through my career, I have repeatedly been asked why one vegetable crop or another failed to perform to expectations. Almost always, those failures could be traced back to planting at the wrong times.

The Texas climate changes rapidly, so the best planting windows of time slam shut very quickly. That's why we have gone to such detail in giving specific guidelines in these pages.

For fall plantings

With fall plantings you must allow extra time (a) because fall temperatures are cooler, so most crops mature more slowly, and (b) because you're interested in more than "days to first harvest." You want more than just one harvest. Allow an extra 6 to 8 weeks. Note: Some varieties are not recommended for fall plantings.

20 to 22 weeks prior to first freeze date

Pumpkins
Tomatoes
Watermelons (small to mid-sized varieties)

16 weeks prior to first freeze date

Beans (green, bush)
Cucumbers
Corn
Melons
Peppers
Potatoes, Irish
Squash, summer

14 weeks prior to first freeze date

Broccoli
Brussels sprouts
Cabbage
Cauliflower
Kohlrabi

10 to 12 weeks prior to first freeze date

Carrots
Collards
Kale
Lettuce, leaf
Mustard
Spinach

Six to eight weeks prior to first freeze date

Beets
Bulbing onions
Garlic
Radishes
Turnips

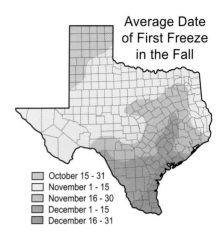

Average Date of First Freeze in the Fall

- October 15 - 31
- November 1 - 15
- November 16 - 30
- December 1 - 15
- December 16 - 31

FAQ

Q How can I succeed with a fall garden in the face of summer heat?

A Here are some tips:

- Plant the recommended varieties at the right times. (See charts).

- Buy transplants that have become acclimated to full sun at the nursery.

- Set transplants out in the evening.

- Water immediately after planting.

- Provide temporary shelter from sun by constructing a small A-frame covering from two shingles or folded cardboard. Remove as plants become acclimated, usually after five to seven days.

- If sowing seeds, use corner of hoe to cut a shallow furrow, then fill it with loose potting soil. The soil mix will retain moisture, and it won't form a hard crust that might inhibit germination.

Your plants are *too dry* if they are wilted and if the soil is dry to the touch. Leaves will often be scorched from their margins and tips inward. Lower leaves will drop first. It is critical that you apply water immediately, or your produce may be damaged or lost.

Your plants are *too wet* if they are wilted even though the soil contains plenty of moisture. The plants will often be wilted, even in the early morning. The soil may have a soured smell. Some plants such as tomatoes may develop adventitious roots along their lower stems. This is an urgent situation. Lack of oxygen is as harmful to plants as it is to animals. Do what you can to correct the poor drainage as quickly as possible.

Slow, thorough soakings are best for vegetables.

Ongoing Care of Vegetables

Keep your vegetable crops growing vigorously. Plants that are allowed to languish will never reach their full potential.

Watering

Water is the main component of almost all fresh produce. Your plants are too wet if they are wilted even though the soil contains plenty of moisture.

There is no standard amount of water that should be applied, nor is there any predictable timetable on which you should irrigate a vegetable garden. There are simply too many variables (temperature, wind, humidity, soil type, etc.).

Learn to "read" each of your vegetable crops, and check the plants daily as they begin to grow actively. When the soil surface begins to feel dry to the touch, it is (or soon will be) time to water. Water deeply and thoroughly, then wait for the soil to begin to dry before watering again.

Best ways to water the garden

Some ways of irrigating a vegetable garden are better than others.

- Drip irrigation and soaker hoses provide deep waterings specifically to the root zones with no loss to evaporation or runoff.

- Furrow watering alongside each row provides deep watering, but it does not provide uniform amounts of water if the garden is on a slope.

- Berms that create basins are effective ways to water tomatoes, melons and other individual plantings.

- Overhead irrigation, whether by automatic systems or hose sprinklers, is not a good plan. It risks spread of disease and can result in leaf scorch should sunlight hit the wet foliage. There is also a good bit of loss to evaporation with overhead watering.

Fertilizing the garden

Begin any garden feeding program by having the soil tested prior to your first plantings. (Mid-winter is best, before the spring rush of home gardeners and farmers.) Your county office of the Texas A&M AgriLife Extension Service can direct you to the Texas A&M Soil Testing Laboratory.

Don't be surprised if the tests show your soil to be high in phosphorus and potassium and lacking only in nitrogen. That is especially common for clay soils. Those tests then may direct you to apply a high-nitrogen or even all-nitrogen fertilizer with half or more of its nitrogen in slow-release form, even for fruit-producing vegetables and root crops.

Applying the fertilizer

Plants are most efficient at taking nutrients in through their roots; therefore, soil applications are much more efficient than foliar feeding.

Granular fertilizers are the standard. As mentioned, they are likely to be high-nitrogen or all-nitrogen. First application should be made two or three weeks after the crop has started growing actively. Use your hoe to cut a shallow V-groove parallel to, and 6 or 8 inches out from each row, then sprinkle ("side-band") the plant food into the groove at the recommended rate. Water deeply to soak the plant food into the ground.

You can also use a hand-held spreader to distribute the granules over the garden, although that is not as precise as side-banding, and it risks leaf burn if granules are left on the foliage in the presence of moisture and sun.

If you prefer to use organic fertilizers, you'll still want to have the soil tested every couple of years. Organic fertilizers are typically of lower nutritional analysis, so it may take a couple of years to build up your plot's fertility. Work fresh organic matter, manure and other organic fertilizer into the soil each time that you rework the garden.

To be productive, a garden must be fed regularly.

Garden Tip

A fact from the soils and plant physiology labs: vegetables do not differentiate whether nutrients are derived from organic or inorganic sources as they enter the plants' roots. All nutrients are broken down into elemental form and brought into the roots in water solution. Which is to say that using organic fertilizers will not actually make the vegetables taste any better. The loving care and regular attention organic gardeners tend to give their gardens is the reason that their produce often tastes better. It has nothing to do with the type of fertilizer that was used.

Young cucumber plant awaits its layer of mulch.

Mulching your garden

Whether it's in flowerbeds or vegetable gardens, mulches bring wonderful benefits. Here are the main ones as they pertain to vegetables. Mulches:

- Conserve water by reducing the soil-to-air contact,

- Retard growth of weeds,

- Keep produce from making direct contact with soil, thereby limiting blemishes and fruit rot,

- Reduce or prevent splashing of soil onto leafy produce, and

- Moderate rate of temperature changes in the soil in the summer.

You'll find many types of suitable mulches. Pine bark chips, hardwood, cedar, cypress and pine needle mulches all work well. You can even mulch with compost from your own bins. As you empty the garden at the end of the season, rototill to blend the organic matter into the soil before replanting.

For all of these organic types of mulches, aim to apply about an inch across the garden. If you make it any deeper, it will soak up rainfall and irrigation to the detriment of the vegetables.

Paper is one option in mulching, although it's short on good looks.

Nurseries also sell special roll-type mulches that can be used between rows of plants in the garden. Some people even use layers of old newspaper as their mulch, but that tends to be unsightly and not as effective as some of the other mulching products in terms of keeping weeds out.

Black polyethylene plastic is not good as a mulch. It prevents movement of air and water into and out of the soil. Plants tend to stay way too wet beneath it.

Without mulch, you may be resigned to hoeing weeds.

Raised bed, good soil preparation, proper watering and feeding, and mulching all combine for a successful home garden.

Surviving the Pests

Insects, diseases and nematodes take a toll on Texas vegetables. However, if you choose your crops wisely and do your homework ahead of time so that you're aware of what problems are likely to show up, you can usually stay ahead of the invasions. Here is a game plan:

- Start with the best varieties. Many will be listed on their seed packets or plant tags as being "resistant" to certain problems.

- Buy high-quality seed or vigorous transplants of those best varieties. Plant at the best time, and keep your plants vigorous by watering and feeding as needed. Healthy plants are less prone to problems.

- Know each of your crops and what problems are likely to appear. Watch the plants daily during the growing season, so that you'll be able to come to their rescue immediately.

- Try mechanical means (hand-picking) or biological controls (predatory insects, etc.) whenever possible. If necessary, step up to organic controls, and if those aren't sufficient, use properly tested and labeled inorganic insecticides or fungicides.

Harvest at Peak of Perfection

Knowing when to harvest each of your vegetable crops is about as important as knowing when to plant them. If you harvest too soon, you lose a part of your plants' production potential. If you wait too long, you run the risk of a loss of vigor of the plants, overly ripe fruit, bitter leafy and root vegetables, bird or insect damage or fungal fruit rot and decay.

The best time to harvest is another crop-by-crop decision that is best discussed for each plant individually. However, in general terms, it's always best to pick your produce before it attains full size.

A scarecrow alone may not be enough to control all the pests that can plague a Texas garden.

Rabbit-proofing the garden

Vigorous vegetables produce the best harvests.

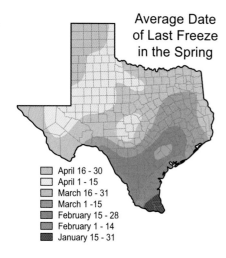

**Average Date
of Last Freeze
in the Spring**

- April 16 - 30
- April 1 - 15
- March 16 - 31
- March 1 - 15
- February 15 - 28
- February 1 - 14
- January 15 - 31

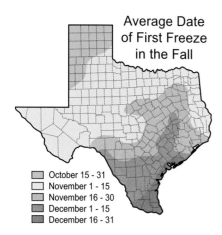

**Average Date
of First Freeze
in the Fall**

- October 15 - 31
- November 1 - 15
- November 16 - 30
- December 1 - 15
- December 16 - 31

Know the proper time to get started.

Guidelines to the Planting Chart

For each crop listed in the planting chart, you will find the following information:

- **Planting date (spring):** Find your county in the map of average dates of last killing freezes of the spring. The numbers in the chart represent the number of weeks before or after that date that each particular crop should be planted in your county. Lettuce, for example, is listed as "-4 to -2," which means that it would be planted two to four weeks earlier than the last freeze date. Beans are planted *on* the average date and up to two weeks after it. Okra is planted four weeks after the last freeze.

- **Planting date (fall):** Find your county on the map of the average dates of the first killing freeze of the fall. The numbers in the chart represent the number of weeks before that date that each particular crop should be planted in your county. While these may seem especially far ahead to you, remember that you want to plant early enough to get a full yield from each of your crops, not just the first picking.

- **Spacing within the rows:** This is the final distance each plant should be from the plants adjacent to it in the row. If you are sowing seeds, you will want to sow 50 to 100 percent more seeds than necessary. While the seedlings are still only a few inches tall, thin them to the recommended spacing.

- **Plants/Seed per 100 feet of row:** This is merely intended to help you know how much of each crop to buy. It's unlikely that you will have 100 feet of any one of the crops, so simply use the number as a starting point.

- **Spacing between rows (inches):** Crowded vegetables quickly become unproductive, and putting rows too close together is one of the fastest ways to fail. Give the plants room to grow, and give yourself room to access them.

- **Days to harvest:** To some degree, this is "days to first harvest," but it's been broadened somewhat to accommodate differences in varieties, also to give you an idea of the length of the harvest season.

- **Insects of major concern:** If a crop is at risk for a particular pest, it is so noted here. More information on the pest(s) can be found in the instructions for each crop later in this chapter.

- **Diseases of major concern:** If a crop is at risk for a particular disease, it is so noted here. More information on the problem(s) can be found in the instructions for each crop later in this chapter.

- **Dependability score:** This is a completely arbitrary rating scale in which more challenging or less rewarding vegetables have fewer stars, while the most dependable types get more. Successes and failures will vary across the state, too, so don't use this rating as your only factor in choosing your crops.

- **Comments:** More specific information is given here, and still more will be found in the instructions for each crop later in this chapter.

Know your crops and how likely you are to succeed with each before you make your final planting decision.

Vegetables CROP AND COMMENTS	PLANTING DATE SPRING Weeks before (-) or after (+) average date of last killing freeze in your county	PLANTING DATE FALL Weeks before average date of first killing freeze in your county	SPACING IN ROWS (INCHES) Final spaces, after seedlings have been thinned	PLANTS OR SEEDS PER 100 FEET	SPACING BETWEEN ROWS (INCHES)	DAYS TO HARVEST	INSECTS OF MAJOR CONCERN	DISEASES OF MAJOR CONCERN	DEPENDABILITY SCORE
Asparagus Perennial; plant dormant roots; first harvest will be third spring	-8	N/A	15-18	65-80 plants	60-72	730	No	No	★★
Beans (green) Bush beans faster, easier than poles	0 to +2	14 to 16	4-5	1/2 to 1 lb. seeds	24-36 (bush), 36-48 (pole)	50-70	Yes	No	★★★★★
Beets Harvest when roots are 2 inches in diameter	-4 to -2	8 to 10	3-4	1 oz. seeds	14-24	45-60	No	No	★★★
Broccoli Easy if planted early; cabbage loopers	-6 to -4	12 to 14	18-24	50-65 plants	30-36	60-80	Yes	No	★★★★
Brussels sprouts More challenging than other cole crops	-6 to -4	12 to 14	18-24	50-65 plants	30-36	80-110	Yes	No	★★
Cabbage Easy if planted early. Cabbage loopers	-6 to -4	12 to 14	18-24	50-65 plants	30-36	70-80	Yes	No	★★★★
Carrots Plant round or stubby varieties	-4 to -2	10 to 12	2	1/2 oz. seeds	12	50-60	No	No	★★
Cauliflower Cabbage loopers; blanch heads	-6 to -4	12 to 14	18-24	50-65 plants	30-36	60-70	Yes	No	★★★
Chard, Swiss Highly nutritious; plant early for best growth and flavor; keep plants growing actively; ornamental types also available	-6 to -4	10 to 12	6-8	2 oz. seeds	24-30	60-80	No	No	★★★

Vegetables

CONTINUED

CROP AND COMMENTS	PLANTING DATE SPRING Weeks before (-) or after (+) average date of last killing freeze in your county	PLANTING DATE FALL Weeks before average date of first killing freeze in your county	SPACING IN ROWS (INCHES) Final spaces, after seedlings have been thinned	PLANTS OR SEEDS PER 100 FEET	SPACING BETWEEN ROWS (INCHES)	DAYS TO HARVEST	INSECTS OF MAJOR CONCERN	DISEASES OF MAJOR CONCERN	DEPENDABILITY SCORE
Collards Excellent in fall garden	-6 to -4	10 to 12	18-24	1/2 oz. seeds or 50-65 plants	30-36	60-75	Yes	No	★★★
Corn Plant large square blocks to ensure good pollination; corn earworm	0 to +2	14 to 16	10-12	3-4 oz. seeds	30-36	60-80	Yes	No	★★★
Cucumbers Dry plants produce bitter fruit	0 to +2	14 to 16	24-48	1/2 oz. seeds	24-30	50-70	Yes	No	★★★★
Eggplants Requires warmth, so spring plantings better	+2 to +4	16 to 18	18-24	50-65 plants	30-36	50-70	Yes	No	★★
Garlic Harvest in spring when tops fall over; 10-foot row probably adequate	N/A	6 to 8	2-4	300-600 cloves	14-18	180	No	No	★★★
Horseradish Plant from root cuttings; can be invasive	-4 to -2	N/A	12	48-60 plants	48-60	365	No	No	★★
Kale Cabbage loopers; fall plantings best	-6 to -4	10 to 12	8-12	1/2 oz. seeds	30-36	60-80	Yes	No	★★★
Kohlrabi Cabbage loopers	-6 to -4	12 to 14	6-8	1/2 oz. seeds	24	30-60	Yes	No	★★★
Lettuce Grow leafy types; attractive, easy and quick	-4 to -2	10 to 12	2-3	1/2 oz. seeds	15-18	45-60	No	No	★★★★
Melons (cantaloupes and watermelons) Require large space; squash bugs	0 to +2	16 to 20	60-120	1 oz. seeds	60-120	70-100	Yes	No	★★★
Mustard greens Best suited to fall gardens	-4 to -2	6 to 8	6-10	1/2 oz. seeds	12-18	45-60	No	No	★★★
Okra Cotton root rot, nematodes	4	N/A	15-18	2 oz. seeds	36-48	60-80	No	Yes	★★★
Onions Spring: bulbing onions from transplants; fall: green onions from seed	-8 to -6 (transplants)	6 to 8 (seed)	2-3	400-600 transplants	16-24	80-100	No	No	★★★★
Peppers Large types may not set fruit in summer	+2 to +4	16 to 18	18-24	50-65 transplants	36-48	60-80	No	No	★★★★
Potatoes, Irish Buy certified seed potatoes; must have perfect drainage	-6 to -4	14 to 16	10-12	35-40 seeds	30-36	60-80	Yes	No	★★★★

Crease seed packet to aid in planting.

Leaf lettuce mixture is quick and easy.

Proper spacing, both within and between rows is critical.

Vegetables
CONTINUED

CROP AND COMMENTS	PLANTING DATE SPRING Weeks before (-) or after (+) average date of last killing freeze in your county	PLANTING DATE FALL Weeks before average date of first killing freeze in your county	SPACING IN ROWS (INCHES) Final spaces, after seedlings have been thinned	PLANTS OR SEEDS PER 100 FEET	SPACING BETWEEN ROWS (INCHES)	DAYS TO HARVEST	INSECTS OF MAJOR CONCERN	DISEASES OF MAJOR CONCERN	DEPENDABILITY SCORE
Pumpkins For Halloween, plant small or mid-sized varieties late June	0 to +2	Late June	48-60	1/2 oz. seeds	72-96	80-100	Yes	No	★★★
Radishes Fast crop; become hot-flavored when weather turns warm	-4 to -2	6	1-1/2-2	1 oz. seeds	8-12	30-45	No	No	★★★
Southern peas Also known as black-eyed peas, cowpeas	+4 to +6	N/A	6-10	1 lb. seeds	48-60	80-100	No	No	★★★
Spinach Plant to mature during cool weather	-4 to -2	10 to 12	2-3	1 oz. seeds	16-24	45-60	No	No	★★★
Squash Very productive; squash bugs; may require hand-pollination	0 to +2	16 (summer) 22 (winter)	30-48	1/2-1 oz. seeds	48-60 (summer squash) 60-72 (winter squash)	50-60 (summer squash) 80-100 (winter squash)	Yes	No	★★★★
Sugar snap peas Plant in late winter, so harvest will be finished before hot weather	-8 to -6	8 to 10	1-2	1 lb. seeds	30-48	60-80	No	No	★★★
Sweet potatoes Sandy soils; sweet potato weevils	+4 to +6	N/A	12-16	75-100 slips	48-60	90-120	Yes	No	★★★
Tomatoes Plant only small and mid-sized varieties	0 to +2	22	30-36	33-40 plants	48-60	60-90	Yes	Yes	★★★★★
Turnips Best in cool weather; harvest at 2 to 2-1/2 inches	-4 to -2	6 to 10	2-4	1/2 oz. seeds	15-18	45-60	No	No	★★★

Asparagus is perennial. Plant at edge of garden.

Asparagus harvest begins two years after planting.

Yellow wax beans are simply variations of bush green beans.

Asparagus ★★

Distance between plants in row: 15 to 18 inches, staggered in double rows in beds 28 to 30 inches wide.

Distance between rows: 60 to 72.

Transplants per 100 feet of row: 65 to 80.

Seeds per 100 feet of row: N/A.

Spring planting date: January, from dormant two-year-old roots.

Fall planting date: N/A.

Fertilizing: High-N or all-N, 1 to 2 pounds per 100 square feet of bed space. Apply just before growth starts for spring (February). Repeat immediately after you stop harvesting spears (mid- to late April).

Insects of concern: None.

Diseases of concern: None.

When to harvest: Do not harvest for first two years after planting. Harvest new spears in early spring, either with a specialty asparagus knife or with a very sharp paring knife.

Comments: Asparagus is a perennial vegetable, which means it should be planted into well-prepared garden soil, where it can grow undisturbed for 10 or 20 years. Harvest spears for only four to six weeks, then stop and allow all of the stalks to grow. They will produce fern-like foliage, which should remain in place until killed by first hard freeze in late fall. Cut to ground once all shoots have turned yellow, then brown.

Beans (green or yellow wax) ★★★★★

Distance between plants in row: 2 to 3 inches; thin to 4 to 5.

Distance between rows: 24 to 36 inches for bush beans, 36 to 48 for pole beans.

Transplants per 100 feet of row: N/A.

Seeds per 100 feet of row: 1/2 to 1 pound.

Spring planting date: On, or up to two weeks after, average date of last killing freeze.

Fall planting date: 14 to 16 weeks before average date of first killing freeze.

Fertilizing: High-N or all-N, 1 to 2 pounds per 100 square feet of bed space. Apply when plants are 6 to 8 inches tall.

Insects of concern: Aphids early in season. Spider mites in late spring, as plants are beginning to produce beans. Follow latest control recommendations of Texas A&M AgriLife Extension Service.

Diseases of concern: None.

When to harvest: When beans are half their potential mature size (generally 4 to 6 inches long), it's time to begin harvesting. Letting them grow longer will result in fibrous, less appealing beans. Keep maturing beans picked off plants to encourage additional production.

Comments: One of our most rewarding vegetables. Especially good for a young child's first garden. Bush beans are easier, faster than pole beans. Lima beans are not well suited to Texas conditions.

Pole beans and hollyhocks

Beets ★★★

Distance between plants in row: 2 to 3 inches; thin to 3 to 4.

Distance between rows: 14 to 24 inches.

Transplants per 100 feet of row: N/A.

Seeds per 100 feet of row: 1 ounce.

Spring planting date: Two to four weeks before average date of last killing freeze.

Fall planting date: Eight to 10 weeks before average date of first killing freeze.

Fertilizing: High-N or all-N, 1 to 2 pounds per 100 square feet of bed space. Apply two weeks after planting. Repeat monthly until harvest. Boron deficiency may appear where soils are alkaline, causing black, corky spots within the roots. To correct, apply 1/2 teaspoon of borax mixed in 5 gallons of water to 100 feet of row.

Insects of concern: White grub worms, wireworms, root knot nematodes and other soil-borne pests. Follow latest control recommendations of Texas A&M AgriLife Extension Service.

Diseases of concern: None.

When to harvest: First harvest comes when roots are golf ball sized. Remove every other root. Harvest remaining beets when they are 2 inches in diameter. Allowing them to grow larger will result in fibrous beets that are lacking in flavor.

Comments: One of our few vegetables that actually do better in slightly alkaline soils.

Beets must be harvested before roots become large.

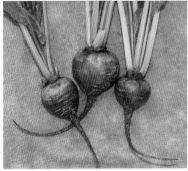

Golden beets provide a colorful alternative.

Large broccoli head is ready to harvest.

Broccoli ★★★★

Distance between plants in row: 18 to 24 inches.

Distance between rows: 30 to 36 inches.

Transplants per 100 feet of row: 50 to 65.

Seeds per 100 feet of row: 1/2 ounce.

Spring planting date: Four to six weeks before average date of last killing freeze.

Fall planting date: 12 to 14 weeks before average date of first killing freeze.

Fertilizing: High-N or all-N, 1 to 2 pounds per 100 square feet of bed space. Apply two weeks after planting. Repeat monthly until harvest.

Insects of concern: Cabbage loopers are green larvae that feed voraciously, leaving holes in leaves. Watch for white butterflies that are adult form of looper larvae. They will lay eggs, and the green loopers will soon follow. *Bacillus thuringiensis* is most reliable control. Aphids may congregate on tender new growth at time of harvest. Rinse thoroughly to eliminate them.

Diseases of concern: None.

When to harvest: Allow florets to grow almost to full size. However, do not allow them to mature enough that yellow flowers begin to open. Use sharp knife to harvest.

Comments: Most commonly grown from potted transplants. Leave plants in place after first cutting so that additional small heads can develop.

Brussels Sprouts ★★

Distance between plants in row: 18 to 24 inches.

Distance between rows (inches): 30 to 36 inches.

Transplants per 100 feet of row: 50 to 65.

Seeds per 100 feet of row: 1/2 ounce.

Spring planting date: Four to six weeks before average date of last killing freeze.

Fall planting date: 12 to 14 weeks before average date of first killing freeze.

Brussels sprouts develop along central stem.

Fertilizing: High-N or all-N, 1 to 2 pounds per 100 square feet of bed space. Apply two weeks after planting. Repeat monthly until harvest.

Insects of concern: Cabbage loopers are green larvae that feed voraciously, leaving holes in leaves. Watch for white butterflies that are adult form of looper larvae. They will lay eggs, and the green loopers will soon follow. *Bacillus thuringiensis* is most reliable control.

Diseases of concern: None.

Ongoing care: Remove leaves from lower half of plant when sprouts begin to form. Remove growing tips from the plants at same time.

When to harvest: When small heads are still tight, in the 1- to 1-1/2-inch range.

Comments: Most commonly grown from potted transplants.

Violetta Chinese cabbage is colorful.

Cabbage ★★★★

Distance between plants in row: 18 to 24 inches.

Distance between rows: 30 to 36 inches.

Transplants per 100 feet of row: 50 to 65.

Seeds per 100 feet of row: 1/2 ounce.

Spring planting date: Four to six weeks before average date of last killing freeze.

Fall planting date: 12 to 14 weeks before average date of first killing freeze.

Fertilizing: High-N or all-N, 1 to 2 pounds per 100 square feet of bed space. Apply two weeks after planting. Repeat as heads start to form.

Insects of concern: Cabbage loopers are green larvae that feed voraciously, leaving holes in leaves. Watch for white butterflies that are adult form of looper larvae. They will lay eggs, and the green loopers will soon follow. *Bacillus thuringiensis* is most reliable control.

Diseases of concern: None.

When to harvest: As early as when heads are size of large grapefruit, until heads are full-sized. Waiting too long results in split and sunscalded heads.

Comments: Most commonly grown from potted or bare-rooted transplants. Watch for white butterflies that are adult form of looper larvae. They will lay eggs, and the green loopers will soon follow. *Bacillus thuringiensis* is most reliable control.

Young cabbage transplants are ready for planting.

Cabbage head is ready to harvest.

Round and stubby-rooted carrots produce best in Texas.

Carrots ★★

Distance between plants in row: 1 inch; thin seedlings to stand 2 inches apart.

Distance between rows: 12 inches.

Transplants per 100 feet of row: N/A.

Seeds per 100 feet of row: 1/2 ounce.

Spring planting date: Two to four weeks before average date of last killing freeze.

Fall planting date: 10 to 12 weeks before average date of first killing freeze.

Fertilizing: High-N or all-N, 1 to 2 pounds per 100 square feet of bed space. Apply monthly.

Insects of concern: None.

Diseases of concern: None.

When to harvest: When roots are half their fully mature size. Allowing them to continue growing beyond that point results in fibrous, flavorless carrots.

Comments: Carrots do far better in sandy soils. Plant only round or stubby-rooted types for best results.

Cauliflower ★★★

Distance between plants in row: 18 to 24 inches.

Distance between rows: 30 to 36 inches.

Transplants per 100 feet of row: 50 to 65.

Seeds per 100 feet of row: N/A.

Spring planting date: Four to six weeks before average date of last killing freeze.

Fall planting date: 12 to 14 weeks before average date of first killing freeze.

Fertilizing: High-N or all-N, 1 to 2 pounds per 100 square feet of bed space. Apply two weeks after planting. Repeat monthly until harvest.

Cauliflower head is ready for harvest.

Insects of concern: Cabbage loopers are green larvae that feed voraciously, leaving holes in leaves. Watch for white butterflies that are adult form of looper larvae. They will lay eggs, and the green loopers will soon follow. *Bacillus thuringiensis* is most reliable control.

Diseases of concern: None.

When to harvest: As heads begin to form, carefully tie leaves up and over them to blanch the heads. Blanching keeps the heads white instead of the normal green color they develop when exposed to sunlight. Cut when heads are 5 or 6 inches in diameter – before quality begins to deteriorate.

Comments: Usually more successful in fall garden. Spring plantings too often fail to produce well due to early summer heat.

Cauliflower head is tied for blanching.

Chard ★★★

Distance between plants in row: 3 to 4 inches; thin seedlings to stand 6 to 8 inches.

Distance between rows: 24 to 30 inches.

Transplants per 100 feet of row: 175-200, but usually grown from seed.

Seeds per 100 feet of row: 2 ounces.

Spring planting date: Four to six weeks before average date of last killing freeze.

Fall planting date: 10 to 12 weeks before average date of first killing freeze.

Fertilizing: High-N or all-N, 1 to 2 pounds per 100 square feet of bed space. Apply two weeks after planting. Repeat every two to three weeks until harvest.

Insects of concern: None.

Diseases of concern: None.

When to harvest: Use thinned seedlings in salads. Harvest larger leaves from outsides of plants.

Comments: Keep plants well fed and consistently moist. Leaves will become bitter if you let the plants' growth slow.

Chard (upper right) and other cool-season vegetables

Swiss chard is handsome, edible.

Young collard greens are off to a good start.

Tassles provide pollen for the corn patch.

Corn silks collect the grains of pollen.

Collards ★★★

Distance between plants in row: 18 to 24 inches.

Distance between rows: 30 to 36 inches.

Transplants per 100 feet of row: 50 to 65.

Seeds per 100 feet of row: 1/2 ounce.

Spring planting date: Four to six weeks before average date of last killing freeze.

Fall planting date: 10 to 12 weeks before average date of first killing freeze.

Fertilizing: High-N or all-N, 1 to 2 pounds per 100 square feet of bed space. Apply two weeks after planting. Repeat monthly until harvest.

Insects of concern: Cabbage loopers are green larvae that feed voraciously, leaving holes in leaves. Watch for white butterflies that are adult form of looper larvae. They will lay eggs, and the green loopers will soon follow. *Bacillus thuringiensis* is most reliable control.

Diseases of concern: None.

When to harvest: If you thin seedlings, cut and use the entire plants. As the remaining plants grow and develop, use lower leaves. Collards are tolerant of temperatures as cold as 20 F, actually becoming sweeter in flavor after exposure to frosts.

Comments: Common and nutritious vegetable in Texas gardens. Because of cold tolerance, collards produce well into winter.

Corn ★★★

Distance between plants in row: 3 to 4 inches; thin to 10 to 12 inches apart when plants are 6 inches tall.

Distance between rows: 30 to 36 inches.

Transplants per 100 feet of row: N/A.

Seeds per 100 feet of row: 2 to 3 ounces.

Spring planting date: On, or up to two weeks after, average date of last killing freeze.

Fall planting date: 14 to 16 weeks before average date of first killing freeze. (Better suited to spring gardens and warm weather.)

Fertilizing: High-N or all-N, 1 to 2 pounds per 100 square feet of bed space when plants reach 6 to 8 inches tall.

Insects of concern: Corn earworm moth lays eggs on developing silks. Resulting larvae invade the young ear and feed on the kernels. Control with a drop of mineral oil applied to the silks after they are fully developed. Mineral oil suffocates earworm eggs.

Diseases of concern: None.

When to harvest: Pull ears when white "milk" squirts from kernels as you press them with your thumbnail. You have only a two- or three-day window. If kernels have passed the milk stage and are sunken, the ear is likely to have lost flavor and it may have become rather grainy. Harvest within an hour of the time you will cook and serve. If that is not possible, refrigerate immediately.

Comments: Choose super-sweet hybrids that reach harvesting age fairly quickly. Plant in square blocks 20 by 20 feet to ensure good wind-driven pollination. When you must plant in rectangles, run rows north and south, so that prevailing south winds can blow through the plantings and carry maximum pollen. When you do not get adequate pollination, the result is poorly filled ears.

Time to apply drop of mineral oil to corn silks to prevent corn earworms.

Cucumbers ★★★★

Distance between plants in row: Sow seeds in clusters of five or six seeds, with the sites spaced 24 to 48 inches apart within their rows.

Distance between rows: 48 to 72 inches. (It helps if cucumbers are planted adjacent to a fence or trellis that can act as a support for their vines.)

Transplants per 100 feet of row: N/A.

Seeds per 100 feet of row: 1/2 ounce.

Spring planting date: On, or up to 2 weeks after, average date of last killing freeze.

Fall planting date: 14 to 16 weeks before average date of first killing freeze.

Fertilizing: High-N or all-N, 1 to 2 pounds per 100 square feet of bed space two weeks after seeds germinate and monthly through harvest.

Insects of concern: Cucumber beetles are striped or spotted insects that chew holes in plant leaves. Squash bugs are gray, shield-shaped

Cucumber is ready to harvest.

Cucumber plants benefit from support.

Harvest cucumbers regularly to keep plants vigorous.

insects that congregate along the lower stem, sucking food reserves from the plant. Spider mites are very frequent visitors about the time cucumbers begin to produce fruit. Watch for tiny tan mottled spots on the leaves. They will usually show first on the lower leaves, and they may appear about the same time that you'll also see them on bean foliage. Thump a suspect leaf over white paper. If you see the tiny pests starting to move, apply a labeled insecticide before they get any worse.

Diseases of concern: None.

When to harvest: Harvest pickling cucumbers before they come close to reaching their full, mature size. Sweet pickles require 2- to 3-inch fruit, while dills traditionally are made from 4- to 6-inch cucumbers. Cucumbers picked for fresh eating should be harvested before they have reached full size, generally by the time they are 6 or 7 inches long.

Comments: Poor fruit set is due to lack of pollination. The plants all bear both male and female flowers, and if you do not have good bee activity, you may have to do the pollinating yourself. The male flowers will have straight stems, while the female flowers will have swollen bases where the fruit will develop. Clip a couple of male flowers off. Peel away their petals, then daub the pollen onto the female flowers.

Eggplants ★★

Distance between plants in row: 18 to 24 inches.

Distance between rows: 30 to 36 inches.

Transplants per 100 feet of row: 50 to 65.

Seeds per 100 feet of row: N/A.

Spring planting date: Two to four weeks after average date of last killing freeze.

Fall planting date: 16 to 18 weeks before average date of first killing freeze. (Eggplants are not recommended in fall gardens due to plants' preference for warm soils.)

Fertilizing: High-N or all-N, 1 to 2 pounds per 100 square feet of bed space applied once every month.

One of many types of eggplants available.

Insects of concern: Spider mites are most common pests, but control is difficult because eggplants are sensitive to many insecticidal sprays. Read and follow label directions carefully.

Diseases of concern: None.

When to harvest: Eggplants should be harvested with a sharp knife or shears, not by pulling or breaking. Do so when the fruit are approximately two-thirds their mature size. (Mature fruit sizes vary dramatically between varieties.) At proper harvest time, the surface of the fruit should spring back when depressed.

Comments: Eggplants are related to tomatoes and peppers. In many respects, the care that you give them should be similar.

Garlic harvest in May

Garlic ★★★

Distance between plants in row: 2 to 4 inches.

Distance between rows: 14 to 18 inches.

Transplants per 100 feet of row: 65 to 85 cloves.

Seeds per 100 feet of row: N/A.

Spring planting date: N/A.

Fall planting date: Six to eight weeks before average date of first killing freeze.

Fertilizing: 2 to 3 pounds of 10-10-10 or 15-15-15 (or similar) food per 100 square feet once plants are growing vigorously in fall. Repeat in early spring.

Insects of concern: None.

Diseases of concern: None.

When to harvest: When tops begin to fall over in spring. Dig, dry and hang in garage until ready to use.

Comments: Plant from cloves from the grocery.

Cloves from garlic ready for planting in fall.

Only a few plants of garlic supply a family's needs.

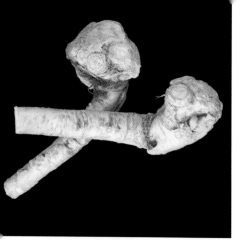

Horseradish roots pack quite a wallop.

Toscano kale is attractive and quite edible.

Horseradish ★★

Distance between plants in row: 12 inches.

Distance between rows: 48 to 60 inches.

Transplants per 100 feet of row: 100.

Seeds per 100 feet of row: N/A.

Spring planting date: Two to four weeks before average date of last killing freeze.

Fall planting date: N/A.

Fertilizing: High-N or all-N, 1/2 to 1 pound per 100 square feet of bed space every six to eight weeks until harvest. These are light feedings intended to keep the plants from overproducing lush foliage.

Insects of concern: None.

Diseases of concern: None.

When to harvest: Growth is most vigorous in late summer and early fall, so delay harvest until October, November. Dig roots only as needed, as quality is superior when fresh. Save smaller roots for replanting back into garden in spring.

Comments: Horseradish plants can become invasive. You may need to take action to contain them by means of an in-ground barrier.

Kale ★★★

Distance between plants in row: Sow seed 1 to 2 inches apart; thin to stand 8 to 12 inches.

Distance between rows: 30 to 36 inches.

Transplants per 100 feet of row: 75 to 100.

Seeds per 100 feet of row: 1/2 ounce.

Spring planting date: Four to six weeks before average date of last killing freeze.

Fall planting date: 10 to 12 weeks before average date of first killing freeze.

Fertilizing: High-N or all-N, 1 to 2 pounds per 100 square feet of bed space. Apply two weeks after planting. Repeat monthly until harvest.

Young kale plants are getting a good start.

Insects of concern: Cabbage loopers are green larvae that feed voraciously, leaving holes in leaves. Watch for white butterflies that are adult form of looper larvae. They will lay eggs, and the green loopers will soon follow. *Bacillus thuringiensis* is most reliable control.

Diseases of concern: None.

When to harvest: As you thin seedlings, cut and use the entire plants. Kale is winter-hardy in Texas, actually becoming sweeter in flavor after exposure to frosts.

Comments: Common and nutritious vegetable in Texas gardens. Fall plantings work best. Because of cold tolerance, will produce well into winter.

Purple kohlrabi shines alongside Rhubarb Swiss chard

Kohlrabi ★★★

Distance between plants in row: Sow seed 1 to 2 inches apart; thin to stand 8 to 12 inches.

Distance between rows: 24 inches.

Transplants per 100 feet of row: N/A.

Seeds per 100 feet of row: 1/2 ounce.

Spring planting date: Four to six weeks before average date of last killing freeze.

Fall planting date: 12 to 14 weeks before average date of first killing freeze.

Fertilizing: High-N or all-N, 1 to 2 pounds per 100 square feet of bed space. Apply two weeks after planting. Repeat monthly until harvest.

Insects of concern: Cabbage loopers are green larvae that feed voraciously, leaving holes in leaves. Watch for white butterflies that are adult form of looper larvae. They will lay eggs, and the green loopers will soon follow. *Bacillus thuringiensis* is most reliable control.

Diseases of concern: None.

When to harvest: Before plants reach full size. Flavor and texture are best when fleshy above-ground storage stems are 2 to 3 inches across.

Comments: Both white- and purple-top types are available. They are also attractive in color beds.

Swollen stem of purple kohlrabi is ready for harvest.

Luscious leaf lettuce can be pluck-harvested, one leaf at a time.

Special mixes of leaf lettuce varieties are sold.

Simpson-type of leaf lettuce

Red leaf lettuce is quite ornamental.

Romaine lettuce does well in cool weather.

Lettuce ★★★★

Distance between plants in row: Sow seed 1/2 to 1 inch apart, thin to be 2 to 3 inches apart.

Distance between rows: 15 to 18 inches.

Transplants per 100 feet of row: N/A.

Seeds per 100 feet of row: 1/2 ounce.

Spring planting date: Two to four weeks before average date of last killing freeze.

Fall planting date: 10 to 12 weeks before average date of first killing freeze. Season can be extended by planting in patio pots into mid-fall, so plants can be brought into protection from first freezes.

Fertilizing: High-N or all-N, 1 to 2 pounds per 100 square feet of bed space. Apply two weeks after planting. Repeat every three weeks until harvest.

Insects of concern: Aphids may congregate on new growth. Apply labeled insecticide, or merely wash pests away with water.

Diseases of concern: None.

When to harvest: Leaves have best flavor while plants are growing vigorously. Use outer leaves, so that plants can keep growing.

Comments: Plant only fast-maturing leaf lettuce varieties. (There are many.) Iceberg head lettuce is not suited to Texas home gardens. Keep plants moist and well nourished at all times. Allowing growth to slow, even for only a few days, results in bitter leaves. The various types of lettuce are handsome additions to color beds.

Melons ★★★

Distance between plants in row: Sow seeds in clusters of five or six seeds, with those sites spaced 60 to 120 inches apart within their rows. Thin to two or three plants per cluster as soon as seeds have germinated and plants are growing vigorously.

Distance between rows: 60 to 120 inches.

Transplants per 100 feet of row: N/A.

Seeds per 100 square feet: 1 ounce.

Spring planting date: On, or up to two weeks after, average date of last killing freeze.

Fall planting date: 16 to 20 weeks before average date of first killing freeze.

Fertilizing: High-N or all-N, 1 to 2 pounds per 100 square feet of bed space two weeks after seeds germinate and every six weeks through harvest.

Insects of concern: Squash bugs are gray, shield-shaped insects that congregate along the lower stem, sucking food reserves from the plant. Eliminate the egg masses from the backs of the plants' leaves by crushing them with your thumb. Prop a shingle up alongside the plants in hot weather. The adult squash bugs will congregate beneath it during the sunny part of the day. You can remove the prop and crush the pests by stepping on the shingle. Insecticidal dusts may offer some help, especially with young squash bug nymphs.

Diseases of concern: None.

When to harvest: (Cantaloupes) Stem slips away easily from the fruit. Blossom end of the fruit will begin to soften, and netting on the skin will become more evident. (Watermelons) Some gardeners watch the white spot on the bottom of the fruit. When it begins to turn yellow, they will harvest the melon. Others use the two tendrils that are on the stem adjacent to the melon as their guides. When the tendrils turn brown and dry, the melon is probably ready. And of course, there are those who thump the fruit with their fingers. If it makes a dull sound, the fruit is probably ready. If it has a high-pitched ring, they wait a few more days.

Comments: There are dozens of types of melons, and all are well adapted to Texas conditions. However, most grow to become very large plants, and for that reason, they are probably not the best plants for small urban gardens. Children want to grow their own watermelons, but parents may want to steer them toward crops that have better yields in more confined spaces. Also note that if you do not have good bee activity, you may need to hand-pollinate your melon flowers. (See details under "Squash.")

Netting of cantaloupe hints that it's ready to harvest.

What youngster isn't ready for watermelon!

For those who prefer not to eat their watermelon with both hands ....

Mustard greens are best in fall garden.

Mustard ★★★

Distance between plants in row: 2 to 3 inches. Thin to 6 to 10 inches between plants.

Distance between rows: 12 to 18 inches.

Transplants per 100 feet of row: N/A.

Seeds per 100 feet of row: 1/2 ounce.

Spring planting date: Two to four weeks before average date of last killing freeze.

Fall planting date: Six to eight weeks before average date of first killing freeze.

Fertilizing: High-N or all-N, 1 to 2 pounds per 100 square feet of bed space. Apply two weeks after planting. Repeat monthly until harvest.

Insects of concern: None.

Diseases of concern: None.

When to harvest: If you thin seedlings, cut and use the entire plants. As the remaining plants grow and develop, remove leaves from stems carefully, leaving stems intact to continue growing and producing more leaves.

Comments: Mustard greens develop a peppery taste when grown in warm weather. For that reason, they are better suited to the fall garden. They are tolerant of cool weather, so they will produce well into late fall and early winter.

Okra is productive in hot Texas summer weather.

Okra ★★★

Distance between plants in row: Sow seeds 6 to 8 inches apart. Thin seedlings to 15 to 18 inches.

Distance between rows: 36 to 48 inches.

Transplants per 100 feet of row: N/A.

Seeds per 100 feet of row: 1 ounce.

Spring planting date: Four weeks after average date of last killing freeze.

Fall planting date: Not common in fall gardens due to plants' preference for warm conditions. Better to plant during summer as garden space becomes available, rather than waiting to plant a fall crop.

Fertilizing: High-N or all-N, 1 to 2 pounds per 100 square feet of bed space applied after you thin the seedlings. After harvest begins, apply 2 pounds of same fertilizer per 100 square feet. Water deeply to encourage good root growth.

Insects of concern: None.

Diseases of concern: Cotton root rot in areas with alkaline soils. There is no chemical control for this soil-borne fungus. Replanting okra into that part of the garden will be futile. Root knot nematodes are microscopic soil-borne worms that sting okra plants' roots and cause abnormal galls. They cause plants to be stunted and unproductive. We do not have good chemical remedies. Check Texas A&M cultural recommendations online.

When to harvest: Pods mature quickly. Harvest before they are more than 3 to 3-1/2 inches long. They quickly become fibrous, and allowing them to remain on plants longer also reduces production of more pods.

Comments: Okra is popular in many southern recipes, and it can be rewarding in the home garden. Just be mindful of its need for heat, and keep harvesting it regularly to keep the plants vigorous. The plants grow to be several feet tall, so plant them on the north side of your garden, so they won't shade other vegetables nearby. Okra is best in relatively large gardens.

Tasty green onions are favorites for eating raw.

Onions ★★★★

Distance between transplants in row: 2 to 3 inches.

Distance between rows: 16 to 24 inches.

Transplants per 100 feet of row: 400 to 600

Seeds per 100 feet of row: 1 ounce

Spring planting date: (Transplants) six to eight weeks before average date of last killing freeze.

Fall planting date: (Seeds) October through December. Sow seeds 1 inch apart. When plants are 6 inches high, thin to 2 to 3 inches. Use the extra plants you remove as green onions. These seed-grown onions will be harvested at the same time as your late-winter onion set plantings. Most people find it easier simply to buy the transplants.

Onions must be planted long before spring.

Onions harvested in May.

Shallots are yet another onion relative.

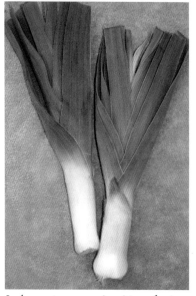
Leeks are strong-growing sisters of onions.

Fertilizing: Spread 2 to 3 pounds of complete-and-balanced analysis such as 10-10-10 or 15-15-15 over 100 square feet of garden before planting. Rototill into top 3 to 4 inches of soil.

Insects of concern: Tiny onion thrips may appear. Apply labeled insecticide.

Diseases of concern: Some fungal problems may occasionally show up, particularly in wet seasons and with poorly draining soils.

When to harvest: Onions seeded in fall or transplanted in late winter should be ready for harvest in May and June. If you want green onions, harvest when they are pencil-size and until they start to form bulbs. If you are growing them for dry-bulb onions, they will be ready when the stems begin to fall over. Carefully dig the onions out of the soil and lay them out on the ground for a day or two to dry. Trim them to remove their tops and continue drying them out of direct sunlight in baskets, boxes or on papers. Store them in a cool, well-ventilated place such as a carport or garage. They can also be put into the crisper in your refrigerator.

Comments: Transplants set out in late winter are the best way to grow onions. Consult Texas A&M horticulture websites for current variety recommendations for your area.

Onion relatives

It's quite a clan – one of many assorted flavors. There's an onion cousin for almost any purpose. Here are a few of their siblings.

- **Green onions** ("multiplier" onions) can be planted from seed sown in fall. They will produce during the fall, winter and even into the spring. They can also be planted from sets.

- **Shallots** are planted in fall in South Texas, or very early in spring in North Texas using sets from nursery, seed source, or grocery. Harvest the tops and use them as a substitute for chives. The plants will form small bulb clusters in spring. Separate them and allow to dry three or four weeks before using.

- **Leeks** are planted in fall. Sow seed 3 to 4 inches apart in rows, with 8 to 15 inches between rows. Plants require six to eight months to mature. As they grow taller, pull loose soil up around their stems to blanch them. Harvest when stems are 1/2 inch to 2 inches in diameter.

Peppers ★★★★

Distance between plants in row: 18 to 24 inches.

Distance between rows: 36 to 48 inches.

Transplants per 100 feet of row: 50 to 65.

Seeds per 100 feet of row: N/A.

Spring planting date: Two to four weeks after average date of last killing freeze.

Fall planting date: 16 to 18 weeks before average date of first killing freeze.

Fertilizing: High-N or all-N food two weeks after planting and monthly until harvests are completed. 1 tablespoon per plant at first feeding. 2 tablespoons per plant at each successive feeding.

Insects of concern: None.

Diseases of concern: None.

Cultural concerns: Fruit may suffer sunscald in hottest summer weather. Fruit may develop blossom-end rot (similar to tomatoes) when plants are allowed to get too dry between waterings. Nematodes may sting plants' roots and cause stunted growth and root galls. Bell peppers and other large types may stop setting fruit when daytime highs climb into the 90s. Again, they react similarly to tomatoes.

When to harvest: Pick fruit as soon as they reach desired size and color. Bells can be harvested slightly immature, or they can be left on the plant to turn red, orange, yellow or purple, depending on the variety. Other types will also change colors as they mature. They may turn to yellow, gold, red or purple.

Comments: Entire books have been written on the subject of "Peppers." It's a very large group of vegetables, with flavors ranging from completely mild all the way to screaming hot. Peppers are quite attractive when their fruit is ripening. Space-conscious gardeners will often plant peppers in color beds in their landscapes.

Bell pepper colors change as fruit ripens.

Small peppers are colorful and flavorful – hot, mild and everything else.

Young pepper plants get a good start.

A variety of new potatoes will be delightful at the table.

Young potato plants are growing in wooden frame boxes.

Potatoes are fresh from the Texas farm.

Potatoes ★★★★

Distance between seeds* in row: 10 to 12 inches.

Distance between rows: 30 to 36 inches.

Transplants per 100 feet of row: N/A

Seeds per 100 feet of row*: 35 to 40.

Spring planting date: Four to six weeks before average date of last killing freeze.

Fall planting date: 14 to 16 weeks before average date of first killing freeze.

Fertilizing: 12-12-12 or similar analysis soon after plants begin growing and again when they are 4 to 6 inches tall.

Insects of concern: Colorado potato beetle, flea beetle, aphids, wireworm.

Diseases of concern: To keep the seed pieces from rotting rapidly soon after planting, let them dry for a few days. They will form a callous layer, at which point you can dust them lightly with a labeled fungicide and then plant them.

When to harvest: New potatoes are ready about the time the plants come into flower. Baking potatoes will be ready about the time the tops die to the ground. Harvest them with a spading fork, taking care not to damage the tubers. Allow them to dry for a few days, then store them cool and dry.

Comments: Potatoes can be very rewarding. They're a popular vegetable anyway, and when you taste the wonderful flavor you'll get from a garden-fresh crop, you'll want to grow them every year.

* Of "seeds," and getting started…

The term "seeds" with potatoes always refers to pieces cut from certified seed potatoes from a nursery or feed store, not from true seeds. Certified seed potatoes are tubers that have not been sprayed with growth inhibitors. Use a sharp knife to cut the certified seed potatoes into seeds. Each seed must have at least one eye, or bud. Those eyes will be the source of the potato plants' new stems. Many gardeners prefer to leave two or three eyes per seed.

After you have cut the seeds from the potatoes, let the pieces dry for several days to form a callous layer on the cut surfaces. Once they have calloused, dust them lightly with a labeled fungicide prior to planting.

Prepare the planting bed carefully. Potatoes must have perfect drainage, so plant them in beds that are raised by 10 or 12 inches. Rake the soil smooth across the tops of the beds. Use your hoe to dig a 3-inch-deep trench down the center of each bed, then drop the seeds in place every 10 to 12 inches and rake the trench full of soil once again. As the potatoes begin to grow, use your rake to pull additional soil up around their stems.

Young potatoes feed heavily as they begin to grow. Use the corner of a hoe to cut shallow trenches 2 or 3 inches deep and 3 or 4 inches down both sides of the row of sprouting plants. Put 2 or 3 pounds of a complete and balanced fertilizer such as 12-12-12 per 30 feet of planting row (half on either side). Apply 1 more cup of the same fertilizer per 30 feet of row when the plants are 4 to 6 inches tall.

White pumpkins are a fall novelty.

Pumpkins ★★★

Distance between plants in row: Sow seeds in clusters of five or six seeds, with those sites spaced 48 to 96 inches apart within their rows. Thin to two or three plants per site as soon as seeds have germinated and plants are growing vigorously.

Distance between rows: 96 to 120 inches.

Transplants per 100 feet of row: N/A.

Seeds per 100 feet of row: 1/2 ounce.

Spring planting date: On, or up to two weeks after, average date of last killing freeze. (Those fruit will ripen in mid-summer.)

Fall planting date: Late June or early July in order to have fruit by Halloween. (Choose small or medium-sized fruit only.)

Fertilizing: High-N or all-N, 1 to 2 pounds per 100 square feet of bed space two weeks after seeds germinate and monthly through harvest.

Insects of concern: Squash bugs are gray, shield-shaped insects that congregate along the lower stem, sucking food reserves from the plant. Eliminate the egg masses from the backs of the plants' leaves by crushing them with your thumb. Prop a shingle up alongside the

Freshly harvested Texas pumpkin

Ornamental gourds mature about same time as fall pumpkin harvest.

plants in hot weather. The adult squash bugs will congregate beneath it during the sunny part of the day. You can remove the prop and crush the pests by stepping on the shingle. Insecticidal dusts may offer some help, especially with young squash bug nymphs.

Diseases of concern: Powdery mildew may cause a white dusting on leaves. Apply fungicide if it appears to be serious. Keep water off foliage whenever possible.

When to harvest: Pumpkins are ready when their fruit has changed to deep orange, the skin has toughened and the vines have started to dry. Clip their stems as you harvest the fruit to lessen the chance of disease invasion.

Comments: Like most other cucurbits, pumpkins demand a great deal of space. Harvests are not always predictable, and plantings must be timed correctly to have pumpkins for Halloween. It's best to avoid the really large types in almost all of Texas. They require too long to mature and ripen, and the Texas summer will take a toll. They should be reserved for gardeners in the Panhandle and High Plains, where night temperatures are usually cooler. Also note that if you do not have good bee activity, you may need to hand-pollinate your melon flowers. (See details under "Squash.")

Radishes ★★★

Distance between plants in row: 1/2 to 1-1/2 inch; thin seedlings to stand 1-1/2 to 2 inches apart.

Distance between rows: 8 to 12 inches.

Transplants per 100 feet of row: N/A.

Seeds per 100 feet of row: 1 ounce. (A 10-foot row is normally more than adequate for a family of four.)

Spring planting date: Two to four weeks before average date of last killing freeze.

Fall planting date: Six weeks before average date of first killing freeze.

Fertilizing: High-N or all-N, 1 pound per 100 square feet of bed space. Apply soon after seeds have sprouted and started to grow. Only one application per crop will be needed.

Insects of concern: None.

Diseases of concern: None.

Radishes can be harvested within four to six weeks after planting.

When to harvest: When roots are half their fully mature size. Letting them grow larger results in tough, fibrous and bitter radishes. When harvesting, pull the radishes. Clip off the extended roots and most of the tops. Rinse and towel dry the

nd place them into plastic bags in the refrigerator. They will be usable for a couple of weeks.

Comments: Radishes are among the very first of spring vegetable harvests, usually only four to six weeks after planting. It's wise to make a succession of plantings weekly for several weeks.

Southern Peas ★★★

Distance between plants in row: 2 to 3 inches; thin to 6 to 10 inches.

Distance between rows: 48 to 60 inches.

Transplants per 100 feet of row: N/A.

Seeds per 100 feet of row: 1 pound.

Spring planting date: Two to six weeks after average date of last killing freeze.

Fall planting date: Heat-loving, so not recommended.

Fertilizing: High-N, 1 pound per 100 square feet of bed space. Apply when plants are 6 to 8 inches tall. Do not overfeed, lest plants produce all leaf and stem growth and no flowers and fruit.

Insects of concern: Spider mites in summer, as plants are beginning to bear southern peas. Follow latest control recommendations of Texas A&M AgriLife Extension Service.

Diseases of concern: None.

When to harvest: Harvest southern peas as soon as the pods have reached full size. Leaving them on the vine will stop further production.

Comments: Including such names as black-eyed peas, purple hull, crowders and cream peas, these popular southern vegetables are actually beans. They are well suited to the hot Texas summer. They're good replacements for early spring leafy and root vegetables going into the summer.

Southern peas fill the garden in summer.

Yields of black-eyed peas are excellent.

Spinach is best when harvested young.

"Straight-neck" summer squash is fast and easy.

Zucchini squash is very productive.

Spinach ★★★

Distance between plants in row: 1 to 2 inches.

Distance between rows: 16 to 24 inches.

Transplants per 100 feet of row: N/A.

Seeds per 100 feet of row: 1 ounce.

Spring planting date: Two to four weeks before average date of last killing freeze.

Fall planting date: 10 to 12 weeks before average date of first killing freeze.

Fertilizing: High-N or all-N, 1 to 2 pounds per 100 square feet of bed space. Apply two weeks after planting. Repeat every three weeks until harvest.

Insects of concern: Aphids may congregate on new leaves. Apply labeled insecticide, or merely wash off with water.

Diseases of concern: None.

When to harvest: Leaves have best flavor while plants are growing vigorously. Harvest partially matured leaves for best flavor. When plants begin to bolt into flower, harvest the entire plants. Rinse and store them in the refrigerator.

Comments: Spinach is highly nutritious, and it's increasingly popular in cooking and used fresh in salads. Care for it much as you would leaf lettuce, although it won't mature as quickly. Its main challenge is with Texas heat. Plant spinach early, so it will be finished before it turns hot. Keep the planting growing vigorously to avoid bitter leaves.

Squash ★★★★

Distance between plants in row: Sow seeds in clusters of five or six seeds, with those sites spaced 42 to 48 inches apart within their rows. Thin to two or three plants per cluster as soon as seeds have germinated and plants are growing vigorously.

Distance between rows: 48 to 60 inches for summer squash. Vining winter squash plants cover more ground and should be planted 60 to 72 inches apart.

Transplants per 100 feet of row: N/A.

Seeds per 100 square feet: 1 ounce (summer squash); 1/2 ounce (winter squash).

Spring planting date: On, or up to two weeks after, average date of last killing freeze.

Fall planting date: Summer squash 16 weeks before average date of first killing freeze. Winter squash 22 weeks before average date of first killing freeze.

Fertilizing: High-N, 1 to 2 pounds per 100 square feet of bed space two weeks after seeds germinate and again six weeks later.

Insects of concern: Squash bugs are gray, shield-shaped insects that congregate along the lower stem, sucking food reserves from the plant. Eliminate the egg masses from the backs of the plants' leaves by crushing them with your thumb. Prop a shingle up alongside the plants in hot weather. The adult squash bugs will congregate beneath it during the sunny part of the day. You can remove the prop and crush many of the pests by stepping on the shingle. Insecticidal dusts may offer some help, especially with young squash bug nymphs.

Squash vine borers are white larvae that tunnel within the stems of the plants, soon killing them. There is no control once they are within the stems. Preventive applications of insecticides, especially *Bacillus thuringiensis,* will help.

Diseases of concern: Mildew may appear on leaves. Treat with

Butternut and acorn, both winter squash, and yellow summer crookneck squash.

Garden Tip

The terms "summer" and "winter" squash can be misleading. Summer squash (crookneck, zucchini, Patty Pan scallops) are generally bush-form, and their fruit is harvested before it is mature. They begin producing by late spring. Winter squash fruit (acorns, butternuts and others) are generally produced on trailing vines. They take much longer to reach maturity, often late summer into fall. They are not harvested until their skins have become hardened and the vines have started to die. They store well for weeks into the fall and winter.

Male squash flower will provide pollen.

Daub pollen from male flower onto female.

Patty Pan and other types of summer squash are among best crops for Texas.

Zucchini squash may out-produce your ability to consume it.

labeled fungicide, and keep foliage as dry as you are able.

When to harvest: Summer squash are harvested when they are about half grown. Straightnecks and crooknecks should be 4 to 5 inches long. Zucchinis are best picked at the 6- or 7-inch length. Keep maturing fruit picked off the plants if you want production to continue. Winter squash are harvested when rinds are hard and when yellow spots develop on the bottoms of the fruit. Clip fruit, rather than pulling it from the vine.

Comments: Also note that if you do not have good bee activity, you may need to hand-pollinate your squash flowers. Cucurbits, including squash, melons, cucumbers and even gourds bear both male (straight-stemmed) and female flowers (swollen primordial fruit visible on flowers' stems) on the same plant. Typically, plants will produce male flowers only for the first week or two. But if you're seeing both male and female flowers, and if you're still not getting fruit set, clip a male flower off the plant. Peel its petals away and daub its pollen onto the female flower parts. You'll know within one or two days whether you've been successful. It almost always works.

Sugar Snap Peas ★★★

Distance between plants in row: 1 to 2 inches. Thin to 2 to 3 inches.

Distance between rows: 36 to 48 inches.

Transplants per 100 feet of row: N/A

Seeds per 100 feet of row: 1 pound. To improve production, coat the seeds with a nitrogen-fixing inoculant prior to planting.

Spring planting date: Six to eight weeks before average date of last killing freeze.

Fall planting date: Eight to 10 weeks before average date of first killing freeze.

Fertilizing: High-nitrogen fertilizer beginning two weeks after germination. Continue until harvest.

Insects of concern: None.

Diseases of concern: None.

When to harvest: When pods are full-sized, but before individual peas begin to swell beyond BB-size. That is usually five to seven days after the blooms drop.

Comments: The several outstanding varieties of sugar snap peas that

Sugar Snap pea pod is ready for harvest.

have been introduced over the past several decades have brought an entirely new option to cool-season vegetable gardening. These are harvested and eaten whole, pods and all. Harvest must be finished before the weather turns hot, so these peas are among the earliest of all vegetables to be planted. They require sturdy supports. Position them so that the vines and the supports do not cast excessive shade on other parts of your garden.

A garden filled with fun – Antique Rose Emporium, Independence (Brenham)

Sweet Potatoes ★★★

Distance between plants in row: 12 to 16 inches.

Distance between rows: 36 to 48 inches.

Transplants ("slips") per 100 feet of row: 75 to 100.

Seeds per 100 feet of row: N/A.

Spring planting date: Four to six weeks after average date of last killing freeze.

Fall planting date: N/A.

Fertilizing: Prior to planting and in early summer with complete-and-balanced food such as 12-12-12. High-nitrogen fertilizer can lead to excessive production of leaves.

Insects of concern: Sweet potato weevils. Plant certified weevil-free slips.

Diseases of concern: None.

When to harvest: Dig carefully around one or two plants to check for development of the roots. When they have reached full size, dig them and lay them out to dry for 15 days on paper in the garage. Store cool (50 to 55 F) and dry.

Comments: Sweet potatoes thrive in hot weather, but they need sandy soils for best growth and root development. Plant in raised beds – good drainage is essential.

Sweet potatoes must have sandy soils.

Mid-sized tomatoes perform well in Texas.

FAQ

Q How do I choose the best tomato transplants?

A Here are a few basics.

- Choose varieties recommended for your area. They will be small to mid-sized types, not large-fruiting varieties.
- Look for stocky, sturdy transplants 6 to 8 inches tall in 4-inch pots.
- Plants with reddish stems have been exposed to cool weather and, therefore are tougher and better acclimated.

Garden Tip

If your tomato transplants are slightly too tall, dig a trench 4 or 5 inches deep in which to plant them. Lay them into their trenches at a 30-degree angle with one-third of their tops sticking out of the soil.

The transplants will form roots along their stems. This is much better than simply digging a deep hole to accommodate the tall stem.

★★★★★

Distance between plants in row: 30 to 36 inches.

Distance between rows: 48 to 60 inches.

Transplants per 100 feet of row: 33 to 40.

Seeds per 100 feet of row: N/A.

Spring planting date: On, or two weeks after, average date of last killing freeze.

Fall planting date: 22 weeks before average date of first killing freeze.

Fertilizing: High-N or all-N food two weeks after planting and monthly until harvests are completed – 1 tablespoon per plant at first feeding, 2 tablespoons per plant at each successive feeding.

Tomato insects of concern

- **Spider mites** damage begins to appear (late May in South Texas into mid-June in North Texas) as small tan mottled specks on leaves, starting at the bottoms of the plants and flushing upward. Eventually, entire plant is affected and leaves dry, often with fine webbing. You must control these tiny pests early, or they will kill your plants. Watch closely for the initial speckling of leaves. If you're unsure, thump a suspect leaf over white paper. If nearly microscopic specks start to move about on the paper, those are the mites. Apply labeled insecticide to control.

- **Tomato hornworms** are fearsome-looking, finger-sized caterpillars that devour entire portions of a plant within hours. They are difficult to spot initially, but you will see their droppings on the leaves that remain. They usually work singly, so it's generally quickest and easiest to search for and destroy the individual hornworms. They will not hurt you. Or you can apply a general-purpose insecticide such as *Bacillus thuringiensis*.

- **Tomato fruit worms** are exactly the same insect as corn earworms and cotton bollworms. Apply a labeled insecticide at first signs of fruit worms invading your tomatoes.

For best productivity, avoid large-fruiting tomato varieties in Texas. They do not set fruit well in our high temperatures

Tomato diseases of concern

- **Early blight** is a fungal disease that first causes lower leaves to develop thumbprint-sized yellow spots. Those blotches are very characteristic of the disease, and they appear by mid-May in South Texas and late May in North Texas (two to three weeks before spider mites usually appear). Apply a labeled fungicide at first evidence. Keep foliage dry as you irrigate. Left unchecked, the disease will spread up the plant, eventually ruining the fruit.

- **Bacterial soft rot** of fruit causes tomatoes to hang like putrid water balloons. Wearing a disposable glove, carefully remove affected fruit from the plant or from the ground and put them into the trash. Do not handle healthy plant tissues in the process.

- **Nematodes** are microscopic soil-borne worms that sting plants' roots, causing abnormal knot-like galls that interfere with the normal flow of water and nutrients into the stems and leaves. The first symptom of their presence is usually stunting of growth and very poor productivity. If you observe the root galls when you remove the plants, you must take several corrective steps. (1) Plant cereal rye as a cover crop for the garden in October. It will entrap a significant percentage of the nematodes in its root system. Plow it into the garden in late January, as you get the plot ready for the next year's plantings. (2) Be careful, as you are plowing or tilling, that you do not carry soil from nematode-infested ground into "clean" parts of your garden. Till the non-infested portions first. (3) Plant tomatoes in following years in another part of your garden where nematodes have not been a problem. (4) Plant nematode-resistant varieties. This will be indicated on the plants' nursery labels as the initial "N" following their names on the pot tags. (5) If all else fails, move your tomato plantings to a new part of your yard, or grow them in potting soil in large containers (10-gallon and larger).

Tomato plants afflicted with spider mites.

Blossom-end rot is usually caused by uneven water supplies.

Remember! Fall tomatoes are not planted in the fall. They must be planted by late June into mid-July.

Tomato blossoms ready to be pollinated.

FAQ

Q Why are the bottom sides of my tomatoes turning dark brown to black and sunken?

A That is a physiological disorder known as blossom-end rot, and it's caused by allowing the plants to get too dry between waterings. The blossom end of the fruit is the point farthest away from the roots, so it dries out first and gets water last. The problem affects primarily medium-sized and large-fruiting tomatoes and is especially common with tomatoes grown in containers. Try never to let your tomatoes wilt badly. It's worth noting that this problem can also be due to a lack of calcium in the soil, especially in acidic sandy soils. Even then, inconsistent watering can be a source of the trouble.

Thump flower cluster to improve pollination.

Tomato cultural concerns

- **Rolling leaves** will develop when temperatures climb into the 90s. It is a problem that looks bad, but is essentially of no concern.

  Spray drift of broadleafed weedkiller, on the other hand, can give the same kind of rolled leaves, but the condition is also normally accompanied by pointed, elongated leaves on the new growth. Due to tomatoes' sensitivities, herbicide drift can do great damage.

- **Cracking and splitting of fruit** will happen when the tomatoes are exposed to sun and high temperatures. Some varieties are more susceptible than others, and the splitting can result in loss of as much as one-fourth to one-third of the top of each fruit. You may want to avoid that damage by picking the tomatoes just as they start changing color from green to pale pink. You can ripen them indoors on towels or paper with no loss of flavor or nutritional value.

- **When tomato flowers fall off,** you might wonder what is cutting the flowers off your tomato plant before it can set fruit. The two most likely reasons may surprise you:

  Those flowers are not getting pollinated. Tomatoes are self-pollinating. They must have wind motion to shatter the pollen loose within the flowers. If you have your plants against a fence or in some other area where wind movement is blocked, you may find that thumping the fruit clusters with your finger every couple of days will jar the pollen loose, resulting in improved fruit set.

  Far more commonly, however, failure to set fruit comes from poor variety choice. There is a physiological tie between temperature and fruit size for a given variety that determines how successful you will be with that variety. Large-fruiting varieties like Big Boy and Beefsteak will not set fruit when daytime temperatures are above 90 F on a daily basis. That may not matter in the Midwest, but it's a sure recipe for failure for those types in Texas. It's a shame that really large types of tomatoes are even offered for sale in our state. Stick with small and medium-sized types for the best results well into the summer.

When to harvest: Pick fruit as soon as they reach their desired size and color. However, if you need to harvest tomatoes several days early because of sunscald, bird damage, potential first freeze, etc., they will continue to ripen if placed on paper or towels on a counter indoors.

Comments: Tomatoes are the most popular vegetable in Texas. Almost every gardener has room for at least one or two tomato plants, whether he or she lives on acreage, in the suburbs, uptown or in an apartment.

Fall tomatoes can be extremely productive in Texas. But you'll have to plant your transplants early enough for them to have ample time to produce a good yield. Fall tomato plants will be free of spider mites and early blight (two spring nemeses), and the fruit won't crack and split due to high temperatures. New transplants should be set out in late June or early July in North Texas and in mid- to late July in the southern half of the state. Fresh plants for the fall garden have far more vigor than the bedraggled, mite-ridden plants that have had to struggle through the summer. Ask your favorite independent garden center if they'll be carrying transplants at the appropriate time. If not, you can start your own seedling transplants or, just as easily, root cuttings from your best spring plants. It takes four to five weeks to produce the transplants ready for planting. Erect A-frame shades from cardboard or wood shingles to protect them from afternoon sun for the first few days. If you're able to adjust the shade each day so that the plants are exposed to one more hour of daytime sun, they will soon be ready to take the sun on full-time.

Vegetable garden tomato support

Tomatoes from the Sperry garden

Tomato plants are caged to keep off ground.

Tomatoes off to a good start

Tomatoes from a Texas farm in June

Turnips are grown for both roots and leaves.

Turnips ★★★

Distance between plants in row: 1 to 2 inches, thin to 2 to 4 inches.

Distance between rows: 15 to 18 inches.

Transplants per 100 feet of row: N/A.

Seeds per 100 feet of row: 1/2 ounce.

Spring planting date: Two to four weeks before average date of last killing freeze.

Fall planting date: Six to 10 weeks before average date of first killing freeze.

Fertilizing: High-N or all-N, 1 to 2 pounds per 100 square feet of bed space. Apply two weeks after planting. Repeat monthly until harvest.

Insects of concern: White grub worms, wireworms, root knot nematodes and other soil-borne pests. Follow latest control recommendations of Texas A&M AgriLife Extension Service.

Diseases of concern: None.

When to harvest: Turnip plants usually produce greens in 40 to 45 days. Turnip roots take 50 to 60 days. Harvest turnip greens by pulling the entire plant when the leaves are 4 to 6 inches long. Turnip roots can be harvested when they are 2 to 2-1/2 inches in diameter. If left longer, they become tough and fibrous.

Comments: Turnips need cool conditions to maintain high quality.

Collin County garden is reaching peak productivity.

The Cloister Garden at Festival Hill in Round Top is perhaps the most famous herb garden in Texas.

Herbs in the Texas Garden

You can't call yourself a gardener if you don't have a plot, row, pot or cranny filled with luscious herbs. They're fragrant, they're flavorful, and they're fun. Every landscape and garden has room for herbs. Here are some basics to get you started, then if your fancy gets tickled, you'll take it from there.

The one little word *herbs* is actually a big umbrella – it's home to thousands of species from hundreds of plant families. It's just a catch-all term for a giant gathering of unrelated plants. So making any general statements about herbs is very difficult, but here are a few basic growing requirements that will almost always apply:

Plant in full or nearly full sunlight. Almost all types of herbs do their best growing in full sunlight, or perhaps with a few hours of protection from the hot afternoon sun in the summer.

Prepare a well-draining, highly organic soil. Think of the best garden soil or potting mix that you've ever used, then set out to prepare it for your herb beds and containers. It will contain 50 or 60 percent sphagnum peat moss, compost and other organic matter. Sure, some herbs will make do with less bed preparation, but almost all will perform to their maximum given the best soil mix.

This way to the herbs!

Raised bed of mixed herbs

Aloe vera belongs in every herb garden

Basil grows well in pots.

Purple basil is delicious and lovely.

Exercise great care in watering. We grow most herbs for their foliage, flowers and seeds, and none of those will flourish unless we keep the plants watered properly. Herbs that are deprived of adequate water soon become weak and unproductive, so maintain recommended levels of soil moisture.

Feed your herbs regularly. Again, your goal is to maintain vigor. Apply a high-nitrogen or all-nitrogen fertilizer every four to six weeks. Actually, you can almost always use the same product you apply to your flowers and vegetables. Unless a soil test suggests otherwise, it will probably be the same fertilizer you use for your lawn and landscape as well, although it's always a good idea to check for any label restrictions. Herbs in containers will need more frequent feedings with a diluted solution of a high-nitrogen, water-soluble plant food.

Mulch your herb beds. Reduce the impact of splashing rains that might damage herbs' leaf qualities. Cut down on weed growth. Use mulches for all of their benefits. They're especially helpful in herb beds.

Harvest herbs at the peak of perfection. You'll refine this statement crop by crop, because each type that you grow will have its own set of rules on when and how it should be harvested. Get to know the best ways to store each type of herb.

Specifics on a few of our favorite herbs

- *Aloe vera.* While this doesn't really qualify as an edible herb, it certainly deserves to be included here somewhere. It has become one of our favorite tropical succulents, used for giving instant relief from burns, also in a wide assortment of cosmetic and other healthcare products. Every gardener has room for one or two aloe plants. Once a particular *Aloe vera* plant becomes mature, it may grace you with a lovely flower spike. Grow it in a pot, so you can bring it indoors during freezing weather.

- **Basil.** This warm-weather annual is grown for its rich and varied flavors. The plants are also very attractive in pots and mixed in with flowers. Start from nursery transplants after all danger of frost and freeze has passed – basil is one of our most cold-sensitive herbs. Flower buds stop further growth of the stems and leaves, so keep them pinched off. Harvest basil leaves and small stems as you need them; clipping often will encourage denser growth. Use fresh whenever possible.

- **Chives.** These small clumping onion relatives are frequent and cheerful visitors to herb gardens. They stay short, and their lavender flowers are cheerful over an extended period of time. Use them to border beds and to add interest to containers. Cut the plants back frequently to encourage thicker growth. Use the fresh leaves finely chopped and sprinkled over salads, meat and potatoes.

- **Coriander (cilantro).** This fast-growing, cool-weather annual is seeded directly where it is going to grow. Plant in fall in a sunny location. It grows to 24 inches, but the leaves can be harvested when the plants are only 6 to 8 inches tall. Gather its seeds as they ripen. It is used in Mexican recipes, also in making of sausages.

- **Dill.** This popular, fine-textured herb grows quite large, so plant it where it won't encroach on other vegetables. It prefers cool weather, so sow from seed in fall or early spring. Keep the plants growing briskly by watering, fertilizing and harvesting regularly. Dill bolts in hot weather, often before cucumbers mature, so investigate ways to preserve/refrigerate some of your yield for pickling time. Harvest fronds, slender stalks, and flower heads when flowers begin to open. Harvest seeds when they turn brown. Dill is used in a variety of ways: obviously for pickles, also in cheese, breads, potato salad and butter sauces.

- **Fennel.** This tall, drought-resistant herb grows to 3 to 5 feet tall. Seed it where it will grow. Rows should be 36 to 42 inches apart, and plants 10 to 12 inches apart within the rows. All parts of the plant may be used. Stems are harvested before the flowers bloom. If leaves are preferred, harvest them when flowers start to bloom for best flavor. Seeds are harvested as soon as they ripen. It is treated as an annual in most of Texas.

Chives make handsome garden border.

Dill

Cilantro

Fennel is grown for leaves, roots.

Swiss chard contrasts with bronze fennel.

Parsley is handsome in garden borders.

Scented geraniums come in dozens of forms.

Herbs at a nursery

- **Scented geraniums.** While their sisters, the flowering geraniums, may be a bit flashier, this large group of fascinating and highly fragrant plants can also add greatly to your outdoor experience. We grow them for their foliage. You'll find a wide assortment of fragrances, leaf forms and growth habits in Texas nurseries. Their leaves are used in potpourri, baking, jellies and teas. The fragrances, including apple, lemon, lime, orange, apricot, pineapple, rose, chocolate and coconut, among dozens of others, come from oils in the plants' leaves and stems. Some types can grow quite large (2 to 3 feet wide and tall), while others stay more compact. They adapt very well to pots. That allows you to move them indoors during winter's freezing weather.

  Note: the scented geranium known as "mosquito plant" or "citronella plant" has not been shown to repel mosquitoes from areas where it is grown.

- **Lavender.** These staples of sachets and potpourris – English, French and Spanish lavenders – are not always easy to grow. Gardeners in Coastal areas of the state will have trouble keeping them for more than a season, but Central and North Texas gardeners can grow them successfully. They require good drainage and ample light/heat. Some gardeners plant them in hills, mulch them with rocks, and lavish them with neglect. They make good container companions for plants with similar cultural requirements.

- **Lemon balm.** This easy-care perennial has attractive mint-like foliage. Leaves have a pleasant lemony fragrance, useful with fruit salads, vegetables and meats. Leaves can be brewed and used with teas. It grows 2 feet tall and wide.

- **Marjoram.** The plants grow 12 to 24 inches tall. Their small leaves are light green on top surfaces and grayish on their reverses. Set transplants out after the last killing frost, either into beds or pots. Technically a perennial, marjoram is not winter-hardy in most of Texas. For maximum flavor, leaves should be harvested just before the plants bloom. They dry well for use later in cooking.

- **Mints.** Perhaps our largest group of herbs, mints come in dozens of flavors. All are perennials. They can be started from seed, but cuttings are preferred. Well-stocked nurseries may have as many as 25 different fragrances in the potted collections of mint transplants. Many mints are quite invasive, so take precaution to keep their root systems from spreading into adjacent beds. An 8-inch root barrier is usually sufficient, or you can grow the plants in pots. Keep flowers pinched off. Harvest stems and leaves frequently to keep the plants growing vigorously. Mints thrive in wet soils, so moisture is especially important in growing them successfully.

- **Oregano.** Most types are perennials, and most have green or golden foliage. They grow to be 24 to 30 inches tall, often serving as a hardy groundcover in the kitchen garden. As with other herbs, keeping flowers pruned off stimulates fresh leaf growth. Leaves can be harvested at any time that the plant is not blooming. Oreganos have many craft and culinary uses.

- **Parsley.** This is a handsome herb that is available in several different leaf forms. It makes an attractive flowerbed border, and it's also a favorite food source for caterpillars of black swallowtail butterflies, so be forewarned not to spray them. Parsley is biennial, bolting to flower and dying quickly the second growing season. As a result, you'll want to start with new plants each spring.

- **Rosemary.** This group of fragrant and well-loved plants (mostly winter-hardy to Zone 8 and southward) has become mainstream in Texas landscaping. Prostrate types sprawl, growing only 12 or 15 inches tall, while upright types are shrub-like, growing 3 to 5 feet tall and wide. The upright types tend to be somewhat more winter-hardy. All types produce bluish-green leaves and small, cheerful flowers along their stems in late winter and early spring. Given excellent drainage, rosemaries are trouble-free and Texas-friendly. They're delightful along garden walks and steps, and they're favorites in the kitchen.

Spearmint

Garden Tip

To keep mint in bounds, some gardeners cut the bottoms out of 5- or 7-gallon plastic nursery pots, sink the pots into the soil so their tops are almost flush with the soil surface, and then fill the bottomless pots with a good garden soil mix. The pots' walls stop the spread of the mint plants.

Rosemary

Greek oregano

Chocolate mint

English thyme

Lemon thyme

Gray-green leaves of sage are useful in landscaping.

- **Sages.** These are easily grown in most of Texas, but beware of waterlogged soils when growing them along the Gulf Coast. Their foliage is usually gray-green or variegated, making them handsome plants in the landscape. Start from nursery transplants in the spring. Replace the plants as they become woody, usually after three or four years. Harvest the leaves as you need them. Best leaf flavor is achieved when the plants begin to bloom.

- **Salad burnet.** A perennial herb, it grows 16 to 24 inches tall. Leaves add a cucumber flavor to salads. Start from transplants or by division. Keep soil moist, and harvest young leaves for best flavor.

- **Tarragon.** This perennial herb is an artemisia that becomes somewhat shrubby, growing to 2 feet tall. It's grown for its fine, dark green leaves. They achieve best flavor just as the plant is coming into flower. As with most ornamental artemisias, you'll want to replant it every three or four years.

- **Thyme.** There are many forms of this perennial herb. Common thyme grows to 12 inches tall, producing purple flowers and gray-green leaves. Other types are quite low and spreading. All need moist soils that are perfectly drained, and many require mulching during winter. The trailing types are well adapted to patio pots and baskets. Harvest leaves by clipping the tops of the plants just before they come into bloom.

Nurseries now offer herbs almost year 'round.

Index